The Price of Sex

The Price of Sex
Prostitution, policy and society

Belinda Brooks-Gordon

WILLAN
PUBLISHING

Published by

Willan Publishing
Culmcott House
Mill Street, Uffculme
Cullompton, Devon
EX15 3AT, UK
Tel: +44(0)1884 840337
Fax: +44(0)1884 840251
e-mail: info@willanpublishing.co.uk
website: www.willanpublishing.co.uk

Published simultaneously in the USA and Canada by

Willan Publishing
c/o ISBS, 920 NE 58th Ave, Suite 300
Portland, Oregon 97213-3786, USA
Tel: +001(0)503 287 3093
Fax: +001(0)503 280 8832
e-mail: info@isbs.com
website: www.isbs.com

Hardback
ISBN-13: 978-1-84392-088-5
ISBN-10: 1-84392-088-3

Paperback
ISBN-13: 978-1-84392-087-8
ISBN-10: 1-84392-087-5

British Library Cataloguing-in-Publication Data

A catalogue record for this book is available from the British Library

Project management by Deer Park Productions, Tavistock, Devon
Typeset by GCS, Leighton Buzzard, Beds
Printed and bound by T.J. International, Padstow, Cornwall

Contents

Acknowledgements

Many people commented upon the text or the research and ideas behind this book, so I thank Charlotte Bilby, Julia Bindman, Ben Bowling, Linda Cusick, Rosie Campbell, Marc Desautels, Janet Foster, Clive Hollin, Richard Kemp, Mary McMurran, Ken Pease, Rowan Pelling, Michael Rice, Helen Self, Keith Soothill, Betsy Stanko, Donald West, and members of The Cambridge Socio-Legal Group. This book began as a doctoral research project. The research was funded by the Economic and Social Research Council (award no. R00429724404), a Wingate Scholarship, and a grant from The Ian Karten Educational Trust, while Churchill College, Cambridge, provided both support and a home. Loraine Gelsthorpe supervised the PhD part of the research and her calm sensitivity and friendship was and is valued. I was helped too by librarians at the Radzinowicz Library at the Institute of Criminology, Cambridge, Helen Krarup, Mary Gower, and Stuart Feathers. Acknowledgement is due to David Howarth for pointing me in the direction of Gusfield's work on symbolic law. I also acknowledge a special debt of gratitude to Andrew Bainham who read chapters of the book and discussed legal cases and the civil liberties issues involved in the policing of prostitution.

During the writing of the book I was diagnosed with systemic lupus (SLE) and I am grateful for the support I received from colleagues and friends at Birkbeck College, most notably Stephen Frosh, Lynne Segal, and Simon Green. The efficiency and calmness of Liz Skinner and Nollaig Frost made the multiple administrative and teaching demands more manageable.

The chapter on violence was written with Hilary Kinnell so I owe a large debt of gratitude to Hilary whose activism along with that of Helen Self, Julia Bindman, and my fellow members of the prostitution legislation reform group remains an inspiration.

My thanks extends to all those at the Metropolitan Police Vice and Clubs Unit at Charing Cross Police Station who made every effort to help with the research, especially Ch. Supt. Martin Jauche and Insp. Brian Ward. Also, to everybody at Paddington Green Police Station, Insp. David Stone and Sgt. Paul Rodford, whose enthusiasm and co-operation was of great value. Not least, thanks are due to Dick Miles whose efforts opened the first door.

A network of friendships sustained me during the data collection and writing up of the book, including Paul Bird, Mike Ginnelly, David and Amy Price, Eleanor and Richard Burack, Simon Delow, Zenobia and Paul Kaura. I am mindful of the succour I received from confidantes Alix Pryde and Alison Wakefield. My siblings Andréa, Ingrid, and Graham have provided sympathetic support and practical help. My children Miles and Isobel, whose acceptance and love of their mother, despite my absences and eccentricities, make me feel most fortunate even when I feel most undeserving.

This book is dedicated to my mother Margaret Brooks, whose unswerving support and love has blessed all of my life. Her travels in Africa and the Americas make the journey researching and writing a book seem like a stroll in the park. Her humour, spirit and resilience are never far from my thoughts. The final word of thanks goes to Mark Holmes, my life partner, with whom a new depth of delight, friendship, kindness, and love emerged when it got the chance second time around.

Belinda Brooks-Gordon
June 2006

Introduction

As a society we are buying more sex than ever before. Adult sex shops now take their place amongst retailers on the high street and lap dancing clubs compete for an increased share of the leisure economy. Hotel chains offer sexually explicit films as part of their standard service and adult films can be beamed into suburban homes from space satellites. While the party-selling of adult toys to women in their own homes has become a mainstream activity, telephone sex lines have proliferated and, at the traditional end of the sexual service economy, prostitution has experienced new growth.

Alongside the growth in the size and the variety of the sexual leisure economy has been a recent increase in measures, as part of a government drive against all sexual offences, against the behaviour of men and women involved in prostitution. The sex industry has become so broad and sexual offences have become such a social spectre, however, that it has become increasingly difficult for policy makers and practitioners to untangle the complex and inter-related nature of the sex industry and sexual offences. Recent attempts by the authorities to provide legal responses to areas of prostitution show evidence of fragmentation and failure. For example, attempts to curb the 'demand' side of prostitution, by proactive policing of the men who buy sex have failed the neighbourhoods and social groups they were intended to appease. Such measures have also created further levels of violence, dependence and immiseration for those at the most vulnerable end of the industry. These effects have been compounded by the introduction of measures to combat anti-social behaviour and their use against those involved in prostitution which has led to the further criminalisation, and loss of rights, of those involved. This approach by government invited concern from professional bodies such as the Law Society for being piecemeal. The law on prostitution required comprehensive review, and root and branch reform. These problems, which prompted the government review and consultation paper *Paying the Price* in July 2004 to result in the government's published strategy on prostitution in January 2006, constitute the true price of commercial sex.

This book demonstrates how the implementation of recent measures in response to the perceived problems of, and abuses in, prostitution have not only failed in their objective, but have created unanticipated problems and wider abuses due to the complexity and interdependence of the various strands of the sex industry to wider social issues.

The book focuses on key areas of contemporary debate about the sex industry, including the demand by customers who buy sex, the policing of women who work in the street sex industry, and the violence that pervades prostitution. I show how these issues have been regarded in policy through the government's disparate measures to regulate prostitution through sex offences legislation, anti-social behaviour measures, and on the ground through policing practice that is at the heart of policy implementation. The book explores the complexity of sexual offences with regard to prostitution and brings lucidity to the debate by focusing on these main areas of policy, showing the link between them and their practical implementation in the context of the burgeoning sex economy. The book traces the recent policy history of the contemporary sexual leisure industry and at the same time presents a complete and straightforward guide to all the various laws that relate to prostitution. Ultimately it presents a picture of how a social policy might be formulated to minimise harm and enhance public understanding.

Chapter 1 shows how the public perception of sex work has changed throughout history for a number of reasons, including changes to family structure, the workforce, and expectations of sexual relationships. Prominent factors now include kerb-crawling and the stringent policing of it in some areas with its associated costs, the costs to the sex workers and to community relations in terms of social tension (Hubbard 1999). A third issue is the vulnerability of women in prostitution. Health workers and non-governmental organisations involved in HIV prevention have long concluded that prostitutes are more at risk from client violence than they are from HIV (McKeganey and Barnard 1996). The chapter thus summarises the problems and issues which led to the Sex Offences Review in 2000. The chapter then examines attempts to curb prostitution and kerb crawling through piecemeal and contradictory legislation, such as the Criminal Justice and Police Act 2001 which came into force before the end of the Review. The chapter explores, for example, environmental measures such as traffic calming, kerb crawler schools, and re-education. It also explains why previous responses failed as they failed to take account of the reasons that impel people into sex work, failed to take account of who the clients are or what psychosexual needs people are trying to satisfy when buying commercial sex. The chapter thus provides the background and policy behind the proposed legislative change in the provisions of the government strategy on prostitution in January 2006.

Chapter 2 provides comprehensive coverage of offences surrounding sex work. It discusses all the disparate laws that relate to prostitution and the sex industry – for example what is criminalised what is not criminalised, and why. The laws currently used include ancient planning laws, laws originally framed to deal with the 1950s fear of homosexuality, and laws such as the recent criminalisation of prostitutes' cards in a public place. In addition, the increased use of civil sanctions in anti-social behaviour orders (ASBOs) for prostitution-related 'offences', although originally applied to neighbour disputes, have severe criminal consequences for sex working women if breached. Legislation also allows the taking of DNA from kerb crawlers to add to the national DNA database. The chapter includes an analysis of contemporary policy as it relates to prostitution, including the Sexual Offences Act 2003, the Green Paper *Paying the Price* in 2004 and the government consultation that resulted in *A Coordinated Strategy on Prostitution and Summary of Responses to Paying the Price* in January 2006, and the Regulatory Impact Assessment that followed.

In Chapter 3 I examine 'sexual demand' to explore the prevalence, nature and extent of clients in the UK with an emphasis on kerb-crawling. The chapter will draw on original empirical research of over 500 cases of men who were stopped for prostitution-related 'offences' and behaviours. It will provide a demographic profile of exactly who buys sexual services, where the men come from, what they actually pay for, and what psychosexual needs they are trying to meet by paying for commercial sex. It will explore the cost of contemporary response in terms of the effects of displacement of prostitution-related activity, the vulnerability of women and children, and the civil liberties of men who are stopped by police for prostitution-related behaviours.

Chapter 4 illustrates the practical problems in contemporary policy by exploring the difficulties and complexities involved for those policing and enforcing the law as it is presently drafted. An understanding of policing responses will be presented through the use of a case study of the vice unit response in a large metropolitan city. The chapter examines the competing demands and pressures on police officers to illustrate the complexity of policing prostitution and will illuminate how policy is enacted on the ground. Competing pressures include the demands made by residents to rid their neighbourhoods of 'vice' due to the perceived behaviour of prostitutes and clients, and the vulnerability of street prostitutes and juveniles at risk (JARS). The chapter also explores contemporary police responses to violence against women using data from the case study. The use of police views on all these issues will provide insight into the perceived legitimacy of punitive laws on sex work.

The issue of violence and victimisation is a central aspect of life for many women in sex work and Chapter 5 explores this issue. Not only is violence against sex workers endemic, there have been a large number of high profile murders of sex workers. The chapter examines the victimisation of women by punters and also from pimps to provide an insight into the prevalence, nature and extent of victimisation and violence against women working in the sex industry. Previously unpublished empirical data, gathered from a large number of prostitute women by a large non-governmental organisation involved in helping prostitute women, will be used. The popular conception of 'sex slavery' will be explored and whether this concept is helpful to the empowerment of women in the sex industry will be discussed. Human rights issues, and the social and human costs of ignoring rights, are also discussed alongside the emergence of sex workers' labour rights.

The theoretical orientation and methodological approach taken in the book is explained in Chapter 6. An outline of the methods used to collect the empirical data used in the book is provided. For example, the choice of site as well as the negotiation of access to carry out the research is discussed. The theoretical orientation, choice and integration of methods, as well as the sampling selection, strategies and influences upon data-collection and analysis are explored. The various ethical problems encountered in such research are commented upon, and the chapter concludes with some reflections upon the research experience which are theorised and set against current social policy.

The final chapter reviews the main points of the book. It evaluates the empirical findings in Chapters 3 to 5 and outlines the implications of these for theory before examining the implications for legal policy and policing practice. Human rights issues, and the social and human costs of ignoring rights, are also discussed alongside sex workers' labour rights following the affiliation of the International Sex Workers' Union with Britain's largest trade union in 2002. The book concludes by outlining what a law governing prostitution *should* look like.

This book offers a critical perspective on prostitution policies and the legal chaos which surrounds the sex industry and the law today. The book provides an accessible introduction to the key debates on sexual offences and prostitution. It presents new insight into the main issues in contemporary society such as human rights and labour rights as they apply to sex work. In addition, the book advances debate on sex work and sexual offences by offering a social policy formulation based on the principles of harm reduction and public education. This book is a useful text for practitioners seeking to understand more about sexual offences and prostitution, and for undergraduate students of criminology, forensic psychology, law, and social policy. It will be valuable for researchers and academics in the more specific fields of policing and sexual offences as well as those in gender and women's studies. Its accessible insight into the key debates in this popular area is also likely to appeal to more general readers interested in the area.

*This book is dedicated
to my mother
Margaret Brooks*

Chapter 1

How prostitution became a legal problem

Payment for sexual services remains at the centre of debates about sexuality, morality, and public order. More recently, it has again become part of a debate on immigration. The exchange of money for sex not surprisingly attracts wide interest amongst policy-makers and academics. However, most attention is given to exploring why women become sex workers or how they manage their involvement in it (for example, Sanders 2004; Home Office 2004; Phoenix 2004). Yet the sex work market also consists of clients and regulatory controls – generally carried out by the police. To focus only on sex workers leaves two sides of the commercial and regulatory triangle under-explored and under-theorised. At present, much debate on police and clients runs ahead of theoretical understanding or factual evidence about those who take part in commercial sexual transactions. This has implications for policy measures which may not only be ineffective, but may have unintended consequences. Investigations of commercial sex clients and their regulatory control is thus badly needed to inform policy and academic understanding.

This chapter outlines the background to contemporary prostitution policy by providing an outline of historical trends and shifts in moral, ideological, social and legal structures that relate to the buying and selling of sex. I show how perceptions of prostitution have changed historically for a number of reasons including changes to family structure, the workforce, and expectations of sexual relationships. I suggest that the overall socio-legal trend has become one of greater criminalisation of the client, and while greater understanding appears to be shown to the sex worker in a rhetoric of 'vulnerability', in effect the increasing criminalisation of the client has been to the detriment of the sex worker.

Prominent factors now include kerb-crawling and the stringent policing of it in some areas with its associated costs, the costs to the women, and to community relations in terms of social tension (Hubbard 1999). Narratives of sexual violence developed by the tabloid news media have been constantly re-used so that women working in prostitution are defined through a specific narrative of slavery and exploitation. 'Exploitation' however lacks definition in law and this has become even more of a problem in the Sexual Offences Act 2003. The issue of the vulnerability of women in prostitution is however an important one that cannot be reduced to 'exploitation' (however it is defined) and health workers and non-governmental organisations involved in HIV prevention have long concluded that sex workers are more at risk from client violence than they are from HIV (McKeganey and Barnard 1996) as do the women themselves (Sanders 2004). This chapter thus summarises the problems and issues around sex workers and their clients which led to the Sex Offences Review in 2000.

The chapter then examines the prevalence of prostitution within the wider context of the sexual leisure industry and the attempts to curtail prostitution and kerb-crawling through piecemeal and contradictory legislation, such as the Criminal Justice and Police Act 2001 which came into force before the end of the Review. It also explains why previous responses failed as they failed to take account of the reasons that impel women into prostitution, and failed to take account of who the men are or what psychosexual needs these men are trying to satisfy when buying commercial sex. The chapter thus provides the background and policy behind the legislative change in the provisions of the Sexual Offences Act 2003 and the Government Consultation Document *Paying the Price* in July 2004.

An historical overview

While there are some earlier historical accounts, it is only since Roman times that multiple records from differing sources have enabled us to understand attitudes to commercial sex; this period then becomes our starting point. Prostitution was an accepted part of life in the Roman Empire, and Roman scholars upheld a view that these men were protecting their marriages and those of their peers (Otis 1985). The idea is exemplified in the writings of Cato, who stipulated that 'blessed be they as virtuous, who when they feel their virile members swollen in lust, visit a brothel than grind at some husband's private mill' (Burford 1976: 18). Leaving aside the misogynistic metaphor of a married woman as a man's 'private mill', this is suggestive of the perceived righteousness of men who became the clients of prostitutes. These clients were ranked into a hierarchy, with the lowest economic classes such as slaves or soldiers visiting brothels, which catered specially for them (Bullough and Bullough 1987). Under Roman law, such men were not allowed to marry,[1] and under such circumstances it seems unsurprising that the purchase of sex was neither stigmatised nor considered reprehensible for these men. While it would appear that the women who provided sex were, along with their families, considered 'disgraced' (Bullough and Bullough 1987: 31), their male clients were accepted and encouraged in classical societies.

By the Dark Ages, the power of the Church was held to be absolute, and historians suggest that prostitution became defined by promiscuity rather than payment (e.g. Karras 1996). It appears that there was no immorality connected to the buying or selling of sex, but that promiscuity or sexual licence was considered immoral, and thus needed to be controlled (Ringdal 2004). Alongside this, a double standard that privileges male sexual desire is apparent in the writing of Church 'fathers' such as St. Augustine, St. Jerome and St. Basil, who claimed it was not the man's fault if he strayed sexually, but the woman's fault, if he or she did (Bullough and Bullough 1987).[2] This was because women, whom Medieval medical theory considered to be more lustful and to have a stronger sex drive than men, were expected to be more able to control any such sexual impulse. For men, on the other hand, a 'hydraulic' model of masculine sexuality seems to have dominated; a model in which 'people believed that pressure builds up and has to be released through a safety valve (marriage or prostitution), or eventually the dam will burst and men will commit seduction, rape, adultery, and sodomy' (Karras 1996: 6). St. Thomas Aquinas, for example, suggested that a man who wanted 'unnatural' (that is, non-procreative) sex acts should fulfil such desires with an already corrupt woman, rather than corrupt his wife. Whilst the sexual licence and freedom of women was regulated whether it was commercial or not, men were almost encouraged to engage in commercial sexual activities.[3] In addition, there is little evidence to suggest any regulation of these men other than banning some groups of men from being clients. These groups of men included Turks, Moors and Jews,[4] or certain employees banned by employers who feared their property would be stolen to pay for such pleasure.[5]

Throughout the Middle Ages, it is reported that towns began variously to regulate or outlaw commercial prostitution. Towns that outlawed prostitution either banished brothels to outside the town or punished the whores, there is no evidence to suggest that they punished any clients[6] (Karras 1996). In towns like Southwark where legal brothels or *stews* existed, they were regulated for the customers' protection. This was so that the men could not be compelled to purchase food or transport at inflated prices (Karras 1996).[7] Prostitution continued to be considered an appropriate outlet for men who did not have access to women through marriage, and Otis (1985) suggests that prostitution became institutionalised because men not only married late, but also outnumbered women owing to the disproportionate mortality of women, especially among the poor. Norbert Elias (1994) illustrates the conventional approach towards the prostitute client in Medieval society by providing an example from the *Colloquies* of Erasmus. In this text, the conversation between client and prostitute is provided as reading matter in a children's book on manners. Elias highlights the difference between Medieval manners and those of today by suggesting that 'to an observer from modern times, it seems surprising that Erasmus in his *Colloquies* should speak at all to a child of prostitutes and the houses in which they live' (1994: 144), but argues that this was a situation for which the Medieval boy child would be expected to learn specific manners. A further example concerns the Emperor Sigismund, who in 1443 publicly thanked the city magistrate at Bern for putting the brothel so freely at the disposal of himself and his attendants for three days (Elias 1994). In this way, it is possible to see what an everyday occurrence the purchase of sex appears to have been for Medieval men.

Who were the main clients? It is suggested by Karras (1996) that clients in England at this time were commonly apprentices, servants, foreign merchants travelling without their wives, and clergy[8] and Rossiaud (1988) describes a similar clientele in Medieval France.[9] From these two studies it appears that these men came from a broad spectrum of the population – a further indication that this practice was normalised across the community. Rossiaud also claims that visiting prostitutes or maintaining a concubine was acceptable so long as the man was free from ties, especially if the 'common' woman was from outside the village and therefore less likely to service his brothers and family (1988). Paying for sex *only* became an offence if the client was married, this was because he would be committing adultery (fornication) and thus breaking the sacrament that marriage became by the fifteenth century. Adultery was an arrestable offence, and like other sexual offences, was dealt with by the ecclesiastical courts under canon law.[10] There were two other types of court that upheld law at this time: county courts and manorial courts, but neither of these was involved with regulating clients. The only other form of censure of male clients who were violent towards the women, was public humiliation, often by hoisting the coat of arms of a man who attacked a prostitute onto a pole in front of a public house. In Genoa, for instance, any customer who hit a prostitute was obliged to pay her medical expenses and pay damages to the manager for work-time lost because of injury (Otis 1985). Thus clients were only regulated when they committed an act of adultery or violence, and that these were limited to financial payment or humiliation for the harm done. The commercial sex client's behaviour, otherwise, was sanctioned by law, religion and community norms. A transitory change in sexual morality seems to have occurred in the late Middle Ages, which subsequently influenced the way the purchaser of sex was regarded at the end of the fifteenth and throughout the sixteenth centuries. This moral climate is reflected in edicts from Reformation leaders and in the canons of the Council of Trent.[11] Concubinage was condemned and laws were imposed against male adultery (Otis 1985). The city authorities in Puritan London enforced strict sexual morality and, while brothels apparently still existed, many such as those in Southwark were closed down by 1546. Although this move to close brothels in the sixteenth century was part of a general reaction against the sexual activity of young unmarried men,[12] it was the prostitutes rather than their clients who were regularly punished by being whipped and pilloried (Briggs *et al.* 1996). The Counter-Reformation too, took a stand against youthful fornication and Otis argues that brothels were no longer considered as a necessary escape-valve for male sexual appetites, but as centres of evil where young men might learn of lust and corruption (1985). Thus the commercial client, even under conditions of prohibition, was seen as a weak soul to be saved from the depravity of women in brothels rather than as someone actively seeking their services.

The morality enforced on the male client nevertheless proved to be short-lived and, as Roberts reports, clients in late Elizabethan times outnumbered prostitutes especially in places like Southwark, where they are said to have 'constantly roved the area in pursuit of pleasure' (1993: 123). From 1640 onwards, Covent Garden was a popular haunt for clients 'active' beneath the arches of the Piazza in the centre, as were the new coffee houses that established themselves throughout the seventeenth century.[13] By the 1700s, large numbers of unmarried men were a consequence of the tradition of the landed families to leave their wealth to the male heir, leaving less money for younger sons, many of whom had to forego marriage (Stone 1977). The purchase of commercial sexual services by such men was consequently looked upon benignly. They were not, however, the only client group, and married men also appeared to be frequent purchasers of sexual services according to noted diarists of the time – although it is hard to discern from historians such as Stone (1977) what the general attitudes towards married clients were, especially since the main examples given are such inveterate rakes such as Pepys and Boswell. One suggestion that emerges very clearly from such diaries, and which is an important factor in understanding wider social attitudes to the men who purchased sex in the eighteenth century, is that it was often condoned within a marital relationship as a form of contraception. Women who did not want more pregnancies were more likely to legitimate their husbands' extra-marital sexual activities with prostitutes (Stone 1977). Given the dangers of childbirth, this tradition continued until the following century, with Victorian husbands justifying their activities with prostitutes on this basis.

Victorian attitudes towards prostitutes and clients

It is well documented that it was a tradition throughout Victorian England for upper-class men to have their initial sexual experiences with prostitutes (Humphries 1988), the first of which typically took place while away at university. These men received little more than a reprimand, however, if caught by the authorities.[14] In their comprehensive history of prostitution, Bullough and Bullough (1989) suggest that Victorian clients mainly came from the middle and upper classes. A conflicting view is put forward by Briggs *et al.* (1996), who argue that 'rich young libertines and philandering middle-class husbands were a real but comparatively insignificant presence in the market. Most clients were poor men paying very small sums to even poorer women' (1996: 199).

Although attempts to reconstruct the Victorian client are difficult because of the inadequacies of records, Hall (1991) contends that it is nonetheless apparent that vast numbers of men of all classes paid for sex, and that the attitudes of legislators and judges provide important insight into how such men were regarded by society and the law. Examples of these attitudes can be seen in debates recorded on the

Criminal Law Amendment Bill of 1920, where it was proclaimed by Lord Dawson that men up to the age of 25 years were powerless against the 'allurements' of girls under 17 (Hall 1991: 48). This construction of the male client as a helpless victim could also be seen in literature and the arts.[15] The image of the innocent male seduced by the self-seeking immoral female permeated the discourse on prostitution in Victorian England (and Ireland) to become enshrined in the Contagious Diseases Acts of 1864, 1866, and 1869 (Walkowitz 1992). These Acts defined venereal diseases as transmitted by women, and forced the women to undergo medical checks to protect their male clients' health (Faugier and Sargeant 1997) as the perception of the prostitute as 'abnormal' and criminal remained pervasive (Lombroso 1885). Their clients by contrast, were ignored in regulatory practice and were portrayed as behaving naturally in the eyes of the medical establishment and the law. The client's legal position remained relatively stable because it was not against the law for a man to solicit a woman for sex. Only if he caused any nuisance by soliciting could he be 'bound over' to keep the peace for which an old statute, the Justices of the Peace Act 1361 was used. This has since been considered an uncertain and inadequate statute for dealing with the matter, and in 1983 Susan Edwards observed that it was rarely invoked and men remained free from censure.[16] Such freedom from censure occurred also because medical opinion continued to stress the need not only for men to be able to satisfy their sexual urges, but to do so in specific ways. Indeed, as the Victorian bourgeoisie began to medicalise sexuality and move it into the home, modern sexology began to penalise and stigmatise certain behaviours.[17]

Havelock Ellis promoted the scientific study of sexuality from the 1890s (Segal 1994) and Walkowitz (1992) suggests the role of positivist science emerged as the authoritative discourse and epistemology, which led to a differentiated account of gender that pathologised female sexuality (stressing sexual purity in women) and at the same time, naturalised male sexuality. The general feeling amongst Victorian doctors and organisations who saw male masturbation as self-abusive and destructive, provided the ground for accepting men's continued use of prostitutes throughout the Victorian period. This was because the purchase of sex was considered preferable to the perversion of self-abasement or its main alternative – the debasement of pure women. Following this period, however, a significant social movement was to alter general social expectations, which in turn changed the way in which the conduct of male clients was perceived.

Modernity and changing ideals

The period 1890–1930 is generally taken as embracing the major transformations of social and philosophical thought, aesthetic codes and practices that have shaped our modern consciousness (Wolff 1994). It is within this period that we can see significant social changes with regard to the payment for sex, as the concept of conjugal love was progressively promoted, not least by Havelock Ellis in his pamphlet *Sex in Relation to Society*.[18] It became less acceptable for a man to go to prostitutes and Hall argues that many more men chose not to indulge in such a 'crude financial transaction' (1991: 51). This change in attitude is also convincingly illustrated in the correspondence Marie Stopes received from men, following the publication of her book *Married Love* in 1918. These men wrote to express their sexual anxieties and to request advice and information. One man wrote: 'The idea of going to prostitutes was always repugnant to my ideas because I could not bring myself to the idea of sleeping with a girl whom I did not love and who did not love me'. Another man illustrates commercial sex as the commonly accepted expedient: 'of course the usual advice is to seek the prostitute but I do not want that' (Stopes 1918). Men also began to see it as a slight on their attractiveness if they had to pay for company rather than attract it. The subsequent lower demand for services reduced prostitute numbers, and by 1930 convictions of prostitutes had gone down to 1,110 in England and Wales from a previous high of 2,350 the decade before (Briggs 1996: 185).

Despite this conceptual shift in attitude towards men who purchased sex, involving an apparent valorisation of conjugal sex, some feminists, most notably Millet (1970), identify conservative trends in sexuality between 1930–1960 as being due to the widespread influence of Freud.[19] However, whilst interpretations of Freud's writings may have influenced explanations as to why men paid women for sex, this is not without some difference of opinion as to the value of Freud's explanations. On the one hand, Millet (1970) condemns Freudian ideas in which she contends that 'women are inherently subservient, and males dominant, more strongly sexed and therefore entitled to sexually subjugate the female, who enjoys her oppression and deserves it'[20] (Millet 1970: 203). On the other hand, feminists such as Segal (1994) credit Freud for the impact of his writing on the liberation of sexuality from essentialist biological discourses. Indeed, it is argued that Freud contributed towards a theory of sexuality that is socially constructed (in that no part of a person's sexuality – paid or otherwise) can be separated from the influences on early psychic life. Chodorow's (1994) interpretation that the stronger sex drive of the man, when faced with the sexual repression[21] of his bourgeois wife (which developed during childhood) would also account for his turn elsewhere for sexual satisfaction (that is, towards sex workers). It is further suggested by Chodorow (1994) that other Freudian concepts such as the masculine Oedipus complex also offered an explanation in that it would lead to the contempt for women (as penis-less) creatures within the complex. In this way Freudian theory arguably explains the role of the client, who, because of his contempt and fear of woman, can only fully express himself sexually with an inferior (that is, a sex worker). Psychoanalysis therefore, as a discipline, whilst seemingly ignoring the role of the client,[22] *has* arguably had a profound influence (whether conservative or otherwise) on *the way in which* the role of the client was interpreted at this time.

In the decades before and after World War II, it is reported that prostitutes continued to be seen as deviant pathological individuals, but the resort to prostitution for the male client, whilst still seen as inevitable, given the dominance of male sexuality, became less socially acceptable than ever before (Sullivan 1997). In 1948, Kinsey, Pomeroy and Martin (controversially) reported that over two-thirds of white males had visited sex workers at least once, and 15 per cent had visited on a regular basis. Generational differences were also noted, with young men having only two-thirds of the contact with sex workers that older males had experienced at the same period in their lives. Higher education was negatively correlated with contact with sex workers. It was presumed therefore, that the trend of visiting sex workers was diminishing in younger generations, especially within higher social classes who might have had greater access to education (Kinsey *et al.* 1948). In 1955, a study called *Women of the Streets* was published which portrayed the 150 sex workers interviewed as understandably alienated, but otherwise honest and hardworking. Their clients however, were described as cheating on their wives, and being dishonest in other ways (Roiph 1955). Both studies contributed to the increasing social disapproval of men who paid for sex, and the first statute in England to specifically outlaw the public purchasing of sex by men came in a section (section 32) of the Sexual Offences Act 1956.[23] It became an offence for 'a man persistently to solicit or importune in a public place for immoral purposes'. The aim of this statute was to penalise the soliciting of females either by the punter or by a pimp who touted for clients, but the Divisional Court later held that 'it does not apply to the man who accosts women for sexual intercourse' and so, with few exceptions, it was applied for homosexual soliciting.[24] Whilst this first legal constraint missed its intended target, the clients of sex workers came under scrutiny in the post-war era more and more, and from the late 1950s, the client increasingly became represented as a legal and sexual deviant for two reasons: the Wolfenden Report (1957) and the so-called sexual revolution of the 1960s.

The impact of the Wolfenden Report[25] was that some private consensual behaviours such as homosexuality and prostitution became regarded as a matter for private morality, and were removed from the law's jurisdiction, except when a 'public nuisance' was created. Shortly afterwards, the Street Offences Act of 1959 increased control over any such public behaviour, and Phoenix (1999) argues that prostitution became conceptualised as being 'publicly offensive'. The Act also prompted a change in the conceptualisation of the client, making him more visible and problematic as the main offences included: loitering and soliciting by a 'common prostitute' in a street or public place for the purposes of prostitution (section 1(1)); solicitation of men for immoral purposes (section 32); kerb-crawling (section 1(1)); persistent solicitation of women for the purposes of prostitution (section 2(1)). The Act therefore controlled the manner by which sex workers and clients contacted each other, and heralded the 'negative regulationist approach' that has arguably framed the British law on prostitution today (Phoenix 1999).

Discursive changes have also taken place in law-makers' understanding of those who purchase sex, these views have been underpinned by shifts in the sexual culture and subsequent understanding of what constitutes 'normal' sexuality (Sullivan 1997). The 'so-called' sexual revolution, with better contraception and greater acceptance of women's sexual freedom outside marriage meant that the average 'normal' male should have no need to visit prostitutes.[26] More companionate forms of sexuality with an emphasis on love and mutual sexual desire became dominant social themes, and Sullivan (1997) argues that paying for sex increasingly became seen as a deviant sexual practice. Accordingly, by the 1960s, social scientists began to attempt to question what *kind* of men would consider paying for sex, not least Mancini (1963), who could only explain the commercial sex client in terms of deviance. It was argued that the men who go to prostitutes were unable to find sexual satisfaction elsewhere:

> They are so physically unattractive, that only a prostitute would consent to having anything to do with them ...; others

demand some unusual technique that they cannot get from a normal woman and are moreover attracted by the atmosphere of prostitution which excites them. Then there are the abnormal, the psychiatric cases, the impotent, the maniacs or sadists, the lovers of the whip, boots and other perversions. (Mancini 1963: 70)

Thus the conservative view of men who paid for sex were considered to have aberrant sexual desires that could not be accommodated within a 'normal' relationship, or as social misfits who could not forge relationships with 'normal' women – perhaps even because of a lack of English in the case of immigrant men (Sullivan 1997). However, within some circles, such as those that were artistic or bohemian, it remained a regular practice. The writer Graham Greene, for example, was open about the amount of time he spent with sex working women.

The transformation of intimacy in post-modernity

By the late 1960s, social expectations of relationships changed views still further about men who paid for sex. The sexual 'libertarianism' proclaimed by movements of the 1960s and the emergence of 'plastic sexuality'[27] arguably sustained a rise in the ideals of romantic love as a socially desirable *normative* state. Ostensibly, a change took place in the expectation of relationships, in what Giddens terms 'the transformation of intimacy'(1992: 34), and Beck (1992) refers to as the 'idealisation of modern love'[28] and sexual exclusivity the ideal (Giddens 1992). Monogamy came to refer not to the relationship itself, but sexual exclusivity as a criterion of trust. This model has circulated globally and as Connell (1998) points out, although it has not displaced indigenous models, it has interacted with, and heavily influenced them. It has had a hegemonic influence on social attitudes and the law. To go outside a monogamous 'relationship' and purchase intimacy or sexual practices violates these idealistic cultural customs.

Throughout the following decades, media portrayals of male clients have strengthened negative attitudes *and* subsequent legislation against the male client. This is evident in the media anxiety surrounding the case of a single client whose dangerousness to vulnerable women was documented throughout the 1980s (Jouve 1986; Smith 1989; Segal 1990). Between 1975 and 1981, 13 women (of whom 7 were sex workers) were killed by Peter Sutcliffe in the north of England.

The case of the 'Yorkshire Ripper' led to women's fear and anger, which Walkowitz (1992) argues fuelled an anti-violence campaign. The Criminal Law Revision Committee of 1975 had already begun to address the issue of kerb-crawling as the continued newspaper notoriety accorded to Peter Sutcliffe, contributed to the public condemnation of men who purchase street sex.[29] In Cambridge, a small conference explored the issue of sex offenders, and one of the speakers, Lloyd Trott, concluded that an accurate typology of prostitutes' clients was necessary and that 'much of the other research will be pointless if the role and needs of clients continue to be ignored' (1979: 134). Whilst the Sutcliffe case highlighted the vulnerability of sex working women, and progress was made in some respects when the Criminal Justice Act 1982 (which amended the 1959 legislation to abolish the use of imprisonment for women convicted of soliciting), Trott's advice to consider commercial clients continued to be ignored. The law thus proceeded to criminalise the client despite scant knowledge about him.

In 1984, the Criminal Law Revision Committee published its Sixteenth Report and the Sex Offences Bill was first brought to Parliament by MP Janet Fookes (Criminal Law Revision Committee 1984) and the Sexual Offences Act 1985 followed.[30] The Act specifically created an offence for any man who:

> solicits a woman for the purposes of prostitution from or near a motor vehicle, persistently ... or in such a manner likely to cause annoyance to the woman solicited, or nuisance to other persons in the neighbourhood' (section 1); or, in a street or public place 'persistently solicits a woman for the purpose of prostitution (section 2).

These offences were triable summarily only and subject to the maximum fines, and in the following year, 1986, 220 men were charged, of which 189 men pleaded or were found guilty (Home Office 1986). The statute thus created a new category of offence, that of kerb-crawling, and the legal position of men changed in England and Wales. [31] In practice, the legislation was hard to enforce because the police had difficulty gathering evidence (Edwards 1993). Not surprisingly therefore, there were moves to make it easier to prosecute by removing the need for the police to prove the man's 'persistence'.

In 1990 Sir William Shelton introduced a Sexual Offences Bill to Parliament that sought to remove the requirement that kerb-crawling be 'persistent or likely to cause annoyance or nuisance' from the law (Hansard Parliamentary Debates, 6 July 1990, col. 1291). The Bill was ostensibly brought about in response to 'constituency feeling and fear', but was talked out by Ken Livingstone who rightly pointed out that toughening approaches against kerb-crawlers might increase the victimisation of both men and women. He feared that the Bill would provide a Trojan horse with which to bring in a new 'sus' law to use against Black, Irish, immigrant and working-class men police might want to charge for quite unconnected purposes. Using the persuasive arguments of the Campaign against Kerb-crawling Legislation[32] it was thought that the Bill would add to prostitutes and other women's vulnerability to violence by: 'forcing working women further underground: curtailing the time available for prostitute women to 'sus out' clients nervous about arrest before going with them; committing more police time and resources to prostitution rather than rape and other violent crimes' (Hansard Parliamentary Debates, 6 July 1990, col. 1291).

There were two important issues around this Bill that illustrate social attitudes to the purchase of sex. One was the strong support the Bill received from the House, most robustly from the Minister of State, David Mellor, as well as MPs Teresa Gorman and Kate Hoey, which indicates a political *interpretation* of public feeling. The second issue revolves around the fact that the subsequent national and local media attacks on Ken Livingstone illustrate the media opinion of the time against the kerb-crawler. Media coverage ran to large columns in all the national broadsheets, up to half a page in some papers (see, for example, The Times, 12 May 1990: 4; Daily Mirror, 12 May 1990: 9). Whilst the front page of the Daily Express unhelpfully suggested that 'MP is condemned for putting women at risk' (12 May 1990), even the local press, usually sympathetic to Mr Livingstone, reported that 'Mr Livingstone filibustered until the set time for the end of the debate' (Kilburn and Willesden Recorder, 16 May 1990: 2). The dust slowly settled on the Shelton Bill and the issues were not taken up by others.

The impact of the HIV crisis on perceptions of prostitution

In the final two decades of the last century there were three other major social issues which have seemingly impacted on how sex workers and their clients have been perceived: the HIV crisis; an increasing awareness of the feminisation of poverty, and increased awareness of child sexual abuse and the subsequent rhetoric of fear. During the 1980s, the media linked HIV infection to sexual excess, 'perversity' or abnormality (McDowell 1998). Whilst homosexuality was linked to HIV via sexual activity and the heroin addict through intravenous drug use, sex working women were linked through their involvement in prostitution in order to support drug use. HIV infection was associated with behaviours deemed to be deviant and illegal and transmission of the disease was considered for criminalisation (Young 1996).[33]

The client became linked with not only deceiving others, but also travelling from one site of infection to another, linking the world of the 'morally correct' with the underworld of the 'sexually deviant' as Alison Young (1996: 200) suggests bisexual men were. Metaphors of a 'war' against disease and a 'war' against crime intersected and by 1990, the number of men proceeded against for kerb-crawling was 1,470 (Edwards 1993). Four years later, and in parallel with an apparent slowing down of the spread of HIV and its accompanying media panic, the figures of men charged with soliciting dropped to 1,185 (Home Office Criminal Statistics 1994). Writing at the end of the 1980s, Bullough and Bullough (1987) argued that proportionately fewer men were buying sex than in the past and with less frequency. The reasons cited were *inter alia*, women's greater sexual freedom, greater occupational choice, the availability of contraception, the increasing availability of divorce so that non-compatible couples need not stay together, the rise in non-marital live-in relationships, and the erosion of the 'culturally supported' myth that men enjoy, need or want sex more than women. These reasons also help to explain the increasingly punitive conservatism that developed against commercial street clients.

The feminisation of poverty

At the same time, the 'feminisation of poverty' – the social change and lack of welfare policies in the wake of the Thatcher-Major regimes that extended the social hardship of women (Glendinning and Miller 1992) played a part in the way that sex working women are socially constructed. By the late 1990s, 9 out of 10 lone parent families were headed by a woman, with many single parent women forced to rely on benefits or low pay in the part-time work sector with a lack of childcare facilities, and struggling daily to avoid hardship and debt (Franks 1999). The English Collective of Prostitutes argued that 75 per cent of women sex workers were lone mothers (ECP 1997: 90). The choice of sex work began to be seen as rational 'resistance', if not courageous choice, in the face of poverty (Scambler and Scambler 1997).[34] Recent research showed that a large proportion were lone parents who entered prostitution to care financially for their children, often the result of the father leaving the relationship and not providing maintenance for the child. For those not used to life on welfare benefits the drastic reduction in quality of life was too severe and prostitution was a financial solution (Sanders 2004: 48). The unfortunate client however attracted vilification for being seen to cash in on the economic disadvantage of these women rather than as an honest partner in a consensual commercial contract.

The growing rhetoric of public protection

Awareness of the economic situation and lack of employment choices of women has been accompanied by a growing awareness of the victimisation of vulnerable children. The involvement of children in prostitution as a strategy for survival has been illustrated in a series of reports by the Children's Society and Barnardo's.[35] These reports revealed children let down by the State in care systems, excluded from school, in violent domestic situations, and at risk at the hands of punters and pimps, and they provide grounds for radical separatist women's groups and the moral right to consider clients' involvement in prostitution in a more abusive vein irrespective of his own situation. With support from the Association of Chief Police Officers (ACPO), Government guidelines recommended that the police respond to juveniles in terms of the Children Act 1989 rather than the criminal law – emphasising that children should be given protection from harm and abuse and the *'primary law enforcement effort must be against abusers'* (emphasis added) (Home Office 1998: 4). In this they meant the pimps and the traffickers who coerce and abuse children, but the ordinary punter who seeks a consensual contract with another adult has increasingly and erroneously been conflated with such characters.

A wider social factor that has possibly impacted on this concerns the emergence of a 'risk culture' – a culture in which Beck (1992) contends that as wealth production and patterns of society have changed along with new forms of pluralised unemployment (with all the associated hazards and opportunities), efforts to lessen risk have become paramount (1992). This is linked with notions of a culture of anxiety and fear of crime (Hollway and Jefferson 1997) as public fear has increased further in the wake of cases of predatory paedophiles.[36] Public protection has become an increasing feature of criminal justice policy and the political ticket on which Nash (1999) argues that more punitive policies have been brought in. The Home Office White Paper *Protecting the Public* declared that: '... the public should receive proper protection from persistent violent and sexual offenders' (1996: 48). Within this wider political and legislative climate of increasing punitiveness, tougher approaches have been implemented which target those committing acts including violence, sex or drugs (Nash 1999).

A new approach was tried, however, under the guise of 'kerb-crawler rehabilitation schools' to target ordinary punters. In the early 1990s 'schools' for clients began to gather momentum – particularly in the US; the first school developed in the UK was in 1998 (Bindel 1998; 1999). The idea of schools is essentially that 'clients/offenders' might be rehabilitated or 'educated' out of their desire to pay women for sex. Kerb-crawler rehabilitation schools are based on the erroneous premise that prostitution is a crime, and secondly that it has many victims – the prostitute, the neighbourhood, non-paid partners of clients. Thirdly, it is believed that individual men are responsible, and that it is possible to educate these men out of buying sex with a day's 'schooling'. The schools largely involve one day workshops during which clients (some of whom are not convicted) are warned of the penalties of reoffending, lectured on the effects of prostitution and soliciting on neighbourhoods, and alerted to various health dangers concerning sexually transmittable diseases. There are also presentations from prostitute 'survivors' who tell embittered stories of abuse and their repulsion for clients, and from families who have experienced the death of a child through prostitution (Monto 2000). In a punitive American legal climate, where criminalisation is the reigning paradigm (see Weitzer 2000, for an account of the politics of prostitution in America) these schools gathered momentum in the 1990s. They were piloted in the UK in 1998 (Bindel 1998; 1999).

John's schools – the start of a dangerous approach

On a theoretical level it is argued that the school curriculum ignores gender and power issues, and the economic marginalisation of women sex workers. As one critic put it: 'such procedures ... abstract prostitution from its systemic and structural roots and treat it merely as a question of individual morality' (O'Connell Davidson 1998: 199). On a practical level, these schools and the intensive policing that goes with them have been dangerous for sex workers, who report increased likelihood of arrest themselves. Many of the women have reported that they have worked longer hours or in more isolated areas (away from their usual forms of support such as outreach teams and other sex workers to whom they could run for help) as well as lessening their power to intuit safety in the first stages of the negotiation with a client. There have been further criticisms that the operation of the schools diverts resources from other developments revolving around women's safety needs, and that the course content – designed to humiliate and shame clients – has had the effect of increasing violence towards women sex workers.[37] Moreover, the practice of sending unconvicted men to such 'schools' raised human rights issues regarding the right to a fair trial. In the UK, health organisations, social justice organisations, and academics expressed concern about such schools shortly after their inception (Kinnell 2000; Self 1999a). Following a groundswell of critical opinion the UK schools ceased to exist although some schools remain in the US (Monto 2000), and attempts to revive them in the UK occur periodically. Recent examples occurred in Hampshire by the Probation Service (see Shell, Campbell and Caren 1999) and in Hull (Home Office 2004b). The latter consisted of only 13 people being 'educated' for half a day.

As the penalties for all areas covered by sex offences legislation were moved 'up-tariff', so has kerb-crawling, and on 1 April 1997 kerb-crawling became a recordable offence. Subsequent legislation has allowed the police to obtain non-intimate samples for DNA analysis from offenders who are charged, reported or cautioned for any recordable offence. This came in section 4 of the Criminal Evidence (Amendment) Act 1997[38] and the legislation is deliberately inclusive, and specifies that: 'sexual offences include all offences with any sexual connotation whatsoever' (S.I. 1997/566). Since September 1998, samples have been taken from all men charged with kerb-crawling under sections 1 and 2 of the Sexual Offences Act 1985, and these samples are maintained on the national database. Human rights debates stemming from the implementation of the Human Rights Act 1998 include DNA sample-taking, particularly with regard to Article 3 concerning degrading and inhumane treatment and Article 8 concerning the right to private and family life. The formulation of policy remains on thin ground theoretically and empirically with regard to the taking of DNA from men who hire women for sexual purposes.

A new Trojan horse?

By the turn of the century, the protection of the public and the fear of dangerous offenders had reached the top of the criminal justice agenda (Nash 1999). The perceived importance of public protection heralded the Sex Offenders Act 1997 and the creation of a sex offender register, placing the onus on the police to assess and manage risk.[39] The rhetoric of public protection is also enshrined in proposals of the Crime and Disorder Act 1998 (for example in sections 2 and 3 regarding sex offender orders, in which the police also have to assess risk).

The political mood shifted dramatically in the last two decades and the power of summary arrest over kerb-crawlers in the legislation enabled the police to take men into custody and question them rather than having to summons men to appear in the magistrates' court to answer a charge. In practice, the officers have also searched the men's homes (Brain 2002) and, more controversially, took non-intimate DNA samples for the national DNA database. A public consultation exercise began in January 1999 for a wholesale review of sexual offences and the commissioned literature review made a recommendation that 'Greater consideration be given to appropriate legal responses to both "forced" and "voluntary" prostitution'.[40] This insightful distinction was blurred in the subsequent report, *Setting the Boundaries*[41] into the recommendation for a further review of prostitution more generally.[42] While the Home Office lamented the piecemeal way in which laws had been applied to prostitution, it continued to produce legislation in an extemporised fashion. Anti-social behaviour orders (ASBOs), brought in under section 1 of the Crime and Disorder Act 1998 had the effect of re-introducing imprisonment for women sex workers.[43] In 2001 the Government strengthened the Sexual Offences Act 1985 when the police were given the power of arrest over kerb-crawlers. In addition, the placing of prostitutes' cards in a public place – 'carding' – was made into a new criminal offence. These amendments in sections 46 and 47 of the Criminal Justice and Police Act 2001 were enacted before any intervention had been trialled or evaluated.[44] Against those convicted of kerb-crawling, fines were increased to a maximum of £1,000 and conditional cautions were introduced as part of the Criminal Justice Act to 'make it a condition that "offenders" are forced to face up to the consequences of their behaviour.' Further measures enabled courts to be notified of provisions under the Powers of Criminal Courts (Sentencing) Act 2001 to consider driver disqualification for as long as the court considered appropriate.[45]

The Government White Paper *Protecting the Public*[46] put forward a number of proposals on prostitution which included the gender equalisation of the law, and a promise to examine the scope for a full-scale review of the issues surrounding prostitution. The Sexual Offences (Amendment) Bill took forward in legislation many of the proposals in *Protecting the Public*. During its passage questions were asked in both Houses, but particularly in the Lords, about the conflation of women and children in sex work, and also the confusion of trafficking and exploitation with voluntary prostitution, in the Bill.[47] The Home Affairs Committee (HAC) published a report on the Bill on 10 July 2003.[48] One-sixth of the published submissions were from interested groups dissatisfied by the angle taken by the Government's enquiries into the laws on sex work. Yet the Government's reply contained no mention of prostitution, but focused on other controversial areas of the Bill.[49] Interested parties began to complain of the difficulties in accessing information from the Government on the timing or remit of the consultation[50] and only persistent direct questions such as those by Lord Faulkner[51] delivered any information about the progress of the review. A further White Paper *Respect and Responsibility*[52] underlined the Government's commitment to the increasing penalties against sex workers' clients on the grounds of 'nuisance' to residents and the vulnerability of sex workers.[53] The Sexual Offences Act 2003 came into effect in May 2004.[54] In it, were a number of proposals which criminalised the client further. For example, kerb-crawling was made gender neutral so that it applies to women as well as men. The Act includes an offence of accepting a sexual service from a person under 18 and many increased penalties such as offences of causing or inciting (adult) prostitution for gain. Offences include trafficking into, within and out of the UK for sexual exploitation. It also provided the option of withdrawing driving licences from kerb-crawlers. The sections on prostitution, when taken with the new and very widely drawn definitions of 'prostitution', 'payment', 'gain', and 'sexual' and sections on voyeurism create further creeping inroads into the lives of sex workers and their clients (see Bainham and Brooks-Gordon 2004; Self 2006).

The increased criminalisation of commercial sexual activity seems contradictory when set against a contemporary climate in which most sexual activity has become commodified. For example, contemporary culture has not only seen the proliferation of high street sex shops, lap-dancing clubs, but sex toys are now sold in provincial department stores, hotel chains offer adult-only films as part of the standard in-room film package, and one of the main terrestrial channels, Channel Five, devotes its evening coverage to programmes about, or containing, sexual activity outside monogamous relationships. Sex trade terminology has become standard on prime-time TV in programmes such as *Pimp My Ride*, pop videos show rappers groping near-naked women, the women in *Big Brother* recently enacted a porn scene, and it has been argued that even shampoo commercials address the product's orgasmic potential (Everett 2005). The wider sexual leisure industry has increased exponentially in all spheres, yet a dual standard exists for honest clients wanting to pay a consenting adult for an hour or so of the real thing. It remains to be seen how much further this dichotomy will be pushed as the Sexual Offences Act 2003 was rapidly followed by the Government Consultation Document *Paying the Price* in July 2004. This document put forward a number of proposals which will be discussed in depth in chapter 2 alongside the extant legislation on prostitution and subsequent government strategy.

Chapter summary

An historical outline can thus reveal the 'trends and shifts in moral, ideological and symbolic images and associations' relating to this aspect of sex work (O'Neill 1997: 19), and can provide a glimpse of how the disciplines of philosophy, theology, canon and civil law have variously approached the question of prostitution. The role of the contemporary 'punter' is essential to an understanding of prostitution, for it is often argued that if men did not create a demand for it, prostitution would cease to exist (see, for example, Kinnell 1989; Sharpe 1998). This chapter has outlined the social and legal construction of the status of men who have purchased sexual access to women's bodies throughout history. This has moved from acceptance in Roman times; through the Dark Ages and Medieval period(s) whereby clients were normalised and acknowledged, the institutionalisation of sex work in the fourteenth and fifteenth centuries, and (despite a transitory prohibition period in the sixteenth century), to a time when the purchase of sex was readily justified and re-established. Such clients were highly visible in the seventeenth century, and their activities looked upon benignly and accepted as birth control throughout the eighteenth century.[55] More recently, the Victorian man who went to prostitutes was normalised in the discourses of medicine and the law. However, a transformation took place in the twentieth century, and as Norbert Elias (1994) points out, practices that were once typical and acceptable, are now deviant. In the past two decades the client who buys sex publicly has become criminalised to the degree that purchase of sexual access to a woman's body is not only perceived as criminally and sexually deviant; by the beginning of the new millennium, the client was also considered to be a seemingly dangerous figure.

Despite some historical and cultural variation, this historical map captures broad structures of change, and notions that the client's deviance was perhaps first viewed through a social, and then legal lens, although, as Johnson (1997) suggests, rhetorical, psychoanalytical and political structures are so profoundly implicated in one another that it is impossible to disentangle and uncover which came first. In common with many legal developments, due to periods of repression and liberalisation, the criminalisation of the client has not taken place in continuous linear fashion but has happened at an uneven pace. As a result, the client's legal status is discussed more in terms of trends than absolutes, and I argue that the overall trend has been one of increasing criminalisation while that of the sex worker has been one of increased vulnerability as her clients' illegal status results in a concomitant loss of rights to the sex worker (see Agustín 2005).

Despite 'up-tariffing' in terms of the categorisation of kerb-crawling and punitive interventionist policies and strategies, the commercial sex client has become increasingly problematic to criminal law, not least because the majority of legal interventions have taken place in the absence of empirical research on this group of men. Focusing on sex workers and their clients, I have briefly traced the historical development of social attitudes and the law in order to examine shifting social and legal conceptions in relation to men's use of sex workers. This serves to highlight the changing direction of the present law. I have summarised the problems and issues that led up to the Sexual Offences Review in 2000, the Sexual Offences Act 2003 and which culminated in the Government review of prostitution in July 2004. Chapter 2 outlines the laws that relate to prostitution and regulate the men and women who transact commercial sex and explores the Government review of prostitution and subsequent strategy document of January 2006.

Notes

1 Slaves were not allowed to marry at all, and soldiers were not allowed to marry during their twenty-year period in the army.

2 This double standard of morality, and women's subordinate status in society, appears to have persisted also throughout Islamic countries, India, and China between Roman and Medieval times. Perhaps one of the key elements to remember is that attitudes towards prostitutes and their clients have been recorded by men, some of whom were likely to have been clients themselves.

3 At this time a whore was someone who engaged in sex in a reprehensible way, for example, with a large number of men, with a priest, or with a man other than her husband. This wider use of the term is reflected in court records which show women prosecuted as whores who were not commercial prostitutes, and there is no difference in Medieval English between the words that mean 'common women' for women common to all, and those who charge money (Karras 1996: 131).

4 This was because the Church feared apostasy in the sexual intimacy between Christians and other groups. Jewish writers too, were opposed to such intimacies between Jews and Gentiles (Bullough and Bullough 1987: 127).

5 For example, the Fuller's Company of London in 1488 ordered their apprentices 'not to use or haunt the stews side' or red light area for this reason (Karras 1996: 76).

6 The towns of Oxford and Cambridge categorised such women (including commercial prostitutes) as 'immoral'. In 1317 and 1327 the king required the local authorities of Cambridge to banish whores, and in 1459 the Chancellor of the University received the power to banish them himself.

7 The portrayal of 'Janet of the Stews' in Piers Plowman is an example of a practitioner plying a dishonest trade.

8 A fifteenth century text, *The Speculum Sacerdotale*, implied that unmarried men were most likely to visit prostitutes because they had no wives (Karras 1996: 114). Priests, however, could be punished for doing so in towns where prostitution was legally proscribed. The town of Gloucester in the early sixteenth century for example, ordained punishment 'if any such priests or religious daily haunt queans within any Ward of the town, or walk by night suspiciously, or practice unlawful demeanour with whores, strumpets, or with men's wives' (Karras 1996: 77).

9 Records show that between 1442 and 1492 in Dijon, brothel incidents requiring intervention indicated a population of workingmen, artisans and merchants from 18 to 40 years of age, three-quarters of whom lived in the city: 'foreigners' and outsiders, including domestic servants, soldiers and the poor, form just over one-quarter of the client population (Rossiaud 1988: 38).

10 For example, the synod at Avignon banned the entrance of married men (and priests) to prostitutional bathhouses. The regulations of Aubignan and Loriol in 1487 forbade a prostitute to 'commit adultery with any man, nor any man with her' (Otis 1985: 108).

11 Despite the differences between the Catholic and Protestant ideals of marriage (the Protestant model being neither a sacrament nor indissoluble), both prohibited adultery.

12 In July 1548, a whore of the stews was found *in flagrante delicto* near Finsbury Court with one of the king's trumpeters. It is significant to note that while he was not punished at all, the whore was led to Cheap where 'she was set on the pillory, her hair cut off and a paper sent on her breast detailing her vicious life' (Briggs *et al.* 1996: 44).

13 Wolff (1994) points out that because the public world has been traditionally closed to the 'respectable woman' the only women visible in these places were so-called 'venal' women.

14 Students at Oxford or Cambridge received only a verbal warning if caught with prostitutes, whereas the women were tried and sentenced by vice-chancellors' courts and later imprisoned in either the 'Spinning House' (for example, see the case of Daisy Hopkins 1894) in Cambridge or the Clarendon 'rooms' in Oxford (Humphries 1988).

15 For example, a lecture by Ruskin entitled 'Of Queen and Gardens' in Sesame and Lilies summed the 'masculine fantasy one might call the official Victorian attitude', whilst the prostitute was the period 'avatar of feminine evil' (Millet 1970: 89).

16 Although this statute was later revived; Nottingham Anti-Vice Squad and Bournemouth Vice Squad revived the statute in 1995, for example (Benson and Matthews 1995b).

17 For example, Krafft-Ebing's *Psychopathia Sexualis* ran to 12 editions between 1886 and 1903. In this, Krafft-Ebing stressed the destructive potential of sexuality and pathologised many sexual practices as perversions.

18 This was followed by *The Objects of Marriage, The Erotic Rights of Women* (1918), and *The Play Function of Sex* (1921), all of which provided a groundbreaking attitude towards sexual expectation of marriage. A further revolutionary tract, *The Hygiene of Marriage* was later published by Isabel Hutton in 1923.

19 Two papers in particular that are cited are 'Some Psychological Consequences of the Anatomical Distinctions Between the Sexes' and 'Female Sexuality'.

20 These ideas were subsequently developed in the work of Helen Deutsch (1945) and Marie Bonaparte (1965).

21 Analysed by Freud (1912) in 'Civilized Sexual Morality and Modern Nervousness'.

22 Despite the evidence that some notable Freudians developed their ideas through work on prostitutes and Stanton (1990: 11) suggests, for example

that Ferenczi's theories on the disadvantaged were developed through, and in relation to, his work with prostitutes.

23 This was drawn from section 1(1)(b) of the Vagrancy Act 1898.

24 In case law, it was decided in *Crook v Edmondson* [1966] that it did not apply to a man who accosted a woman for commercial sex, yet 11 years later in *Dodd* [1977] [66 Cr App R 87] it was held to apply where the accused had accosted 14-year-old girls. The offence was triable either way and carried a maximum penalty on indictment of a 2-year custodial sentence (Home Office 1984a).

25 The Wolfenden Report on Prostitution and Homosexuality, published in 1957, offered a new encoding of sexual tolerance (see Self 2003) and numerous liberal legislative changes flowed from it (Weeks 1977).

26 Whilst not the radical alteration of patriarchy it is sometimes claimed to be, Millet (1970) argues that a cultural change occurred regarding a reformation of the abject legal status of women.

27 This term encompasses both the separating of sexual practice from procreation and the plasticity of sexual relationships (Giddens 1992).

28 Although the rise of romance arguably began in the late nineteenth century with the emergence of the novel, the recent apotheosis only occurred with the 'revalorisation of monogamy, loving commitment and heterosexual stability' (Lemoncheck 1997: 3).

29 At the same time, the Criminal Justice Bill 1982 abolished imprisonment for soliciting by women. Imprisonment was continued, however, for the non-payment of fines for soliciting.

30 This was not without opposition; Matthew Parris MP was on the standing committee of the 1985 Sexual Offences Bill and called it 'an ill-drafted and knee-jerk Private Members' Bill to criminalise kerb-crawling' (Parris 2002: 294)

31 The situation in Ireland was somewhat different, and did not change until 1993 in Ireland when the Dail passed the Criminal Law (Sexual Offences) Act (Viney 1996).

32 This was a coalition of anti-rape, black and civil rights organisations, AIDS preventions groups, lawyers, probation officers and Labour party activists.

33 In Sweden, where the roots of the legal system place a strong emphasis on morality, it was illegal to be HIV positive and not tell one's sexual partners.

34 This is not the case in the right-wing press, however, who maintain a less open and sympathetic attitude to both lone parents and sex working women.

35 These included *Young Runaways* (Newman 1989), *Hidden Truths* (Rees 1993), *Running – The Risk* (Stein et al. 1994), *The Game's Up* (Lee and O'Brien 1995), and *One Way Street* (Melrose, Barrett and Brodie 1999), *Stolen Childhood* (1999), *Bitter Legacy* (2002), and *Just One Click* (2004).

36 These include the Dutroux case in Belgium in 1996, the case of Sidney Cooke in 1997, and that of Robert Oliver in 1998.

37 An outcome that might have been predicted by applying defiance theory (Sherman 1992).

38 This empowered any constable to require a person who has been charged with a recordable offence or informed that he will be reported for such an offence, to attend a police station so that a non-intimate sample may be taken. The legislation was ostensibly to 'correct an omission' from the Police and Criminal Evidence Act 1984. Whilst non-intimate samples include, amongst other things, saliva or hair, saliva is the recommended type of sample to take in these instances.

39 Offences that are 'dangerous' include rape, intercourse with a girl under 13 years, intercourse with a girl aged 13–16, incest by a man, buggery, indecency between men, indecent assault on a woman, indecent assault on man (both if under 18), assault with intent to commit buggery, causing or encouraging prostitution of, or intercourse with, or indecent assault on a girl under 16.

40 See M. O'Neill, 'Literature Review: Sexual Exploitation' in *Setting the Boundaries: Reforming the Law on Sexual Offences*, Vol. 2 Supporting Evidence, App.D3 recc. 74, Home Office (2000). For an analytical assessment, see N. Lacey, 'Beset by Boundaries: The Home Office Review of Sex Offences' [2001] Crim. L.R. 3.

41 *Setting the Boundaries: Reforming the Law on Sexual Offences* (July 2000), Home Office.

42 Ibid. (recc. 53).

43 Imprisonment for prostitutes had been removed in section 71 of the Criminal Justice Act 1982. See further, H. Jones and T. Sagar, 'Crime and Disorder Act 1998: Prostitution and the Anti-social Behaviour Order' [2001] Crim. L.R. 873.

44 The legislation did not clear the telephone boxes, but it had the net-widening effect of criminalising a further group of people, and the penalties imposed received criticism in the context of the Human Rights Act 1998. See M. Wasik, 'Legislating in the Shadow of the Human Rights Act: The Criminal Justice and Police Act 2001' [2001] Crim. L.R. 931.

45 This steady flow of legislation was applied to prostitutes' clients without any public discussion. See B.M. Brooks-Gordon, and L.R. Gelsthorpe 'The Hiring and Selling of Bodies', in A. Bainham, S. Day Sclater, and M. Richards, (eds) *Body Lore and Laws* (Hart, Oxford, 2002).

46 Home Office, Cm. 5668 (2002).

47 Amendments were made to separate child and adult prostitution after effective intervention by Lord Faulkner, Lord Lucas, and Baroness Walmsley, and Baroness Noakes (see col. 181, House of Lords Hansard, 13 May 2003). Despite attempts to clarify the law further (in amendments 299, 308 and 308A, 308B in the Sexual Offences Bill Fourth Marshalled

List of Amendments to be Moved in Committee [HL Bill 26–IV]) amendments were not moved.

48 House of Commons Home Affairs Committee, Sexual Offences Bill, Fifth Report of Session 2002–03, HC 639.

49 Home Office, Government Reply to the Fifth Report from the Home Affairs Committee Session 2002–03, Cm. 5986, October 2003.

50 Personal correspondence from UKNSWP and Dr. Helen Self, February 2004.

51 House of Lords, Minutes of Proceedings, Die Veneris, 27 June 2003, col. 2185.

52 Home Office, Cm. 5778 (2003).

53 *Protecting the Public*, op cit., at n.10. para.3.45 to para.3.47.

54 For critiques of the Act, see J. Tempkin and A. Ashworth 'The Sexual Offences Act 2003: Rape, Sexual Assaults and the Problem of Consent' [2004] Crim. L.R 328; J. Spencer 'The Sexual Offences Act 2003: Child and Family Offences' [2004] Crim. L.R. 347; and A. Bainham and B. Brooks-Gordon 'Reforming the Law on Sexual Offences' in B. Brooks-Gordon, L. Gelsthorpe, M. Johnson and A. Bainham (*eds*) *Sexuality Repositioned: Diversity and the Law* (Hart, Oxford, 2004).

55 As Connell (1998) points out, not all men will behave in the same way, the hegemonic form of masculinity might not be the most common form of behaviour. Many men live in a state of some tension with or distance from hegemonic forms of masculinity, and this chapter merely serves to place in context general historical patterns that emerge from the evidence.

Chapter 2

Understanding prostitution policy

The changing nature of the regulation described in the previous chapter has led to fragmentation in terms of the offences that arrived on the statute book over time. This chapter will provide comprehensive coverage of prostitution-related offences. I will discuss the disparate laws that govern sex work and the sex industry – for example, what is criminalised what is not criminalised, and why. The laws have emerged from ancient planning laws and include laws originally framed to deal with the 1950s fear of homosexuality, and laws such as the criminalisation of sex workers' cards in public space. In addition, the increased use of civil sanctions in anti-social behaviour orders (ASBOs) for sex work related 'offences', although originally applied to neighbour disputes, have severe criminal consequences for sex workers if breached. Legislation also allows the taking of DNA from kerb crawlers to add to the national DNA database. This chapter includes a description of contemporary law and policy as it relates to sex work, including the Sexual Offences Act 2003, and the Home Office White Paper *A Coordinated Prostitution Strategy* published in January 2006.[1]

In the second part of this chapter I examine the problems with the Government consultation process using evidence from the Consultation Document *Paying the Price*, the White Paper *A Coordinated Prostitution Strategy*,[2] and its Regulatory Impact Assessment (RIA), as they relate to sex workers and their clients. I draw attention to the considerable body of research evidence on prostitutes' clients which might usefully have informed the consultation process and strategy. Second, I show how the Government's publications disregarded models from other jurisdictions which could offer alternative policy directions, yet promoted principles and intervention strategies, such as kerb-crawler or 'Johns' schools, which are not sufficiently evidence-based. Third, there is a lack of attention to feminist theoretical writings and relevant legal issues such as human rights and legitimacy. Finally, these contemporary policy documents are questioned for the conceptual confusion of some relevant issues in prostitution, which leads to ordinary clients being constructed as 'abusers' and towards enforced medical treatment of sex workers.

Statutes on sex work

The law relating to sex work is not only diverse, but there is also a wide range of local Acts and by-laws which, whilst not limited in their applicability to sex workers, have often been used to regulate purported nuisance aspects of sex workers' behaviour, resulting in inefficiency and inconsistency in application and enforcement (Selfe and Burke 2001).[3] This section draws together and discusses the main offences on the statute books that relate to sex work.

What is a 'prostitute'?

The interpretation in the Sexual Offences Act 2003, s.51 provided the first statutory definition of a 'prostitute'. For the purposes of sections 48 to 50 of the Sexual Offences Act 2003, a prostitute is defined as:

> (2) a person (A) who, on at least one occasion and whether or not compelled to do so, offers or provides sexual services to another person in return for payment or promise of payment to A or a third person; and 'prostitution' is to be interpreted accordingly.
>
> (3) 'payment' means any financial advantage, including the discharge of an obligation to pay or the provision of goods or services (including sexual services) gratuitously or at a discount.

However, as sexual services can encompass work such as lap-dancing, pole-dancing, erotic striptease, and telephone chat-lines, penetrative intercourse is not required for the statutory definition. It is also possible that a person need only sell sexual services once for them to be defined in this way. Prior to the Sexual Offences Act 2003 a 'prostitute' was defined only within clause 122 of the draft Criminal Code Bill. Before this the meaning of prostitution was derived from case law, first in *de Munck* [1918] 1 KB 635 and supported in subsequent case law such as *Webb* [1964] QB 357. However, interpretations have had to be made by trial judges, as other laws on sex work have contained, and as we will see still contain, the term 'common prostitute'. It has been left to judges to interpret what was meant by this. In *Morris-Lowe* [1985] 1 All ER 400, a prostitute was found to be a woman 'who is prepared for reward to engage in acts of lewdness with all and sundry, or with anyone who might hire her for that purpose' by Lord Lane CJ and that a single act of 'lewdness' was not enough to be a 'common' prostitute. For a prostitute to be 'common' it was necessary to commit multiple acts of 'lewdness' (although the requisite number has not been defined). To be a prostitute in the eyes of the law it was necessary in the past also to be a woman. The gender specificity of prostitution however was extended in section 56 of the Sexual Offences Act 2003 to include both sexes.[4] To be a prostitute is not and never has been a crime. Such definition has been considered necessary in order to penalise behaviour around the provision and purchase of sexual services, but the compatibility of such labelling with human rights has to be questioned[5] and the broad definition of a person as a 'prostitute' defined in the Sexual Offences Act 2003 is of questionable compatibility with the right under the European Convention on Human Rights (ECHR) to a fair hearing (see Bainham and Brooks-Gordon 2004).

Street sex work

The offences which govern street sex work are the offences of loitering and soliciting. The main statute here is section 1 of the Street Offences Act 1959, wherein:

> s.1 Loitering and soliciting for purposes of prostitution
> (1) It shall be an offence for a common prostitute (whether male or female) to loiter or solicit in a street or public place for the purpose of prostitution.
> ...
> (4) For the purpose of this section 'street' includes any bridge, road, lane, footway, subway, square, court, alley or passage, whether a thoroughfare or not, which is for the time being open to the public; and the doorways and entrances of premises

adjoining and open to a street, shall be treated as forming part
of the street.

The wording of the Act was made gender neutral by the Sexual
Offences Act 2003, and whilst there was much condemnation of the
discriminatory term 'common prostitute' throughout the Sex Offences
Review, the controversial word was still on the statute book when
the Government Strategy on sex work was published in 2006. By
using the two alternative verbs of 'loitering' and 'soliciting' section 1
creates two offences. To loiter is the harder to define, and it is likely
that a sex worker will wander along the same stretch of pavement
stopping in the hope that a client will come along and ask for
business. It needs no active approach. Selfe and Burke (2001) rightly
point out that the criminalisation of such minimalist behaviour is
difficult to justify. Whereas to solicit requires more physical action
and is more linked to soliciting for other purposes, such as betting,
as it appears in other criminal statutes (see Selfe and Burke 2001 for
case law on this). At present the offence incurs a Level 2 fine and a
second offence incurs a Level 3 fine. Irrespective of the difficulties,
the offences of 'loitering' and 'soliciting' have become linked to the
recent concept of 'anti-social behaviour' in the Crime and Disorder
Act 1998. Section 1 provides:

> s.1 An application for an order under this section may be
> made by a relevant authority if it appears that the ... following
> conditions are fulfilled with respect to any person aged 10 or
> over, namely–
> (a) that the person has acted, since the commencement date, in
> an anti-social manner, that is to say, in a manner that was
> likely to cause embarrassment, alarm or distress to one or
> more persons not of the same household as himself; and
> (b) that such an order is necessary to protect persons in the
> local government area in which the harassment, alarm or
> distress was caused or was likely to be caused from further
> anti-social acts by him.

It became possible for someone loitering and soliciting to receive an
ASBO. ASBOs are civil injunctions which were initially brought in for
neighbour disputes, but have been applied to sex workers in order
to prevent them from working within a given area. These orders can
result in a custodial prison sentence if they are breached (although
imprisonment for repeat offenders was repealed in the Criminal

Justice Act 1982). Amendments to the Police and Criminal Evidence Act 1984 (PACE) in the Criminal Justice Act 2003, s.205 contained an 'exclusion requirement' in relation to a relevant order such as an ASBO. This provision would prohibit a sex worker from entering a place or area specified in the order for a period so specified. Where the relevant order is a community order, the period specified must not be more than two years. An exclusion requirement may operate only during the periods specified in the order, and may specify different places for different periods or days.

Kerb-crawling

The rationale behind the offences of soliciting from a car and kerb crawling is one of 'nuisance' and 'obstruction'. Public decency is an issue that often creeps into the public and media debates. However as social mores of what constitutes public decency have changed rapidly to the degree that mainstream TV now routinely show sexual activities, the public decency argument is hard to sustain. It is really nuisance, and more recently a culture of fear and the myths that surround kerb-crawling that provides the rationale for statutory offences against kerb-crawlers. The offences in the Sexual Offences Act 1985 comprise:

s.1 Kerb-crawling
A person commits an offence if he solicits another person (or different persons) for the purpose of prostitution –
(a) from a motor vehicle while it is in a street or public place; or
(b) in a street or public place while in the immediate vicinity or a motor vehicle that he has just got out of or off, persistently ... or in such a manner or in such circumstances as to be likely to cause annoyance to the person (or any of the persons) solicited, or nuisance to the other persons in the neighbourhood.

s.2 Persistent soliciting
(1) A person commits an offence if in a street or public place he persistently solicits another person (or different persons) for the purpose of obtaining that person's services as a prostitute.

s. 4 Interpretation
(1) Reference in this Act to a person soliciting another person

for the purpose of prostitution are references to his soliciting that person for the purpose of obtaining that person's services as a prostitute.

...

(4) For the purpose of this Act 'street' includes any bridge, road, lane, footway, subway, square, court, alley or passage, whether a thoroughfare or not, which is for the time being open to the public; and the doorways and entrances of premises abutting on a street (as hereinbefore defined), and any ground adjoining and open to a street, shall be treated as forming part of the street.

In case law it was held by the Divisional Court in *Darroch v DPP* (1990) 91 Cr App R 378 that merely driving around and around a red light district, and on one occasion beckoning a sex worker over to a man's car, was not sufficient to constitute soliciting under the kerb crawling legislation. It would be necessary to have more positive indication such as a remarks or requests for sexual services. This offence carries the penalty of a Level 3 fine, but the offence was made arrestable by the Criminal Justice and Police Act 2001. The Powers of the Criminal Courts (Sentencing) Act 2000, s.146 gave the courts the power to remove driving licences. Home Office Circular HOC59/2003 suggested that courts consider using the power to disqualify drivers and this additional penalty of disqualification from driving was implemented in January 2004. In May 2004 the Sexual Offences Act 2003 made this offence gender neutral so that it now captures women who kerb-crawl, as some sex workers do, for clients.

Advertisements for sexual services

Prior to specific legislation for the advertising of sexual services, attempts had been made to prosecute for advertising under the 'soliciting' legislation. For example, *Weisz v Monahan* [1962] 1 All ER 664 was a case whereby the defendant had advertised sexual services in a glass case outside a shop. Since the Criminal Justice and Police Act 2001, s.46 however, the placing of advertisements relating to prostitution has been an offence. This provides:

(1) A person commits an offence if –
    (a) he places on, or in the immediate vicinity of, a public telephone an advertisement relating to prostitution, and
    (b) he does so with the intention that the advertisement

should come to the attention of any other person or persons.

(2) For the purposes of this section, an advertisement is an advertisement relating to prostitution if it –

    (a) is for the services of a prostitute, whether male or female; or

    (b) indicates that premises are premises at which such services are offered.

(3) In any proceedings for an offence under this section, any advertisement which a reasonable person would consider to be an advertisement relating to prostitution shall be presumed to be such an advertisement unless it is shown not to be.

(4) A person guilty of an offence under this section is liable on summary conviction to imprisonment for a term not exceeding six months or to a fine not exceeding level 5 on the standard scale, or both.

(5) In this section – ... 'public telephone' means –

    (a) any telephone which is located in a public place and made available for use by the public, or a section of the public, and

    (b) where such a telephone is located in or on, or attached to, a kiosk, booth, acoustic hood, shelter or other structure, that structure; and

'public place' means any place to which the public have or are permitted to have access, whether on payment or otherwise, other than –

    (a) any place to which children under the age of 16 years are not permitted to have access, whether by law or otherwise, and

    (b) any premises which are wholly or mainly used for residential purposes.

This piece of legislation was extended from public payphones to include telephones in any public structures, and the offence results in six months' imprisonment and/or a fine not exceeding Level 5. This law is an example of the anachronistic nature of laws on sex work. The advertisements can give rise to prosecution, not on the basis of content, or causing offence, but merely on the grounds of being an advertisement for the sale of sexual services. It is therefore illegal to place an advertisement for the sale of something that is not in itself illegal.

Brothels and brothel-keeping

The current laws on brothel-keeping date back to, and have developed from, the Criminal Law Amendment Act 1885, s.13 which proscribed brothels. In many respects this age old suppression continues today in the remaining statutes, the main one of which is the Sexual Offences Act 1956:

> s.33 Keeping a brothel
> It is an offence for a person to keep a brothel, or to manage, or act or assist in the management of, a brothel.
>
> s.33A Keeping a brothel used for prostitution
> (1) It is an offence for a person to keep, or to manage, or act or assist in the management of, a brothel to which people resort for practices involving prostitution (whether or not also for other practices).

To 'keep' a brothel is to conduct business within it and a brothel can be a house, flat, building, or part of a building, provided it is used by more than one sex worker. Most current 'working flats' where women work alone or with a maid have evolved from case law allowing one set of conditions, but not another. In *Donovan v Gavin* [1965] 2 QB 648 the defendant had a house in which he had a ground floor flat, and in which three women rented three separate rooms on the ground floor from which they all sold sexual services. They had front door keys as well as keys to their own rooms. They all had different tenancies started at different times, yet because the space was deemed to have been shared, it was found to be a brothel. In a later case *Strath v Foxon* [1965] QB 67 however, the defendant let the first and second floors of his house to one sex worker and the third floor to another. The only parts of the building that were shared were the kitchen, bathroom, front door, hall and staircase, and in this instance the Divisional Court found that this did not constitute a brothel. Because of this case, the majority of 'working flats' from which sex is sold are in buildings that have been divided into many flats where sex workers work alone or with a maid. This is however a less safe situation than if sex workers were allowed to work together. This is an aspect of sex work which will be explored further in Chapter 5.

What activities have to take place within to constitute a brothel are not statutorily defined. In the past it was sufficient for 'fornication' to have taken place on the premises; latterly the definition of 'prostitution' makes 'payment' a necessity. The reasoning behind the law on brothels was originally to prevent others from living off (in outmoded language) 'immoral' earnings. Now that there are laws against coercion and control, there is little justification for these laws still to be on the statute book. Similarly, for a landlord allowing premises to be used for the sale of sexual services, as in the Sexual Offences Act 1956:

s.34 Landlord letting premises for use as a brothel
It is an offence for the lessor or landlord of any premises or his agent to let the whole or part of the premises with the knowledge that it is to be used in whole or in part, as a brothel, or where the whole or part of the premises is used as a brothel, to be wilfully a party to that use continuing.

s.35 Tenant permitting premises to be used as brothel
(1) It is an offence for the tenant or occupier, or person in charge, of any premises knowingly to permit the whole or part of the premises to be used as a brothel.
(2) Where the tenant or occupier of any premises is convicted (whether under this section, or for an offence committed before the commencement of this Act, under section thirteen of the Criminal Law Amendment Act 1885) of knowingly permitting the whole or part of the premises to be used as a brothel, the First Schedule of this Act shall apply to enlarge the rights of the lessor or landlord with respect to the assignment or determination of the lease or other contract under which the premises are held by the person convicted.
(3) Where the tenant or occupier of any premises is so convicted, or was so convicted under the said section thirteen before the commencement of this Act, and either the lessor or landlord, after having the conviction brought to his notice, fails or failed to exercise his statutory rights in relation to the lease or contract under which the premises are or were held by the person convicted; or
   (a) the lessor or landlord, after exercising his statutory rights so as to determine that lease or contract, grants or granted a new lease or enters or entered into a new contract of tenancy of the premises to, with or for the benefit of the same person, without having all reasonable provisions to prevent the recurrence of the offence inserted into the new lease or contract.

s.36 Tenant permitting premises to be used for prostitution
It is offence for the tenant or occupier of any premises knowingly to permit the whole or part of the premises to be used for the purposes of habitual prostitution (whether any prostitute involved is male or female).

In all of the above statutes, it becomes an offence for any social landlord or tenant subletting to allow sex workers to rent premises. This makes it more difficult for sex workers, who cannot afford their own premises, to rent premises on the legitimate letting market. The law as it stands therefore militates against sex workers' right to self-determination by pushing them *towards* unscrupulous landlords who are prepared to break the law and will often charge exhorbitant rents. It can be argued that the law exists to prevent exploitation and coercion, but in these statutes are created the conditions for exploitative relationships between unscrupulous landlords and sex workers to germinate.

Decriminalisation of these statutes would, in a free market economy, allow property companies and landlords to offer sex workers better rental conditions including lease terms and safer premises, and there would be a decrease in exploitation through the rental market. Despite this, during the enactment of the Sexual Offences Act 2003, not only were the previous statutes not repealed, but the punishment for an offence under section 33A of the Sexual Offences Act 1956 was increased in the Sexual Offences Act 2003 to (i) on indictment seven years, (ii) summarily six months, or a fine not exceeding the statutory maximum, or both.

One strange offence that stands out as particularly clumsy is an offence which dates back to the 1950s fear of homosexuality. Section 6 of the Sexual Offences Act 1967 relates to 'premises resorted to for homosexual practices'. This provides that:

Premises shall be treated for purposes of sections 33 and 35 of the Act of 1956 as a brothel if people resort to it for the purpose of lewd homosexual practices in circumstances in which resort thereto for lewd heterosexual practices would have led to it being treated as a brothel for the purposes of those sections.

While this was extended to encompass either homosexual or heterosexual practices in the Sexual Offences Act 2003, the wording 'resorted to' and 'homosexual' sit uneasily with contemporary notions of gay identity. One recent improvement however to the statute book in this area has been the repeal of section 175 of the Licensing Act 1964 in which it was an offence for the holder of a justices' licence knowingly to allow his (*sic*) premises to be the habitual resort or meeting place of reputed prostitutes. This Act was replaced by the Licensing Act 2003 which came into force on 24 November 2005.

The construction of 'anti-social' behaviour has also been applied to brothels. Section 15 of the Anti-Social Behaviour Act 2003 amended the Housing Act 1996 to insert section 153B to allow injunctions to be used against the inhabitants of unlawful premises. The subsection states:

> (1) This section applies to conduct which consists of or involves using or threatening to use housing accommodation owned or managed by a relevant landlord for an unlawful purpose.
> (2) The court on the application of the relevant landlord may grant an injunction prohibiting the person in respect of whom the injunction is granted from engaging in conduct to which this section applies.

This section allows specified landlords to apply for injunctions where someone has used or threatened to use their housing for an illegal purpose. This could cover, for example, drug dealing or use of the premises as a brothel. It could also be argued that by its very nature, a brothel is 'social'. Most importantly though it is an example of the layering effect that is taking place in the law. This statute does not define what types of behaviour or nuisance are indeed 'anti-social', but that they are already proscribed is enough.

Brothels and 'proceeds of crime'

The Proceeds of Crime Act 2002 established the Assets Recovery Agency and empowered it to take goods and property from individuals. Under section 49 of the Act are 'powers to take possession' and if a defendant has a 'criminal' lifestyle the Act provides powers to take possession of property including bank accounts and confiscate, deal with, manage, even sell, property, including property abroad (section 74) if the property has been obtained or bought with the proceeds of 'criminal conduct'. Under section 242 of the Act property obtained through unlawful conduct 'whether his own conduct or another's' could be taken. The Proceeds of Crime Act 2002 has enabled police authorities to freeze assets of brothel owners, sell the assets for money, and this money is split four ways with the Home Office, CPS, Courts Service and police all getting their share. The Serious Organised Crime and Police Act 2005 set up the Serious and Organised Crime Agency (SOCA) and tightened the Proceeds of Crime Act 2002 further to extend powers for civil recovery of assets (for example, sections 245A, 245B). In section 110 the power of arrest is extended to enable police (or Community Wardens) to arrest without warrant (PACE, s.24A) anyone for any offence, or on suspicion that an offence might be committed, however trivial, and as a result keep their DNA, fingerprints or photographs for any length of time whether or not they are charged or convicted for an offence (sections 116, 117, 119). In the financial year 2004/05 it was reported that £2.5 million in cash was seized from the sex industry and at the time of writing the police are reported to have already taken £1.1m in the financial year 2005-6.[6] There are however concerns of conflict of interest when the police take a cut of sex workers' earnings in this way. The introduction of this law has given the police a powerful vested interest in maintaining the criminality of many sex work related activities.

Children involved in prostitution

The Sexual Offences Act 2003 created, for the first time, a specific set of offences dealing with sexual exploitation of children. In addition, the Children Act 1989 places specific duties on agencies to co-operate in the interests of children involved in prostitution. Home Office guidelines expand and re-inforce this emphasising that children should be treated as victims of abuse. One of most popular misconceptions in debates. Since the Sexual Offences 2003 came into force in May 2004 is that the law needs to be toughened to protect against young people's involvement in prostitution. Below are laid out the numerous statutes that are already in force for such protection.

Meeting a child following sexual grooming

In section 15 of the Sexual Offences Act 2003 it is an offence to meet or to have communicated with another person on at least two earlier occasions, if the person being met is under 16 years old and is not reasonably believed to be 16 years old. It does not matter where the person is met or where the 'relevant' offence is committed or intended to be committed, for example, in another country, if it is an act which would be an offence in England, Wales and Northern Ireland. This includes those offences listed in Part 1 of the Sexual Offences Act 2003. The penalty is 10 years' imprisonment.

Paying for sexual services of a child
It is a serious offence under section 47 of the Sexual Offences Act 2003 to pay for sex with a child. Section 47 provides that:

(1) A person (A) commits an offence if –
  (a) he intentionally obtains for himself the sexual services of another person (B),
  (b) before obtaining those services, he has made or promised payment for those services to B or a third person, or knows that another person has made or promised such a payment, and
  (c) either –
    (i) B is under 18, and A does not reasonably believe that B is 18 or over, or
    (ii) B is under 13.

When the young person involved is aged 16–17 years of age, the maximum penalty is seven years' imprisonment. When the child is aged under 13 years old and the sexual services are non-penetrative, or where the child is aged between 13 years and 15 years, this offence results in a maximum penalty of 14 years' imprisonment. If however, the child is aged under 13 years and the sexual services involve vaginal/anal penetration or oral penile penetration then the maximum penalty is life imprisonment. Sections 48 to 50 of the 2003 Act provide for causing or inciting (section 48), controlling (section 49), or arranging or facilitating (section 50) child prostitution or pornography. A person commits an offence if he intentionally causes or incites another person (B) to become a prostitute, or to be involved in pornography, in any part of the world, or 'controls' the activities in any part of the world. The maximum penalty for the offence is 14 years' imprisonment. The statute in sections 47 to 50 is anomalous to other major statutes involving children as a child of either sex is defined as a child up to the age of 18 years rather than 16 years which is when legal emancipation to leave school, have sexual relations etc, occurs. Offences under section 50, unlike the adult offences in sections 52 and 53, and contrary to the Sexual Offences Review Recommendation, require proof that the defendant has acted for or in the expectation of gain for himself or a third person (Card 2004, para. 7.11).

These laws being merely additions to the existing muddled laws regulating prostitution are considered of doubtful usefulness by some lawyers and child policy experts (e.g. Bainham 2005). And the difficulties inherent in such statutes is that, counter to the prevailing attitudes of treating children in sex work as victims, they could be used to criminalise children already in sex work who encourage other youngsters to work in sex work. Research with young people shows that it is more prevalent for youngsters to become involved in sex work through peers than, for example, trafficking gangs, or enslavement (e.g. Pearce *et al.* 2003; Phoenix 2004). They do however have the advantage of separating children's involvement from that of adults in sex work. This has the advantage of granting adults in sex work, implicitly at least, autonomy and consent to what they do.

Enforcing and controlling

The law that carries one of the heaviest penalties for the *enforced* involvement of adults in sex work is the International Criminal Courts Act 2001, s.51 and this stipulates that:

(1)   It is an offence against the law of England and Wales for a person to commit genocide, a crime against humanity or a war crime.

A crime against humanity means acts committed as part of a widespread or systematic attack directed against any civilian population, with knowledge of the attack. Amongst the acts defined are: rape, sexual slavery, and enforced prostitution (see Ormerod 2005: 515).[7] Crimes against humanity are triable in the international criminal court and carry a 30-year sentence.

To cause or incite someone into sex work for the gain of oneself or another is an offence under section 52 of the Sexual Offences Act 2003. It is also an offence under section 53 of the Sexual Offences Act 2003 intentionally to control prostitution in any part of the world for gain or in the expectation of gain for oneself or another. The penalty is seven years' imprisonment on conviction on indictment for each of these offences. The element of 'control' is required for the offences under section 52 and section 53. It therefore no longer criminalises, as the previous statute (Sexual Offences Act 1956, s.30) used to, innocent parties such as partners and adult children who technically 'lived on' the earnings of those in sex work (see Card 2004 for further on this). This is a more pragmatic approach to the lived experience of many sex workers. The requirement that there must be some element of 'gain' was considered necessary by the Home Office as causing, inciting or controlling adult sex work did not merit criminality without this element. Encouraging a hard-up woman, for example, to pay off her debts by prostitution does not constitute an offence (Card 2004).

Trafficking

The offences for trafficking for sexual exploitation cover both children and adults. They deal with recruiting, harbouring or facilitating the movement of another person for the purposes of sexual exploitation. These include:

- trafficking *into* the UK for sexual exploitation (section 57 SOA 2003);
- trafficking *within* the UK for sexual exploitation (section 58 SOA 2003);
- trafficking *out of* the UK for sexual exploitation (section 59 SOA 2003).

A person commits an offence if, he intentionally arranges or facilitates the travel of another and he intends, or knows another intends or is likely to do something which if done will involve the commission of a relevant (sexual) offence. In sections 57 to 59 of the Sexual Offences Act 2003 a 'relevant offence' means an offence under the Act or an offence under section 1(1)(a) of the Protection of Children Act 1978, anything done outside England and Wales and Northern Ireland which is not an offence within any of the paragraphs (a) to (d) of section 1 but would be if it were done in England and Wales and Northern Ireland. Offences under sections 57, 58 and 59 incur punishment of 14 years' imprisonment. The prosecution is not required to prove the use of force, coercion, deception or abuse of power or of a position of vulnerability because, not unproblematically, the law now assumes that these things will be involved in most cases (Card 2004). Contrary to the recommendation of the Sexual Offences Review, the arranging or facilitating need not be done 'for the purposes of gain' – it is enough that the person trafficked is for 'sexual exploitation'. It is the phrase 'sexual exploitation' that is most problematic here. What constitutes sexual exploitation has not been defined in any of the statutes. This results in a tension between an aggressive lobby, which argues that all sex work is exploitation, and supporters of human rights who argue that the only way to combat exploitation *per se* is with worker rights rather than further criminalisation. While not the only voice questioning[8] the desire of the former lobby to help and save, Agustín (2004a, 2004b, 2005a, 2005b) has produced the only research that explores the intricacies of the migration and trafficking debate with the sensitivity and intellectual rigour its complexity requires. The final decisions, as to what constitutes 'trafficking' and 'sexual exploitation' however will be taken by the courts.

In addition to all of the above offences there are several related inchoate offences. These include the offences under section 62 of the Sexual Offences Act 2003 of committing an offence with *intent* to commit a sexual offence. A person commits an offence under this section if he commits an offence with the intention of committing a relevant sexual offence. This includes an offence of aiding, abetting, counselling or procuring such an offence. Similarly section 63 of the same Act criminalises trespass with intent to commit a sexual offence. Here, a person commits an offence if he is a trespasser on any premises, he intends to commit a relevant sexual offence on the premises, and he knows that, or is reckless as to whether, he is a trespasser. In this section 'premises' includes a structure or part of a structure (including a tent, vehicle or vessel or other temporary or movable structure). A person guilty of an offence under this section is liable on conviction on indictment, where the offence is committed by kidnapping or false imprisonment, to imprisonment for life, or on summary conviction, to imprisonment for a term not exceeding six months or a fine not exceeding the statutory maximum or both; on conviction on indictment, to imprisonment for a term not exceeding 10 years (for a critique of the Sexual Offences Act 2003 in relation to recklessness see Bainham and Brooks-Gordon 2004).

The Sexual Offences Act 2003 dealt specifically with the *exploitation* (albeit without defining it) of people through prostitution. The Act did not, for example, decriminalise loitering or soliciting by children involved in prostitution. Nor did it directly replace the offences of abduction which had been repealed (although one was replaced by one of the preparatory offences (see Card 2004, para. 8.7)). The Act was a piece of legislation that continued the punitive trend against sex workers and their clients that had gathered momentum over the last 20 years. As Peter Glazebrook points out:

> the Home Office, reckless of the shape and intelligibility of the law, has continued to add new offences and heavier penalties to the statute book in a manner reminiscent of the late eighteenth century... And the drafting becomes ever more prolix and convoluted: that of the Sexual Offences Act 2003, for instance is quite appalling. (Glazebrook 2005)

Punitive pressure and the law in progress

At the time of writing there was also a private Bill before Parliament, brought by the City of Westminster Council, the aim of which was to determine and limit the interaction (and the civil liberties) of sex workers and their clients. The Bill is under consideration and while this may never make it onto the statute book it is a good example of the waves of pressure that are applied in further efforts to make the extant laws more punitive.

In Part I of the London and Local Authorities Bill 2006[9], clause 7 deals with advertisements relating to prostitution placed on, or in the immediate vicinity of, a public telephone or public structure. This clause would enable councils, where they find an advertisement relating to prostitution in their area, to require the communications service provider of the telephone number advertised to prevent calls being able to be received by the user of the telephone number. Where a communications service provider fails to comply with the council's request, it would commit an offence liable on summary conviction to a fine not exceeding Level 5. This clause would extend the power of sections 46 and 47 of the Criminal Justice and Police Act 1991 to councils and spread that power over email to make internet service providers liable if they fail to comply with the council's request, to an offence liable on summary conviction to a fine not exceeding Level 5. Similarly repressive strategies have been tried in the past when the City of Westminster Council and British Telecom tried to cut sex workers' telephone services (selective call barring), however on appeal the English Collective of Prostitutes (ECP) had the ban overturned. The City of Westminster Council is trying to address the same issue through internet service providers. The clause as it stands would allow councils to impose additional local conditions on internet service providers, not because the content of an internet site is illegal, but because the owner of the site is connected to 'carding'. However, a written response from the Department of Trade and Industry (DTI) requests deletion of the clause, on the basis that the benefits, if any, of call-barring measures are not proven, the costs have not been calculated, and the issues should be addressed with regard to a national strategy on prostitution.

Clause 44 of the Bill is an amendment of the law relating to sex establishments. The clause introduces in London a new class of establishment, known as hostess bars, which will become subject to licensing as a sex establishment under Schedule 3 to the Local Government (Miscellaneous Provisions) Act 1982. The introduction of the new class of sex establishment is effected by the introduction of a new paragraph 3A into Schedule 3, which sets out a definition of a 'hostess bar'. 'Hostess bar' is defined as meaning: (a) any premises used for a business which consists of the offering, expressly or by implication, whether on payment of a fee or not, of the provision of companions for customers on the premises, (b) any premises in respect of which any impression by whatever means, is given to customers, or potential customers, that a performance, entertainment, service, exhibition or other experience of a sexual nature is available on the premises. A list of exemptions is provided in subsection (2), including premises which are licensed under a number of different licensing regimes. The clause makes a number of consequential amendments to Schedule 3 and clause 45 provides transitional provisions for existing premises which fall within the new category of sex establishments, enabling them to operate without a licence for a limited period after the new definition comes into force so long as an application for a licence is made within a certain time. Clause 46 provides for the repeal of Part IV of the London Local Authorities Act 1995, which makes provision for the licensing of near beer premises, on the introduction of the licensing of hostess bars under the Local Government (Miscellaneous Provisions) Act 1982 as provided for in clause 44. This would give the local council a great deal more power over burgeoning premises in London such as lap-dancing, pole-dancing and table-dancing clubs.

Clauses 73 to 84 deal with special treatment. Special treatment premises currently require licences in Greater London under the London Local Authorities Act 1991. The Bill provides a definition of special treatment, which includes massage, manicure, depilatory waxing, acupuncture, tattooing, cosmetic piercing and chiropody. The purpose of this is to introduce a licensing system for persons who carry out special treatments, but not in premises licensed under the 1991 Act. Chapter 3 of the Bill sets out a personal licensing system. Under the present legislation, if a person wished to make a home visit and carry out special treatment, then the home would have to be licensed. Chapter 3 will do away with that necessity, and enable practitioners to carry out treatment from place to place with a personal licence. Clause 73 makes provision for the application of Chapter 3, which shall come into effect in a borough as from the appointed day.[10] Clause 74 deals with the interpretation of Chapter 3 and includes definitions of 'special treatment', 'visiting special treatment', 'personal licence' and 'temporary licence'. Clauses 76 to 84 set out a licensing regime for individuals who carry out special treatment, and will enable holders of those licences to carry out special treatment in premises which are not establishments licensed for special treatment. Such treatment is referred to as 'visiting special treatment'. Clause 76 provides that it will be unlawful for any person to provide visiting special treatment unless authorised to do so by a personal licence or a temporary licence. The clause stipulates in section 3 of the 1991 Act that a person would have to belong to a body of health practitioners which must have a register of members; requires as qualification for membership qualifications by way of training for, and experience of, the therapy concerned; requires its members to hold professional indemnity insurance; subjects its members to a code of conduct and ethics, including a *prohibition of immoral conduct* in the course of their practice.

Clause 77 makes provision about applications for personal licenses and renewal of such licences. It provides a list of stringent compliance procedures and the grounds on which an application may be refused. It provides that it will be unlawful for any person to provide visiting special treatment (e.g. massage or manicure) unless authorised to do so by special licence or a temporary licence. 'The council may refuse an application on any of the following grounds' including 'the applicant is, on account of misconduct, or for any other sufficient reason unsuitable to hold the licence'. It does not state *what* the misconduct might be but both this and clause 76 'prohibiting immoral conduct' indicate the controls the local authority want to establish on behaviour and how the morality of services are viewed.

Paying the Price

The previous section shows that there were 30 statutes already on the statute book to regulate sex work, the penalties of which go up to 30 years and life imprisonment, when the Green Paper *Paying the Price* was published in July 2004. This heralded the start of a review into prostitution to which 861 responses were received and thereafter the Home Office published *A Coordinated Strategy on Prostitution* (*The Strategy*) in January 2006. Throughout the process a change took place from the initial remit which included safeguards for sex to be sold from private premises (*Paying the Price*: 113), the exploration of safety (tolerance) zones, and the removal of the discriminatory term 'common prostitute'. All this had changed by the end of the consultation to a highly punitive stance in *The Strategy*. This included increased police powers to allow intrusion into private life that emanates from the idea that women experience sex as violence to 'disrupt' off-street places of work, intervention orders for compulsory medical treatment for the civil disobedience of non-compliant sex workers (e.g. drug treatment as a penalty), and penalties against clients (p. 9) who would be forced to have untried psychological treatments without having been convicted. The Consultation Documents were not uncontroversial and the discussion that follows specifies particular areas of concern that involve sex workers and their clients and the effect these may have on policy.

The stated intention of *Paying the Price* is as: 'the starting point for the development of a realistic and coherent strategy to deal with prostitution'.[11] It lays out the Government's intention with regard to prostitution, which is to address the issues of prevention, protection and support, and justice. The strengths of the document include an emphasis on the protection and support for children in prostitution, on multi-agency approaches in response to risk factors amongst vulnerable children, and on human rights abuses in trafficking. *Paying the Price* also promotes the welfare needs of those exiting prostitution and provides a platform for discussing various models throughout the world that manage street and off-street prostitution, and it opens up the debate as regards the legitimacy of prostitution, as well as the frameworks that facilitate safe sex. Concerns were articulated in some quarters about its weaknesses along with its potential for misinformation (Soothill and Sanders 2004). This section focuses on the document's policy perspective as it affects the *clients* of commercial sexual services, and by extension the labour rights and human rights of sex workers. I shall identify a number of omissions in the Consultation Paper which relate to clients. In doing so, I reveal some serious flaws in the basic assumptions, approach, methodology, accuracy, and recommendations made in *Paying the Price*.

Morality and legal development since Wolfenden

Despite the punitive policy trend leading up to *Paying the Price*, it contains no legal history nor does it make use of the past legal debate and legislation on prostitution. For example, Wolfenden made the important distinction between public nuisance and morality and it was accepted that morality should be no business of the law (see Self 2003). Four government committees reported on sex work between 1928 and 1986: the Street Offences Committee in 1928, Wolfenden in 1957, the Vagrancy and Street Offences Committee between 1974 and 1976, and the Criminal Law Revision Committee between 1982 and 1986. They produced seven reports on prostitution between them. In addition, an independent report was produced by the Parliamentary Group on Prostitution, headed by Diane Abbott in 1996 (Self 2005). Yet *Paying the Price* contains none of their findings or pronouncements. In recent history, the most important issue is that the ECHR became enshrined in English law by the implementation of the Human Rights Act 1998 (HRA) in October 2000. Within ECHR, Art. 8 is enshrined the right to respect for private life, and case law[12] has shown this to encompass a person's sex life as the most intimate aspect of private life (Bainham 2002). What is missing from *Paying the Price* is an exploration of how the socio-legal situation is different for sex industry workers *now* than it was at the time of Wolfenden, taking into account the guidelines on the removal of morality, ECHR and HRA, as well as the civil remedies against sexual harassment that all non-sex workers have. However, given that this was supposed to be a complete review of the situation, the first question that should be asked is whether the behaviours involved in the sale and purchase of sexual services *ought* to be the province of the criminal law, or whether that is likely to be a disproportionate response or even counter-productive.[13] It is with this question to the fore that I shall discuss the empirical research on clients as it is represented in *Paying the Price*.

Examining the empirical research base

The idiosyncratic attention given to research evidence is where *Paying the Price* could affect sex workers and clients most detrimentally. There is no systematic review of the literature on clients in *Paying the Price* and the review given omits much useful evidence. There are only six citations for research which contain information on clients.[14] These are, with one exception, books which each contain only a small section on clients. All except one of these were published in the previous century and much has been written since this time. Notwithstanding this, *Paying the Price* neglects key information which the cited studies do contain. Intriguingly, it misrepresents its own Home Office funded research. There are also important classic papers which provide a good understanding of clients which have been overlooked in *Paying the Price*.

Firstly, we know something of the prevalence of commercial sexual encounters from early general sex surveys in the USA. These found that between 15 per cent (Kinsey, Pomeroy, Martin 1948) to 25 per cent (Stanley 1995) of men had paid for sex. Similarly, in the UK, 25 per cent of men surveyed had paid for sex. These figures have remained fairly constant over the years in the USA,[15] UK (Knox *et al.* 1993) and Europe (Prieur and Taskal 1989).[16] The first methodologically rigorous study, the NATSAL survey, found that almost 7 per cent of men in London had paid for sex (Wellings *et al.* 1994). This increased over the last decade to 1 man in 11 in London paying for sex (Wellings 2000).[17] Studies also illustrate that where law enforcement exists customers will travel long distances to buy sex (Winnick and Kinsie 1971) and that a large number of men buy sex when away from home (Simon and Gagnon 1973). Unless the Home Office aims to criminalise 10 per cent of the capital's male population, the alternative, the targeting of interventions to specific demographic groups, necessitates the use of detailed demographic studies of clients and an understanding of their needs. For example, *Paying the Price* refers to 'those who suffer the unwanted approaches of kerb crawlers' (p. 5) as justification for penalising clients. In reality this rarely happens as those seeking commercial sex do not wish to waste time approaching those who are not obviously selling sex and there is no empirical evidence of 'unwanted approaches of kerb crawlers' in the literature on sex work. The issue however, seems to have fuelled some of the debates in parliament against sex workers' clients.[18]

Secondly, from classic papers we understand more of clients and their needs. For example, object relations theory explains the needs of men who sexualise their need for intimacy and comfort (Klein 1928; Chodorow 1978). From in-depth interviews with clients, it has been found that most men were seeking sexual solutions for emotional problems, and that for these men going to a prostitute relieved feelings of despair and intense loneliness (Jordan 1997). This has empirical support from client surveys (e.g. Kinnell and Griffiths 1999). Moreover, men who go to prostitutes enjoy the psychological build-up of planning and preparing to go to a sex worker (Holzman and Pines 1982). Many male clients dislike, and have difficulty with, 'dating rituals' such as clubbing and chatting up (Campbell 1997) and some men create a 'rhetoric of mutuality' to create a fantasy relationship out of the commercial interaction with a sex-working woman (Plumridge *et al.* (1996: 408). Such 'difficulty' may also indicate the pressure put upon men in conventional roles that feminists argue are as damaging to men as to women (e.g. McLeod 1982; Segal 1997). Men also eroticise the fantasy of the dominant woman, and this is one reason men enter into commercial sex contracts (O'Connell Davidson 1998). It might be concluded that the internalisation of masculine stereotypes legitimated men's roles as sexual consumers and it has been argued further that through prostitution these men can claim membership of a dominant masculine community that otherwise eludes them (O'Connell Davidson 1998). While the further systematic study of the accounts of these men will provide useful data on the motivations and behaviour of these men, current understandings do not provide justification for the perjorative way in which male clients are regarded in *Paying the Price*.

Men who are not in relationships have a range of psychological, genetic, economic, social, and geographic reasons for buying sex. These include for example: at the margins, the relative search costs of finding a willing sexual partner in *ad hoc* or formal settings in a given time period, low self-esteem in conventional social gatherings, fear or dislike of emotional entanglements, and perceptions about one's own level of physical attractiveness (e.g. in matters relating to height, build, or looks). Other factors include unsocial working hours, persistent gender imbalances at work, thin markets for potential sexual partners in rural areas, and tight social controls such as community disapproval against pre-marital sexual activity (such as within certain faiths).[19] The question 'Why do men in relationships buy sex?' has been answered recently with a statistical model of economic consumption (Cameron and Collins 2003: 274). The answer includes: (1) the need for variety, (2) sexual frustration with a shortfall of sexual activity in their current relationship, and (3) not wanting a committed emotional relationship which may threaten their current relationship. Men with partners have stated that they wanted only sex with prostitutes and that they got other things like commitment, intimacy and love from others (Cameron and Collins 2003). There is also the fantasy of 'risk', associated with the activity (Holzman and Pines 1982) and while the conceptualisation that these men make of risk including the risk of legal censure, is not yet fully understood, we do know that kerb crawling itself, *because* of the risks involved, is a source of significant ludic utility in a sexual context (Cameron and Collins 2003). Clients purchase sex, at least in part because of the dare of doing it, 'the thrill of being illicit'. This theme is well-developed in the literature (see McKegany and Barnard 1996: 53 and O'Connell Davidson 1998: 9). Mens' decisions to use prostitutes' services are therefore conditioned by: location, disposition, religion, range of opportunities to conceal consumption, and risk.

Third, recent studies of clients have shown some useful demographic profiles that have significant implications for intervention as well as analyses of supply and demand for sexual services (Edlund and Korn 2000), and that sex work is similar to other organisations in terms of stratification, organisation and commodification (Brewis and Linstead 2000). Yet the variance in the demographic profile of clients given in *Paying the Price* is so broad that its utility for policy is questionable; it states that the demographic profile of clients is 'around 30 years of age, married, in full time employment' (p. 17). This is unsupported. The Home Office Consultation Document states that the men were married yet research commissioned by the Home Office *Tackling Street Prostitution* (albeit a small study on 127 men), still found that less than half were married (48 per cent) (Hester and Westmarland 2004). It is an unsatisfactory use of statistics to use less than half the sample to generalise for an entire population. With regard to clients' ages, *Tackling Street Prostitution* states that the mean age was 35 years yet *Paying the Price* quotes this research stating that the age is around 30 years. These are two examples of the Home Office Consultation Paper quoting Home Office research inaccurately. There are also examples of data being cited which do not exist in the publication cited. For example, it is stated that the Home Office *Solutions and Strategies: Drug Problems and Street Sex Markets* document contains demographic profiles of clients. While Section Three of The Executive Summary lists 'characteristics of kerb crawlers'[20] the document itself does not contain this information. The general ignorance and confusion in *Paying the Price* as to who the clients of prostitutes are, and their purpose for the visit has also been shown to exist in other parliamentary debates, media, and policy (Carpenter 2000). Any policy on commercial sex clients necessitates knowing *why* men buy sex, and an understanding of the demographic profile of clients. Clients are ordinary men, no different from customers looking for a hairdresser or doctor, yet *Paying the Price* sets the client apart from the rest of humanity not least by using pejorative terms such as 'the user'.[21] In an attempt to fill the knowledge gaps about why clients pay for sex *Paying the Price* makes fundamental attribution errors.

Analysing alternative policy options

In considering the policy options, only six are deemed possible in *Paying the Price*, and only five models are put forward: the Swedish model (criminalising clients), the Dutch model (managed zones), the Victoria (Australia) model (licensed brothels), the New South Wales model (registration), and the Austrian model (registration). The rationale behind the choice of these models is not provided and lack of balance occurs, firstly in the choice of those listed and secondly in the partial way many are reported. For example, North

America, where prohibition reigns is listed but not, say, Thailand where prostitution is a criminal offence. This is important because in Thailand criminalisation of prostitution has led to corruption, not least within the police force, while at the same time sex work is a mainstay of the Thai economy. Such hypocrisy has allowed corruption to flourish and shows how prohibition nurtures organised crime (Kuo 2002). The inclusion of the US without Thailand illustrates the uneven coverage given to other jurisdictions. It appears that these models are listed according to responses to a survey, which unfortunately is a notorious way of getting a biased sample.

It is possible that the best 'model' for future policy did not respond to the survey. One of the most recent and most relevant models for English law, that of Germany, has been omitted as a viable 'model' and merits only four lines in Annex D (p. 100). It is the most relevant model as it was decided *after* the ECHR was incorporated into English law by The Human Rights Act 1998. In November 2001, the European Court of Justice (ECJ) decided that prostitution is 'a provision of services the remuneration of which … falls within the concept of economic activities' within the meaning of Article 2 of the EC Treaty.[22] In January 2002, the new German Prostitution Act came into force. The Act consists of three articles and covers three distinct areas of law: civil law, labour law, and social insurance law. Besides this it decriminalised brothels which offered good working conditions. Two primary purposes of the Act were to enable prostitutes to enter the social insurance scheme under the profession of prostitute, and second, to perform their business under good and legally secure working conditions (Laskowski 2002). In civil law, under Article 1, section 1, a sex work contract is enforceable. If a client is not able or willing to pay, a sex worker can sue for payment. However the client cannot enforce services promised and does not have any particular contractual rights in the case of default in performance. Under labour law, Article 1, section 1, allows for the employment of sex workers, and contracts between sex workers and brothel owners are valid. Finally, social insurance law guarantees sex workers access to the statutory social insurance scheme. The aim of the German Act is to protect prostitutes from social discrimination by strengthening their legal rights and by reinforcing their right to (legal and sexual) determination. The decisive questions are: are both parties willing to exchange sexual services and money?, and is the exchange possible under fair (legal) conditions? If sex is forced on a person then that is not fair and the criminal law is adequate. But if the decision is made by two adults who are aware of what they are doing then the

State has to respect their decision; it is their private matter. The right to self-determination belongs to the very important constitutional guarantees of civil rights also in substance in Article 8 of ECHR. This was confirmed by the decision of the ECJ above.[23] Taking into account that in the member states, including Sweden, prostitution is not prohibited, most member states will have to respect the court's legal valuation of prostitution as an economic activity within the meaning of the EC Treaty and the Associated Agreements. As a result of this, prostitution has to be classified as work. This will influence the interpretation of Article 15 of the new EU Charter on Fundamental Rights which protects an individual's 'profession and the right to work'. There are no doubts that voluntary prostitution also comes under the Article 15 of the EU Charter. If the decisions of the ECJ influence the member states' legal opinions about prostitution, it will lead to a more rational view of the profession (Laskowski 2002).

The New Zealand law is another recent model that is highly relevant but has been effectively omitted from *Paying the Price*. This comprehensive law came into force in June 2003 and contains sections dealing *inter alia* with: age limits of sex workers, brothel location, coercion, contractual responsibilities, employment rights, gang involvement, immigration provision, 'living on the earnings', media advertising, morality, numbers engaged in sex work, occupational safety and health, public health, safer sex responsibilities, soliciting, and street work (Barnett 2004). One year on, the results for the New Zealand policy are exceptionally promising. Local bodies have been able to set special rules about the situation of sex work establishments, for example with regard to their distance from schools or churches. There have been good results on exploitation as the police have enforced age limit legislation and three brothel owners have been charged with employing under age sex workers. Police time has been saved as arrests against sex workers have ceased. There have been no reports of offensive behaviour by sex workers and adult entertainment adverts have decreased. There is stronger provision in the law against coercion and sex workers are making use of the law to protect themselves from dangerous situations. Sex workers now have employment contracts and have asserted their employment rights. Moreover, there has been no increase in gang involvement. This comprehensive and successful policy on sex work unfortunately merits only two lines in *Paying the Price*.

The Dutch model is also highly relevant because it offers the only European example of 'managed' or 'toleration' zones which have been extensively researched. Yet the Dutch model is deemed a failure in *Paying the Price* because some sex workers work outside toleration zones. Nonetheless, it can be argued that in every economic market a grey market also operates, and this is not a good reason to reject zones as a policy measure that would help significant numbers of sex workers and cut down police time and residents' complaints.[24] *Paying the Price* also suggests that the biggest problem for toleration zones is finding an area in which to site them. 'Nimbyism' occurs when *any* planning issue is considered, from new homes to airport runways, yet with sensitive planning and negotiation, this can be managed successfully (see Larsen 1996 for example). The opportunity for a realistic analysis of zoning has been lost in *Paying the Price* and the baby appears to have been thrown out with the bathwater. Discussion needs to take place about what is an acceptable baseline for a toleration zone and zones need to be trialled with realistic baseline measures. For example, a sex work zone cannot be said to be a failure just because some sex workers fail to work inside it. But rather a zone only fails when there are serious safety concerns such as more murders of sex workers inside it than the number that occur without it. The high levels of murdered sex workers are well-documented and if zoning saves a few of these lives, then zones are a success. Zones should be considered and should be measured with realistic baseline measures.

A misreading of policy occurs in the opposite direction with regard to Sweden. The 1998 Swedish law made it a crime to purchase or attempt to purchase a temporary sexual relationship. In the contemporary European context, this is exceptional. The Swedish Prostitution Act 1999 regards all sex workers as victims, reduced to sexual objects, and exploited by men to satisfy their base sexual needs. The Swedish legislator ignores the fact that there are a lot of prostitutes who decide to earn money by selling sexual services to those who like that kind of sex. In spite of this there is uncritical acceptance of the Swedish model in *Paying the Price* which omits to take account of the enormous problems encountered since the Swedish law was implemented, the wide legal and policy differences between Sweden and England, and the widespread criticism of Sweden's approach in the legal and policy literature (Kulick 2003). Official reports have concluded there has been *no drop* in street solicitation in Sweden. There has been an *increase* in internet advertising. Prostitutes interviewed in the media report that women with drug problems have been driven to desperation or even suicide by the new law, social workers state that it has been harder to reach prostitutes, and police reports state that it has been harder to prosecute pimps and traffickers because clients used to be willing to be witnesses, but are now disinclined to co-operate. Recent reports by the Board of Police concluded that women are now forced to take more clients since prices have dropped and there are more unstable and dangerous clients than before. Police harassment of sex workers has increased, as they can be forced to give testimony, and be searched (Kulick 2003). This has implications for sexual safety as condoms can be used as evidence a person is sex working. The law has been catastrophic for non-Swedish sex workers who are deported and government prosecutors complain that they cannot gain a conviction because sex workers are deported before they can provide even a statement. There has been a negative effect on sex workers reporting violence.[25]

The law was passed in Sweden despite enormous opposition by the National Board of Police, National Social Welfare Board, the Attorney General, and the National Courts of Administration. Importantly, there is a different legal base for the law in Sweden which grew out of agrarian Lutheranism. The wider context of the law is also different in Sweden to any other state in Europe.[26] The Swedish legislation reflects different social attitudes to those held in England. A major difference is that Sweden has a longstanding social-democratic tradition of attempted reform of human nature, resulting in punitive laws relating to regulation of alcohol to work fare for the unemployed (Outshoorn 2001). These are measures which while not unproblematic in Sweden are a wholesale failure elsewhere.

The law of criminalising clients in Sweden arose as a response to Sweden's entry into the EU[27] and prostitution thus emerged as an argument for staying out of the EU. Wider political and moral influences may underpin the policy as the Swedish Government is reported to have teamed up with the White House to fund anti-prostitution campaigns all over Europe.[28] Critics have suggested that this is nothing more than pure moralism combined with a supposed feministic touch and that protecting prostitutes does not require the discrimination of men. If there is a philosophically significant distinction to be made between those who buy sexual services and those who buy services of any kind then that distinction must be given a philosophical rationale.[29] From the point of view which respects a sex worker's voluntary decision to become a sex worker, the Swedish Prostitution Act 1999 has been rejected by legal scholars, it also has to be rejected on the grounds of efficacy, yet it has been unjustifiably accepted in *Paying the Price*.

'Rehabilitation', 're-education' and 'Johns' schools

A measure which is endorsed uncritically in *Paying the Price* is the re-education of and enforcement against prostitutes' clients through kerb crawler 're-education schemes' or 'Johns' schools' which are described as a 'coherent approach' (p. 40). However these schemes were widely criticised when they were infamously trialled in Leeds in England (Campbell and Storr 2001). Such schemes abroad have been roundly condemned, yet none of the criticisms, dangers and costs of these schemes have been put forward in *Paying the Price*. The reverse seems to be the case, and under the heading 'Conditional cautioning' *Paying the Price* states that 'Re-education programmes have proved to be effective' (p. 68). Only the Home Office's own research entitled *Tackling Street Prostitution* suggests that one kerb crawler school may have *appeared* to have a positive effect (Hester and Westmarland 2004); although it does not state what the effect was, nor how it was measured. On closer inspection it is apparent that conclusions were based on just 13 kerb crawlers. While the authors are properly tentative about such a small study and report that the one year follow-up was too short to assess re-offending. Indeed they point out that because re-offence was not recorded in one year in Hull *that this does not mean that the men did not re-offend* in Hull or elsewhere and that only more research with longer term outcomes could assess this.[30] In *Paying the Price*, this tentative interpretation is converted into an unqualified success. There is no further evidence of any literature which supports Johns' schools in the bibliography of *Paying the Price*. The growing literature on their problems shows that they could not be put forward as a viable policy option. Only one of the independent papers cited in *Paying the Price* reports on Johns' schools and it is highly critical of them (Campbell and Storr 2001).

Canada's experience merits only five lines (p. 102) and yet here Johns' schools have been operating for several years and are cause for grave concern (Van Bruschot 2002). The legal literature that is critical of Johns' schools has grown for a large number of reasons. First, the legal basis of them has been called into question. For example, if the central focus of the programme is legal activity (and the purchase and sale of sex itself *is* a legal activity), how can these programmes be legally justified? If clients are being educated out of kerb crawling then rehabilitation and training should focus on where a client *can* go to buy sex legally. While rehabilitation is considered a meaningful response to offending, what exactly, are these men being rehabilitated out of? It seems that in many Johns' schools the aim is to educate clients out of *participation* in commercial sexual activity. Yet participation itself is not an offence. Johns' schools therefore represent a slippage between the offence and the response to that offence. With or without the emphasis on the offence itself these programmes amount to moral regulation. Second, such 'schools' raise serious questions about due process, particularly in the requirement for participants to waive basic procedural rights in return for admission to the school and withdrawal of 'criminal' charges. Erosion of due process occurs when diversion imposes sanctions on those who would *not* be prosecuted or convicted if the case went through the usual course of the criminal justice system. Johns' schools do not accord divertees the rights of due process and risk 'imperilling democratic rights' (Fischer *et al.* 2002). Diversion to a programme is paradoxically conditional upon a formal admission of guilt before any formal determination of guilt has been made and the issue of 'required donations' without any formal finding of guilt is problematic. 'Voluntary acceptance' of diversion or construction of diversion as 'choice' is misleading, even untenable. The nature of choice is further compromised by those who do not know that acquittal would be possible or don't realise that they have a choice. Diversion is therefore not a voluntary choice, but a coercive alternative. Third, Crown attorneys in Canada have expressed general uneasiness about the 'trade of a degree of protection from criminal punishment in exchange for the requirements of the Johns' school' (Fischer *et al.* 2002: 405). Fourth, there are concerns about 'net widening' given the expanded role of the police in such diversion. Police have a stake in the tuition fee from the programmes and they determine how much the activity is policed often using undercover sting operations; this vested interest contributes to the net-widening process. Besides these main points, objections have also been raised because class politics are inherent as programmes focus disproportionately on those in lower social classes, as those who can afford it pay for legal representation and fight the case rather than accepting the 'diversion' option. Furthermore, the key discourse in schools is on moralising, blaming and shaming clients.[31] There is no 'reparation', no 'restitution' or 're-integration' as there would be in other diversion programmes such as restorative justice. Johns' schools not only contribute to the ongoing surveillance of prostitution and its continued stigmatisation, but are also problematic and misguided, to say the least, to expect policing agencies to take responsibility for addressing the root cause of *any* behaviour.[32] Unfortunately, none of these serious criminal justice issues are addressed in *Paying the Price.*

Legal theory and legitimacy

The prohibitionist stance in *Paying the Price* does not take account of legal theory. Analysis of the temperance movement and prohibition in the US, shows how a status law, one based on morality, can only ever be a symbolic law (Gusfield 1966; 1981). The movement on temperance now seems both intolerant and naïve, yet many of the same issues are present in *Paying the Price* where the support of one conception of morality is at the expense of another. The establishment of prohibition laws was a battle in the struggle for status between two divergent styles of life. Protestant American prohibition is similar to Sweden with its agrarian Lutheran roots and issues like prostitution generate irrational emotions and excessive zeal as the attempt to reform the 'pleasure-loving who want stimulation and excitement' is not unlike the concept of temperance. In the years up to 1919 in the US, the majority of States had passed prohibition legislation, yet changes in drinking habits reflected a decrease in the legitimacy of the temperance movement. For one thing, the consumption of alcohol was higher than at any time since 1850, and the increase appears to have involved more persons as drinkers. This rise in alcohol consumption, in terms of kerb-crawlers, would mean an increase in the occasional-use clients, and a lowering in the number of frequent clients. Prohibition was an attempt to succeed in coercive reform and ended up with institutionalised evasion. Such evasion is common over moral issues when people do not agree with the morality enshrined in law[33] and illustrates that measures against the buying and selling of sex may be counterproductive.

A further legal tenet overlooked in *Paying the Price* is legitimacy. For a law to work it must be effective, fair and have legitimacy. Norms only become legitimate when actors view them as right, proper, and appropriate. To be workable, any law must have legitimacy with those who have to police it and the quasi-religious moral view in *Paying the Price* is not a view shared by the police who deal with prostitution on a daily basis, nor shared by an increasingly secular Britain.

The importance of discourse in prostitution debates

A number of scholars have analysed the discourses around prostitution, and within feminist debates there have been three prevalent discourses: (1) A 'traditional moral discourse' which was prevalent in the 1890s and 1900s. This viewed prostitution as immoral and drew on the bible for ideas about sin and unchaste women. It gave the state a pivotal role in eradicating 'vice' and saving 'fallen women' (Outshoorn 2001). In the 1980s this moral discourse was modernised and prostitution was defined as exploitation of female sexuality, but this time the fallen woman was a victim of poverty, or trafficking and deceit. (2) The second, a 'sexual domination discourse' was inspired by radical feminism about victimised women. It defines male demand as creating prostitution (Kesler 2002). The sex industry is discursively framed as connected to the underworld and increasing commercialisation of the sex industry in which the prostitute is in danger. This emerged in the leftist discourses of 1980s, but was later employed in trafficking debates. In the course of the 1990s it became evident that trafficking was a significant issue in prostitution and a discourse developed that *all* women migrating from abroad were victims of unscrupulous traffickers, trafficked into prostitution by false promises. This was turned into a parallel discourse about rich and poor countries. This discourse explains the supply of women from the third to first world divide (Outshoorn 2001), and was taken up by women from the moral right and keenly pursued by the radical separatist lesbian left[34] and academics with a vested interest in victimology. (3) The third is the 'sex work discourse' which links prostitution to the concept of self-determination. It is congruent with an individual rights discourse and liberal contract theory, which distinguishes between forced and voluntary prostitution. This is linked to the realist stance that prostitution will take place as it has in virtually every society at every period throughout history. There is a recognition here that anti-prostitution law has never contributed to the improvement of women.

Within social policy debates on prostitution there have also been three discourses. The dominant discourse in the UK recently has been a 'public nuisance' discourse in relation to kerb crawling, and a 'moral order' discourse in relation to trafficking. These are both present in *Paying the Price*. Further afield debates have taken place in what I would identify as a 'market discourse'. This is a neutral discourse that defines sex work as an economic activity like any other. This discourse was prevalent in the development of German legislation. The difference in the various discourses is in the image they contain. In both the modernised moral discourse and the sexual domination discourse women are victims denied agency and sexuality, while in the sex work discourse and market discourse the prostitute becomes a sex-provider entering into a contract. The latter is important to give women the rights to which they are entitled. In a comparison of the discourses surrounding policies in the Netherlands and the UK it has been shown that in the Netherlands the dominant discourse is the sex work discourse (Kantola and Squires 2004). It is necessary in prostitution policy debate to include measures on pay, time off, workplace safety, working conditions, hygiene, health, and the recognition of the rights of sex workers to refuse drunk or violent clients. In the UK policy debates, however, the sex work discourse and the market discourse are absent, and this unfortunately remains the case in *Paying the Price*. So how does *Paying the Price* use the remaining discourses to construct the issues in the debate?

Discourses within Paying the Price

There is a strong self-improvement motif in *Paying the Price* and the emphasis is on moral perfection. For example, while ostensibly exploring the support of those in prostitution, the document shows a heavy bias towards exiting prostitution or 'positive lifestyle choices towards leaving prostitution'. The document states that 'legitimate' businesses should not be 'tainted' by the association with prostitution (p. 59). This use of language is important because prostitution is *not* a crime. When the Paper asks 'What problems are caused by the existence of the "trade"?'[35], the distancing device of inverted commas is used around the word 'trade' rather than accepting that sex work *is* a trade and is recognised as such by the largest union in the country, the GMB. *Paying the Price* goes on to state that 'Prostitution must not be concealed behind the façade of legitimate business' (p. 6), yet it does not answer the fundamental question why consideration cannot be given to legitimising voluntary prostitution itself. *Paying the Price* is a Consultation Document, but it does not start with the first principle which should be whether this conduct should really be brought within the criminal law (Ashworth 2004). Rather, it discursively constructs sex work as a crime.

A flawed assumption running through *Paying the Price* is the supposition that sex work is a monolithic thing. Sex work is carried out and exists in a variety of contexts and has different meanings for those working in it. Feminist scholars have theorised sex work, and theories that are both sophisticated and practical have evolved, but these have not been taken into account in *Paying the Price*. Indeed, confusion exists in the document about the socio-legal theoretical tradition on prostitution. For example, the scholar Mary McIntosh states the contractarian view of sex work in which it is accepted that:

> Prostitutes need trade union rights and a degree of control over their working situation just as other workers do. But the idea that prostitution itself is particularly degrading is seen as part of the patriarchal hypocrisy about sex that feminism rejects. So contractarians argue that 'sound prostitution' is possible, with a free market in sexual services in which anyone, male or female, may have the opportunity to be a buyer or a seller (McIntosh 1979; 1996: 95).

It is suggested that only by taking full account of these established theories and contexts can solutions be developed to help the condition of *all* of those engaged in sex work.

There is confusion in *Paying the Price* between child and adult prostitution. The cover exemplifies this and shows a sad-faced female child in an image representing 'brokenness'. The picture draws a parallel between woman and child that most women would reject. Although the image is an inappropriate one it *does* indicate how adult women are treated throughout the document. The conflation is stronger still in the language used, which insists all those over 18 years old are also 'victims' and that the realities of prostitution are 'brutal' (p. 6). This construction is not representative of the majority of sex work. Sex work is carried out by adults of all ages (McKeganey and Barnard 1996).[36] This document places no emphasis on the autonomy or empowerment of adult women and chapters 2, 3, are 4 are focused almost totally on children. The American scholar, Chapkis (2003), cautions feminists to look critically at policy documents which rely heavily on narratives of female powerlessness and childlike sexual vulnerability. The same narratives blur the difference between voluntary and forced prostitution.[37] The rhetoric of the vulnerability of sex workers is exemplified for example in the Contents headings and the vocabulary used within the chapters to focus on 'the pimp', 'coercion', 'homelessness', 'physical sexual abuse', 'exploitation', and 'abusers'. This is a further means by which clients are demonised in the document. There is confusion in the document with regard to trafficking and prostitution. The conflation of migration abuse, trafficking and sex slavery is a common rhetorical device in prostitution debates and it contributes to sensationalist claims of a massive legal and moral crisis. In a close reading of the Trafficking Victims Protection Act 2000, Chapkis (2003) shows how this occurs through three sleights of hand: relying on repressive moral panic about 'sexual slavery' which in turn relies on slippery statistics and sliding definitions; the notion that *all* prostitution is sexual slavery despite symbolic support to women; re-inforcing the notion that punishment to the 'guilty' is justified by making assistance to the innocent. Yet the victim discourse dominant throughout *Paying the Price* uses graphic accounts of extreme violation and gothic vignettes at the beginning of each chapter distort the issue without taking account of the mundane nature of the majority of commercial sexual exchanges.[38] *Paying the Price* builds and merges these victim discourses as its main rationale and legitimation for pursuing and punishing the client.[39]

The theme of vulnerability in the document marginalises men who sell sexual services to men, and to women, as well as trans(gender) people who sell sex. The literature on men who sell sex has not been acknowledged or explored fully in the document, although not unproblematically, the Sexual Offences Act 2003 made the law relating to prostitution gender neutral (Brooks-Gordon 2003). It is inaccurate to assume that the same conditions exist for men selling sex to men, men selling sex to women, women selling sex to men, and women selling sex to couples. However, in marginalising men in sex work, who generally have greater autonomy than women in sex work, not only is the rhetoric of victimhood reinforced, but the needs of male sex workers are overlooked (Connell and Hart 2003).

A further implicit assumption in the document is that dealing with prostitution in a positive way is not a political option, a political poison chalice even. This may be an erroneous assumption. It is apparent that politicians who spoke or voted against punitive measures for kerb crawlers, or supported the rights of autonomous sex workers in past debates have in various ways gained popularity since. Matthew Parris and Robert Kilroy-Silk for example, were both MPs on the standing committee of the Criminal Justice Bill who argued for the removal of the penalty of imprisonment for prostitutes. Mr. Parris in particular, who as an MP was on the standing committee of the then 1985 Sexual Offences Bill, called it 'an ill-drafted and knee-jerk Private Members' Bill to criminalise kerb crawling' (Parris 2002: 294). The current Mayor of London, Ken Livingstone, spoke *against* harsher penalties for kerb crawlers during the Shelton Bill in 1990 and is a politician whose public popularity has since gone from strength to strength (Brooks-Gordon and Gelsthorpe 2003).

The document discursively creates community as a singular concept and *Paying the Price* misjudges the public view because this concept of community is flawed. The reality of community feeling is not a black and white polaroid punctured by needles and smeared by condoms. One example in London of community support was the Soho community who provided 10,000 signatures on a petition not to evict women sex workers after Westminster Council tried to evict them. Conflict can however arise from status aspirations and discontents; conflict between material goals and aspirations of different social groups (Hofstadter and Lipset 1969).[40] Economics play a large part in prostitution and in the lynch mob behaviour of communities who have allowed vigilantes. Studies of the lynching of negroes by whites in America as a consequence of the low prices of cotton are a classic example. The frustrations of economic setback can give rise to aggressive feelings which are then displaced against the target with the least power to resist (Gusfield 1966). It is not therefore surprising that some poorer communities have exhibited hate politics against prostitutes (Hubbard 1999). For Muslim and Catholic communities where men have less access to pre-marital sex, they fear for the men in the community. In depressed communities where people are managing on insufficient benefits, frustration may be displaced onto sex workers making good money on the street corner who provide a prime example of conspicuous consumption. Within *Paying the Price* also exists the notion that clients exist *outside* the community, that the community dislikes prostitutes, and that the community speaks with one voice. All of these are without foundation (Sagar 2005). It is necessary to get balanced research into communities as too often in criminal justice policy it is the 'squeaky wheel getting the oil' as one police officer has put it, rather than the view of the *whole* community.

The Strategy

Despite, or perhaps because of, the serious flaws in the methodology and assumptions within *Paying the Price*, a large number of sensible and erudite responses ensued, many of which, in addition to being sent to the Home Office, were published in academic journals and online.[41] In January 2006 the Home Office published its White Paper *A Coordinated Prostitution Strategy and a Summary of Responses to Paying the Price* (*The Strategy*).

Indications of what *The Strategy* would deliver were becoming apparent before its publication when, in the lull between Christmas and New Year, on 28 December 2005 the Home Office announced through the media that a policy of zero tolerance would be pursued against clients. 'Prostitution blights communities. We will take a zero tolerance approach to kerb crawling. Men who choose to use prostitutes are indirectly supporting drug dealers and abusers. The power to confiscate driving licences already exists. We want the police to use that power more' (Fiona Mactaggart MP quoted in the Guardian, 28 December 2005, p.1). *The Strategy* was published following this Yuletide invective at the end of January 2006.

The stated aims of *The Strategy* are to: challenge the view that street prostitution is inevitable; reduce street prostitution; improve the safety and quality of life of communities affected by prostitution, including those directly involved in street sex markets; and reduce all forms of commercial sexual exploitation. It also favours enforcement against kerb-crawlers and people who pay for sex or drive around red light districts. The specific proposals include greater police power for enforcement against loitering and soliciting, kerb-crawling, and the disruption of indoor markets, and the document rejects safety zones. There is little good in the document for sex workers other than the recommendation that the definition of brothel be changed to allow two or three workers to work together for safety, and the removal of the term 'common prostitute'.

Enforcement against kerb-crawling

Enforcement against kerb-crawling, although acknowledged in *The Strategy* to be dangerous and increase risk for street sex workers who have less time to negotiate safely or check out a client, is put forward as a key issue. It is acknowledged in the document that relatively few residents are affected. Kerb-crawling is flagged as an environmental nuisance and is couched in terms of 'pollution' such as 'congestion and noise' (p. 33), yet the ironically named 'environmental' measures suggested in *The Strategy* include light pollution and environment-degrading CCTVs on street corners. There is no explanation as to why clients on foot, who are also mentioned, cause an environmental problem. Although it was already been pointed out that there are a whole range of minor public order offences that could be used to prosecute any clients who do cause alarm, distress or harassment (Liberty 2004), a range of 'diversion' strategies are put forward in the strategy through which clients will spiral through the criminal justice system. The first stage will be informal warning, followed by court diversion as an alternative to prosecution to a 're-education programme' funded by the person warned. Alternatively, conditional cautions are put forward with 're-education' being a condition. For those with previous convictions, or those who refuse the 'offer' of the 're-education', prosecution will result. Those who refuse the 'option' of a re-education programme or have past convictions would attend court and all kerb-crawlers, and would have to attend court on the same day; ostensibly to 'ensure consistency in sentencing and use full range of penalties'. But if there is inconsistency in sentencing then this should be addressed in training and in the sentencing guidelines rather than batch-handling to facilitate the last recommendation in *The Strategy* which is to 'name and shame' those convicted in the local media. Labelling theory would suggest that it would encourage further such behaviour once someone has been 'outed'. It is a retributive strategy that could result in vigilantism of the worst sort as occurred in summer 2000 when the *News of the World* swiftly ended its name and shame campaign after a number of vigilante attacks broke out and drove five families from their homes. The suggested enforcement against men who are only cruising around an area and not even kerb crawling represents a hideous intrusion into civil liberties and this has been found in case law (*Darroch v DPP* (1990) 91 Cr App R 378) not to constitute an offence.

The specific proposals also include those on children involved in sex work who will no longer be criminalised. This is not a contentious issue, but the Government seems to keep running around in ever-diminishing circles around an issue which is already heavily legislated. The document goes over much old ground on the issue of children at risk and much of what *The Strategy* puts forward is already in place. Care however must be given to make realistic and not neurotic assessments of risk about children living in a sex work environment, for example when an adult woman is working in sex work to support her children. Freeman (1997) provides examples in the juvenile justice system where well-intentioned measures have had a net-widening effect and instead of enhancing rights, eroded them instead (see Bainham (2005) for discussion of this principle).

Enforced medical treatment of street sex workers

The Strategy contains a set of penalties for street sex workers who, if they do not 'accept' referral to services offering routes out of sex work, will be cautioned with 'pre-charge diversion' (p. 38) which will have conditions attached to them such as attendance on Drug Intervention Programmes (DIPs). Failure to comply will be an offence. The Government's intention is clear: 'The current offence of loitering and soliciting is a very low-level offence and, as such, the court will usually only consider imposing a fine. This is said to have very little deterrent effect and does not address the underlying cause of the offending behaviour. To rectify this situation, the Government intends to publish proposals for legislative reform to provide a penalty specifically tailored for the needs of men and women in prostitution. The intentions will be for the courts to be able to order an appropriate package of interventions to address the causes of offending behaviour where the behaviour is persistent. This will ensure a robust, staged approach to the policing of street offences' (p. 37). New measures in the Drugs Act 2005 are already giving the police enormous power to test for drugs after arrest and continue testing after charge. The Act also includes 'required assessment' which means that those who test positive will have to be assessed for drug use. Failure to comply will be an offence: 'The Government has introduced a new civil order for adults which can run alongside an ASBO. The new Intervention Order will be available from April 2006 and will enable individuals engaged in anti-social behaviour to receive treatment to address the underlying causes of their behaviour where it is drug-related' (p. 40).

Conditional cautions for sex workers are not a convincing step forward. Questions have to be asked about what happens if they cannot agree or keep to the 'care plan'. The new penalties for offence of soliciting and loitering along with the continued use of ASBOs and Acceptable Behaviour Contracts (ABCs) could have a net-widening effect and increase the downward spiral of those who, once criminalised, find it harder to get out of sex work. It is unlikely that new legislation would be required as the Criminal Justice Act 2003, s.209 already contains drug rehabilitation requirements which in relation to a community order or suspended sentence order, means a requirement that during a period specified in the order the person:

(a) must submit to treatment by or under the direction of a specified person having the necessary qualifications or experience with a view to the reduction or elimination of the offender's dependency on or propensity to misuse drugs, and

(b) for the purpose of ascertaining whether he has any drug in his body during that period, must provide samples of such description as may be so determined, at such times or in such circumstances as may (subject to the provisions of the order) be determined by the responsible officer or by the person specified as the person by or under whose direction the treatment is to be provided.

(2) A court may not impose a drug rehabilitation requirement unless–

(a) it is satisfied–
  (i) that the offender is dependent on, or has a propensity to misuse, drugs, and
  (ii) that his dependency or propensity is such as requires and may be susceptible to treatment,

(b) it is also satisfied that arrangements have been or can be made for the treatment intended to be specified in the order (including arrangements for the reception of the offender where he is to be required to submit to treatment as a resident),

(7) ... –In this section 'drug' means a controlled drug as defined by section 2 of the Misuse of Drugs Act 1971 (c. 38).

These provisions were introduced to send those who were persistently carrying out acquisitive crimes to fund drug habits and who wanted help, into treatment. Given the misleading emphasis on drug taking within *The Strategy* on sex work, it is possible that this type of medical treatment will be enforced on sex workers who do not want to exit sex work or drug taking. Further provisions brought in under the Drugs Act 2005 gave the police further power, following a positive drug test, to order a person to be 'assessed'. However the difference between selling sex and acquisitive crime is that the former is not illegal. This so-called 'rehabilitative approach' (p. 39) presents a return to the days of Lock hospitals where people were incarcerated against their will.

Removal of 'common prostitute'

The Strategy suggests removal of the offensive term 'common prostitute' (p. 39). But, as has been pointed out elsewhere, the broad definition of a person as a 'prostitute' defined in the Sexual Offences Act 2003 is of questionable compatibility with the right under the ECHR to a fair hearing (Bainham and Brooks-Gordon 2004).

Re-definition of brothel and information sharing

The Strategy provides for the re-definition of a brothel to enable two or three individuals and a maid to share premises for safety. This is a step forward and a necessary step for the safety of those in off-street locations. It also calls for improvements in information sharing protocols with the expansion of the so-called Ugly Mugs lists. This is to be welcomed so long as it is a two-way process between police and sex workers' groups. Proposals for such information sharing was put forward seven years ago in 1999 so the Government has acted rather slowly on this matter (Brooks-Gordon 1999).

Disruption of indoor sex markets

The Strategy signals the Government's intention to allow police to 'disrupt' indoor sex markets. Such a strategy could be linked to the conflation in the document between migrant workers and trafficked people, for example: 'drop-in services in London find that brothel workers are now almost entirely migrants ... Those involved are often highly vulnerable to exploitation' (p. 11). Under the guise of helping the 'highly vulnerable' such power could turn into a bullies' charter as police officers disrupt (destroy?) off-street locations. The result would be that more people will be thrown onto the street where there will only be penalties and there will be little for them in the way of safety.

Safety zones

The document rejects the option of safety zones: 'we reject the option of managed areas. The clear aim of the Government will be to disrupt street sex markets to significantly reduce the numbers involved in street prostitution' (p. 9). This is a missed opportunity to create safety (tolerance/managed) zones for sex workers, when a rigorously evaluated pilot showed them to be of benefit in Liverpool. All street sex workers should have the option to work in a safety zone. To dismiss safety zones takes *The Strategy* out of line with European policy.[42] Research in Scotland shows that not all street sex workers are drug addicted or were sex working from a young age (McKegany and Barnard 1996). For example, some women were in their 40s when they turned to street work after their husbands' jobs disappeared in the shipbuilding industry. The Government approach to sex work fails to acknowledge that many of the dangers in sex work are preventable rather than being related to coercion and involvement with other forms of crime. Rather, the danger is due to a lack of protection that is taken for granted in other employment sectors (Liberty 2004). It seems neither prudent nor pragmatic to ignore this issue.

A summary of responses?

It is implied in the title that *The Strategy* is a result of the responses yet it does not contain a summary of the responses, which would necessarily include the quantitative compilation of the 861 responses received to the 35 questions asked in *Paying the Price* (p. 133) along with a qualitative analysis of qualitative material received. Rather, *The Strategy* is overtly based on anecdote and opinion rather than any credible evidence base, for example, 'anecdotal evidence suggests' (p. 7, para. 2), and 'anecdotally this has a high deterrent effect' (p. 34). There is also a lack of transparency of methods; unlike the *Setting the Boundaries* report which listed the exact number of responses to each specific question asked so it was possible accurately to assess what level and type of support each proposal had. The Home Office also published a list of individuals in *Setting the Boundaries* who attended consultation meetings and seminars, and while not all views were represented, the process was at least transparent and the findings could be interpreted according to the methodology employed.

The Strategy, however, does not list the individuals who contributed (except MPs whose names are written in full). Rather, only organisations are listed in Annex A. Thus, this lack of attention to detail does not enable the quality of research to be evaluated and it militates against getting hold of the research/response independently. The situation is ameliorated slightly only by the fact that many individuals have published their responses in academic journals and on websites. It is interesting to note that many of the published responses do not accord with the proposals in *The Strategy* (for example, Soothill and Sanders 2004; Self 2004; Cusick and Bernal 2005). The summary of the consultation exercise (Annex B) lists only three meetings, four focus groups, and 'a questionnaire'. It does not state the grounds on which participants were chosen (i.e. the most vociferous or those living in closest proximity to red light districts), the demographic make-up, religion/ethnicity of participants, how the groups were conducted, how these were facilitated, how the data was analysed. Clearly, some views were privileged in their access, for example some groups on 'sexual exploitation' gave their views directly to ministers (p. 5), while other groups struggled to get replies from the Home Office staff despite repeated attempts (e.g. Self 2005). There is a lack of transparency that makes it impossible to interpret or give credence to the findings. One of the most important rules of research is that it should be transparent. Similarly with the 'questionnaire', there is no list of questions in order to see how they were framed, distribution rate, attrition rates, nor the method of analysis. The methodology published in *The Strategy* fails the most basic requirements of social science research.

Anecdote and opinion as consultation summary

The confusion about what is and isn't evidence is also present in the layout. The document text is interspersed by short boxes of text providing a mixture of anecdote and opinion, for example there is a short vignette recommending a 'Change Programme', but offering no evidence to support it. Another text box is placed under the heading 'Ensuring Justice' (p. 55) cites the individual case of Ann (Nancy) O'Brien who was convicted of controlling prostitution in three London brothels and sentenced in November 2005. Her case has been used for 'talking-up' trafficking and it is considered a victory for justice in *The Strategy* that a confiscation order for over half a million pounds sterling was awarded against her. But what was she really guilty of? A quotation in The Times given by one of the officers, Detective Constable Day states that 'she was a pleasant woman who ran a salubrious and up-market brothel. There was no coercion and no sign of trafficked women but she had not paid income tax and was benefitting from the proceeds of crime' (The Times online, 17 November 2005). Given that money confiscated under proceeds of 'crime', is split four ways with the Home Office, CPS, Courts Service and the police all getting their share, the use of this case to increase the case against 'trafficking' is therefore dishonest. The subsequent division of assets is taxation by a dishonest route, by the Home Office who should allow brothel owners to pay tax in the usual way. It is interesting to note that in a document of this type there would ordinarily be a foreword by a minister, usually the Home Secretary. There is no ministerial foreword in this document. Either it was a hastily presented piece of work, or the Home Secretary was distancing himself from it.[43]

Moral tone

One of the most notable aspects of the *The Strategy* is its high moral tone. For example, the executive summary states that one key objective is to 'challenge the view that street prostitution is inevitable' (p. 1). This however is based on moral rather than practical reasoning or precedent. Further on in the document the tone becomes almost messianic, for example, 'we are failing our communities if we simply accept the existence of street prostitution' (p. 13). It presents a rallying call to believers to serve 'our communities' by denying the existence of sex work and that it is heretical to believe otherwise. The document separates sex work from sexual exploitation and yet still rejects that the former 'is an activity that we can tolerate in our towns and cities' (p. 1). However, it is not for the state to determine the morality of sex work and it is most certainly not the purpose of the criminal law.

Measures that provide help and support to street sex workers are rejected as creating a 'comfort zone' or that they attract people into sex work. This amounts to moral condemnation of sex work and is an insult to the national government organisations (NGOs) and voluntary agencies where many people work tirelessly helping those in street sex work, and such terminology would not be used to describe any other form of aid. The document draws moral equivalence between consensual adults exchanging sex for money and sexual slavery or child rape, which is dangerous and offensive.

There is gender discrimination in the way male sex workers are marginalised in the document. The document does not take account of the fact that statute is now gender neutral since: 'the strategy focuses primarily on the needs of women' (p. 9). There is also an anti-men bias in the way clients are referred to and it is viscerally and emotionally anti-men. The Home Office has developed a new ideology which makes victims of women and demons of men (Self 2006).

Media reaction, the 'new puritans' vs the real public

Following the publication of *The Strategy* there was much coverage and comment in the media. Much of this was supportive of the re-drafting of laws to allow two or three sex workers to work together. The majority of newspapers either missed the dangers of kerb-crawler enforcement and re-education programmes or were critical of the perceived 'crackdown'.[44] Many elements of the news media were critical of the Government's missed opportunity to reform the law properly on commercial sex. In this respect attention was directed at the puritanical underpinning of *The Strategy*: 'what really outrages the new puritans is tarting, not trafficking. There is an odd alliance of über-feminists and arch conservatives who deny the right to buy sex. But in a free society is that anyone else's business?'[45] In the days that followed two polls were published, one by the Independent on Sunday (22 January 2006), which asked 'should mini brothels be legal?', 64 per cent replied yes. The second, by MORI, was based on

1,790 British adults, 2/3 (66 per cent) felt that sex work should be legalised (which of course it is), an increase of four points since 2002. Approximately 2/3 (64 per cent) felt that paying for sex should be legal.[46] MORI is a highly reputable company, but its findings of a large sample of the British population are at odds with the Governments' proposals from its own consultation. It is interesting that MORI's wider measure of public opinion elicited a more favourable view of commercial sex than the Governments' dissemination of its four small focus groups.

The Strategy to draw its proposals from the evidence base of properly evaluated independent research either at home or abroad. Its basis owes more to tabloid and sensationalist reports of 'trafficking' and public opinion based on fear of crime rather than a proper understanding of the extant research: 'The essence of the strategy is proactive policing and a robust legal framework with severe penalties' (p. 53). Criminological researchers have routinely found however that, when well-informed, the public are less punitive than the tabloids assert (Roberts and Hough 2005).

Regulatory Impact Assessment[47]

As *The Strategy* was being put forward, a *Regulatory Impact Assessment* (RIA) was sent to ministers to sign. The document is written in convincing language that might sway anybody not familiar with the research, it states for example: 'It is increasingly recognised that those involved in street prostitution exercise little choice'. Notwithstanding the fact that vast tracts of the labour market actually exercise real choice over their jobs, it is one-sided and inclined to favour without reason or evidence a number of controversial strategies. The RIA focuses the strategy to: increase preventative measures, tackle demand, reform law on loitering or soliciting, develop routes out of prostitution, tackling off-street prostitution. It states that: 'The legal framework will enable enforcement action to be taken against all those who use and abuse those involved in prostitution, through specific offences targeted at kerb-crawling, pimping, trafficking, and grooming' (para. 11.2, p. 15). There is not much with which the reasonable person, or minister, would disagree here, but as has been shown earlier pimping has already been dealt with extensively, as has 'grooming' in the preparatory offences in the Sex Offences Act 2003 legislation. There are many errors of fact, for example the RIA states that 'those involved in prostitution who also share injecting equipment are at high risk of HIV infection. There are also reported to be high rates of chlamydia, gonorrhea, abnormal cervical cytology, ...'. This is highly misleading as the medical evidence is that there are low prevalences (0–3.5 per cent) of these amongst sex workers and it is going down which contrasts with increasing rates amongst non-sex workers in younger age groups (Cusick 2006).

Kerb-crawling especially is an area in which the whole consultation process and strategy misleads through lack of evidence and research. The suitability of ABCs and ASBOs as measures to deter kerb-crawling are promoted despite the fact that it is admitted that 'there has been no formal review of their effectiveness' (p. 4). The document gives a clearer indication of the shape of policy: 'there will be a increased focus on those who create the demand for a sex market through more regular and consistent enforcement on kerb crawling' (p. 8). It is admitted in the RIA that 'the potential risk with increasing enforcement is that it could place those involved in prostitution at greater danger [and] that enforcement measures alone will often result only in displacement' (p. 8). The estimates in the RIA are that £176m public money is spent on seeking out and catching behaviours related to the sale of sexual services and that the increase needed has not been costed, but 'would be on this scale' (p. 8). It is claimed that such spending could be cut back if 'tougher enforcement' proved to be a deterrent. History and recent precedents illustrate that such optimism is both misplaced and misleading to the ministers who would be expected to sign off the RIA. The recommendations in *The Strategy* to 'remove the stigmatising term "common prostitute"' (p. 9) and 'The Government will make proposals for the amendment to the definition of a brothel so that two or three individuals may work together' (p. 61), have both disappeared in the RIA. So that by the end of the consultation process, the sensible, safe options have been lost and only the punitive or dangerous strategies remain. So what went wrong?

Politicisation of the police

In the face of such questionable reliability of evidence, it is necessary to look at context. As this chapter has shown, the statute books are bursting with legislation which already confer immense powers on the police in this area yet there was an orchestrated press campaign by the police throughout and beyond the consultation period. The police press machine is sophisticated (see Chibnall 1977) and not only did newspapers reprint the police stories around trafficking scares[48], but television cameras also accompanied police officers on 'raids' on brothels to 'rescue' 'trafficked' women. One such raid took place in Birmingham in September 2005, although it was later found that none of the women were 'trafficked'.

The Strategy bears many of the hallmarks of the police intervention as it repeats much of the published police strategy (Brain *et al.* 2004). This police input into the process of developing *The Strategy* on prostitution is interesting as it came at a time when police involvement in the political process was being heavily criticised during a Bill on terrorism. The interference of the police,[49] and the so-called politicisation of the police, caused great concern amongst MPs who had considered the issues carefully and then found themselves being lobbied by the police using pseudo-scare tactics. There were three issues: (1) MPs were not convinced by the evidence the police put before them, (2) MPs objected in principle to being lobbied by the police who should be neutral and implement changes decreed by Parliament rather than the other way around,[50] and (3) in particular MPs, such as Clare Short, were dismayed by the process, and specifically the 'pseudo-scare' tactics used by the police.

When it came to power in 1997, New Labour did not seem, in principle, to object to the sex industry *per se*. For example, the party accepted from Richard Desmond money known to have been made from pornographic magazines. In addition, political advisor and architect of New Labour, Alistair Campbell, had written a column for *Forum*, a pornographic magazine. It seems strange therefore that the puritanical moral tone of the Government's consultation was so out of step with the actions of the early party in power. The key to *The Strategy* is the curious alliance of views which melds those of the police and the tabloids with those of radical separatist feminists who along with the religious right, had a vested interest in running exit programmes linked to a new moral agenda.[51] And New Labour, bowing to the sensationalism of the tabloid press which uses a combination of gothic personal testimonies and titillation (but at the same time hire sex workers to deliver 'kiss-and-tell' stories on celebrity clients), and prepared to give the police everything they asked for, was prepared to listen to a new moral agenda. None of this would have been able to influence the outcome so heavily had it not also been for the appalling consultation carried out by the Home Office.

Home Office Incompetence

The Governments' documents were all published during a period when the Home Office came under intense criticism from leading criminologists who stated publicly that their research had been misused by the Home Office. Concerns were first raised in June 2003 by a number of researchers engaged in Home Office funded research, some of whom were outraged by the misuse of their research. One subsequently stated: 'It is clear that the Home Office is only interested in rubber stamping the political priorities of the Government of the day' and 'To participate in Home Office research is to endorse a biased agenda' (Hope 2005/06: 37). Another stated 'To participate in Home Office research is to endorse a biased agenda that omits topics of national or global concern in favour of regulating the poor and the powerless' (Walters 2005/06: 6). There followed a rallying call within criminology to boycott Home Office research attesting that 'critical criminological research is vital during the ascendancy of an intolerant, punitive, and moral authoritarian state' (Walters 2005/06: 7). There is no doubt that Home Office credibility has been severely damaged amongst some leading researchers who claim: 'Its research agenda is motivated by outcomes of immediate benefit to existing political demands' (Walters 2005/06: 6). There are other possible explanations. It is also possible that the Home Office staff were too inexperienced or too incompetent to be able to analyse the 861 responses properly. Perhaps not enough resources were allocated to the consultation process. However, as this book went to press the Home Secretary Charles Clarke 'resigned' over a series of Home Office blunders traced back over a number of years. For some, or all of these reasons, it has come to pass that Home Office policy at present is inconsistent, impractical, and it has in recent years, departed from the evidence base. It is sex workers and their clients who will pay the price for such evidence-deficient policy.

Chapter summary

This chapter provides a summary of the extant laws surrounding sex work. The state of the law is still piecemeal, contradictory, it lacks explicit and clear purpose for workable policy on the sex industry, and recognition of sex workers as social and economic actors entitled to the same civil and human rights as other citizens. The situation in 1990 was summarised, thus:

current vice laws in the urban West are not easily summarised or interpreted. Full of contradiction, they embrace notions derived from liberal humanist philosophies about the sexual rights of individuals yet simultaneously assert that certain expressions of sexuality are morally unacceptable. (Hubbard 1990: 14).

Unfortunately, sixteen years later there was a great need for overhaul, but it seems that the Home Office has failed to do what was needed.

This chapter has begun to reveal that as the fifth government exploration of the laws surrounding sex work in 50 years the consultation process was welcomed. However, the Green Paper *Paying the Price* and the subsequent Government Strategy has disappointed researchers, health workers, legal historians, and activists alike. Regrettably, omissions and factual errors are made in the use of research and legal evidence – especially on clients of commercial sexual services. Viable policy alternatives, such as those in Germany and Holland have been dismissed. Inaccuracies about the legal basis of other jurisdictions such as Sweden have led to the flawed representation of them as options, and inadequate research and attention to the literature has led to failed programmes such as Johns' schools being put forward as viable. Furthermore, essential legal issues, such as human rights, legitimacy, and status law, as well as feminist theorisation in the area, need to be considered. It seems also that the various discourses in the documents close down rather than open up, the opportunity for discussion.

It is clear that regulatory approaches are, with very little evidence, heading swiftly in several directions. One of these is the disruption of off-street sex work establishments; a strategy that the Government admit the likelihood that those working in brothels and flats' would 'be transferred onto the streets where they are at greater risk of victimisation' (RIA: 11). The second direction is towards tough enforcement against clients who buy sex whereby men who have not been found guilty will be subjected to untested psychological treatment which will be meted out in a so-called 're-education'. Given this raft of punitive, expensive, and potentially damaging proposals, it is essential to have a full analysis of the research evidence on clients. What is important is to move beyond the general profiles and pejoratives in *Paying the Price* and towards specific demographic profiles and motivations of clients so that sensible interventions can be implemented. Chapter 3 will explore in depth the evidence base on clients.

Notes

1 *A Coordinated Strategy and a Summary of Responses to Paying the Price*. Ref 272136. London. Home Office 2006. www.homeoffice.gov.uk/documents/ cons-paying_the_price.pdf

2 Henceforth called 'The Strategy'.

3 For example, Birmingham City Council uses section 222 of the Local Government Act 1972.

4 A list of the all the offences appears in Schedule 1 of the Act. So, for example, it provides the following: the offence of permitting premises to be used for prostitution (Sexual Offences Act 1956, s.36) is amended so as to provide that it is irrelevant whether any prostitute involved is male or female; the offence of loitering or soliciting for the purposes of prostitution by a 'common prostitute' (Street Offences Act 1959, s.1) was amended so that it is irrelevant whether the prostitute is male or female, and consequential amendments are made to the provisions about cautioning in section 2 of the 1959 Act; the kerb-crawling offence of soliciting a woman by a man for the purposes of prostitution (Sexual Offences Act 1985, s.1) was amended so that becomes an offence for a person to solicit a person for such purposes. The other remaining offences in the Sexual Offences Act 1956, provided by sections 33–35 relating to keeping, or managing or acting or assisting in the management of, a brothel (s.33), letting premises be used as a brothel (s.35) already extend to premises which are used for lewd homosexual practices, as well as to those for lewd heterosexual practices, by virtue of the Sexual Offences Act 1967, s.6.

5 For this reason, in this text I will use the term 'prostitute' only when referring to particular aspects of law. Otherwise the term sex worker will be used as this provides a better understanding of sex as work.

6 At: http://news.bbc.co.uk/.

7 D. Ormerod, *Smith and Hogan Criminal Law*, 11th edn. Oxford University Press, 2005.

8 The Sexual Offences Act 2003, s.78 defines 'sexual' as: For the purposes of this [Act] (excluding s.71), penetration, touching or any other activity is sexual if a reasonable person would consider that: (a) whatever its circumstances or any person's purpose in relation to it, it is because of its nature sexual, or (b) because of its nature it may be sexual and because of its circumstances or the purpose of any person in relation to it (or both) it is sexual.

9 See Appendix 1 for these relevant sections of the London and Local Authorities Bill 2006 in full.

10 The provisions do not apply to the City of London, which has its own legislation relating to special treatment of premises.

11 Home Secretary's Foreword, p. 5.

12 *Niemietz v Germany* (1993) 16 EHRR 97.

13 This point is made with clarity by A. Ashworth (2004).
14 These are: Brooks-Gordon and Gelsthorpe 2003b; Boyle 1994; Faugier and Cranfield 1994; Pease and Pringle 2002; and Sharpe 1998. The first and most recently published is cited wrongly in *Paying the Price*.
15 The National Health and Social Life Survey (1989) found that 16 per cent of men had paid for sex.
16 Further understanding comes from a survey of 1,001 randomly chosen men in Norway of which 13 per cent had paid for sex.
17 The increase could however, be due to sampling error, or merely the fact that throughout the decade more men were prepared to discuss the buying of sexual services.
18 See for example, Ms. Gisela Stuart (MP Edgbaston) (Hansard House of Commons, 3 July 2001, col 46WH, 19 November 2002, column 511).
19 This accounts for the significant number of unmarried Catholic and Muslim men who pay for sexual services in the statistics.
20 Home Office (2004) 'Solutions and Strategies: Drug Problems and Street Sex Markets', p. 1. Home Office.
21 p. 17.
22 ECJ, Decision of 20 November 2001, Case C–268/99, [2001] ECR I-8615, paras 33, 49.
23 It also falls within the meaning of Article 44 of the Association Agreement between the Communities and Poland and Article 45 of the Association Agreement between the Communities and the Czech Republic. The District Court of the Hague referred to the ECJ for a preliminary ruling under Article 234 of the EC Treaty concerning the interpretation of the two agreements..
24 To use the argument that some sex workers do not use zones as a reason to reject zones is perhaps like arguing that the presence of fake designer goods on the street is in itself a reason to prohibit or criminalise the designer goods industry and all who buy from it.
25 The effect of police action on sex worker health and safety occurs across jurisdictions, see for example, Pauw and Brener (2003).
26 For example, it is the only country in Europe, where a national law was passed banning gay bathhouses; where HIV victims can be forcibly incarcerated without trial if doctors believe that they will not tell future partners of their HIV status; where doctors are legally obliged to report an HIV+ person to the authorities; and where HIV victims must report all their sexual relationships. England, by contrast has a powerful gay lobby, a unionised sex industry, and an active collective for sex worker's rights. In addition, the state is not a 'moral' police force telling its citizens what to do sexually.
27 It has been argued that during the two years leading up to the law the fear of 'Eastern bloc' women eager for intercourse in Sweden and pro-prostitution laws in other countries made Sweden fear that it would be penetrated on all fronts. See Kulick (2003).

28 'Importing Policies: Swedish Message', The Economist, 4 September 2004, p. 30.

29 It has been suggested that it is an idealism to argue that sex which is bought is different to sex which is not bought as casual sex between people who have just met may not be so different from the sexual encounter a prostitute has with an entertaining client (Kesler 2002).

30 Hester and Westmarland, op cit.at n.57, p. 45.

31 Fischer et al. (2002) compares the 'educational' aim with the punitive qualities that emerge in practice.

32 In any case, large meta-analyses show that even lengthy two-year programmes by psychologically trained staff have shown little success in changing sexually related behaviour. See Kenworthy et al. (2004).

33 Two other examples have been methods of obtaining divorce and abortion. Here, all parties and witnesses colluded to provide evidence, and doctors would grant medical diagnoses (though false) to sustain a 'legal' abortion. Institutionalised evasion results in loss of status for the government; in the case of prohibition it led to repeal of the 18th Amendment.

34 For whom the logical extension is that all heterosexual sex is demeaning, oppressive, and violent for women. These views owe much to the work of Dworkin (1987) and MacKinnon (1987).

35 para. 2.17, p. 17.

36 For example, the situation of women in their 40s has been highlighted in research who, as husbands' steel industry jobs vanished, started work in street prostitution.

37 This is important because the raft of measures brought in by the Sexual Offences Act 2003 dealt extensively with children in prostitution and the trafficking and exploitation of women and arguably the issues most in need of reform now are those which help women who are voluntarily in prostitution.

38 The distortion, and impact of the distortion, is what H. Kinnell has referred to as 'perverse feminism'.

39 It has actually been sex worker groups and those concerned with the unfairness of recent criminalising tendencies in the law who have striven most for the review.

40 Shown in an analysis of McCarthyism and extreme right wing groups in the 1950s by Hofstadter and Lipset (1969).

41 Examples here include those from Liberty, the Humanist Society, UKNSWP.

42 In April 2000 the Parliamentary Assembly adopted recommendations [1450 (2000)] on the subject of violence against women in Council of Europe member states which included trial tolerance zones (safety parks).

43 It is interesting to compare this in relation to previous recent consultation and strategy documents on sexual behaviour. For example, in the last

consultation exercise on sexual behaviour, *Setting the Boundaries*, the then Home Secretary, Jack Straw, stated in the Foreword that the review was set up: to make recommendations for clear and coherent offences that protect individuals, especially children and the more vulnerable, from abuse and exploitation, and enable abusers to be appropriately punished' (*Setting the Boundaries: Reforming the Law on Sex Offences, Summary Report and Recommendations*, July 2000, p. 1). In the subsequent White Paper, *Protecting the Public*, the next Home Secretary, David Blunket stated that 'Public protection, particularly of children and the most vulnerable, is this Government's priority', but he did also state that 'we cannot hope to provide 100 per cent safeguards and protection. Nor must we intervene in the personal, private relationship of consenting adults' (*Protecting the Public*, Foreword p. 5, November 2002, Cm 5668).

44 Ben Russell, 'Ministers criticised over crackdown on sex trade', The Independent, p. 10 2006.
45 Jasper Gerrard, Sunday Times, 22 January 2006, p. 28.
46 This was carried out for The Observer (http://www.mori.com/polls/2006/sa.shtml, accessed 22 January 2006).
47 See: http://old.homeoffice.gov.uk/docs3/paying_the_price.html, downloaded on 6 February 2006.
48 See, for example, 'Janie's Secret', The Guardian, 5 November 2003, at: http://www.guardian.co.uk/child/story/0,7369,1077799,00.html; 'Home Office Defers Expulsion of Women held in Brothel Raid', The Guardian, 5 October 2005, at: http://www.guardian.co.uk/uk_news/story/0,3604,1584888,00.html.
49 The police wanted to detain suspects for long periods of time without charge.
50 MPs argued that this was the 'tail wagging the dog'.
51 For Alliance of ACPO spokesperson and religious groups such as CHASTE, see www.chaste.org.uk/cst.10scnf. For Police/Women's Groups Alliance, see www.bearhunt.org.uk and Disrupting Sex Markets Conference. For Women's Groups/Religious Alliance present in National Women's Commission see: http://www.thewnc.org.uk/about_us/index.html. None of these groups have been including sex worker groups.

Chapter 3

Understanding sexual demand

Part I: Understanding sexual demand: why do men pay for sex?

> The frequencies of such contacts in any large segment of
> the population have never been investigated ... and this is
> astounding in view of the tremendous interest that so many
> agencies have had in controlling the frequencies of such contacts
> (Kinsey, Pomeroy and Martin 1948: 597).

In chapter 2 the laws that govern prostitution were analysed and the
Government's Strategy outlined. Alongside the historical summary in
the initial chapter, this illustrates how prostitution has long been subject
to moral and social debate. Despite this debate, however, the *extent*
to which men pay money for sex with women is poorly understood
(Wellings *et al.* 1994). In particular, there are few estimates of the
number of men who pay for sex and empirical research on clients
has been a relatively recent, post-war enterprise. A theoretical bias
in socio-legal research has traditionally led researchers to disregard
men's gendered status. While research has begun to address the
gendered status of men in general (for example, Connell 1987, 1995;
Frosh 1994; Edley and Wetherall 1995; Messerschmidt 1997; Collier
1998; Jukes 1999; Segal 1990, 1997) the male client has remained a
marginal figure and studies of men involved in prostitution account
for less than one per cent of all prostitution studies (Perkins 1991).
This occurs also because the nature of the sex industry has led to
clients being so hidden that their characteristics, behaviour patterns
and offences have proved difficult to study empirically (Faugier

1995; McKeganey and Barnard 1996; Campbell 1997). The continued difficulty in accessing clients means that consideration of these men *as clients* remains in its early stages, and a combination of the above factors has resulted in a lack of information on the client; in turn this has hindered the development of theory, policy, and intervention strategies in the area (Høigard and Finstad 1992; O'Neil 1997; Sharpe 1998). In this chapter I review the literature on male sex clients. Firstly, I outline the prevalence of commercial sex clients who have been researched as part of general sex surveys. Secondly, I review studies that have focused specifically on clients.

Prevalence

One of the first attempts to explore the prevalence of male commercial sex encounters was in a general sex survey by Kinsey, Pomeroy and Martin (1948) who speculated that two-thirds of men had paid for sex at some stage in their lives. No more than 15 per cent to 20 per cent of these men, however, regularly paid for sex (Kinsey *et al.* 1948). It was argued that these regular clients were motivated to do so because prostitutes were thought to be an 'easy' and 'certain' sexual outlet; would offer 'variety' and were cheaper than dates; devoid of all obligation, emotional commitment and worries about pregnancy, there was also some evidence of a decline in the use of prostitutes (Kinsey *et al.* 1948: 607). The methods used in the study were notoriously controversial however,[1] and a similarly large-scale, but methodologically superior sexual attitudes survey by the Mass Observation Unit (1949) in Britain (referred to as 'Little Kinsey'), avoided the sampling problems of the original study. This study found that although respondents said they regarded prostitution as 'immoral', one in four of the men interviewed had paid for sex at least once.[2]

A later study in the US showed that the number of young clients had declined since Kinsey, and that customers were married men in their 30s, 40s and 50s (Winick and Kinsie 1971). The authors attributed this decline to the 'loosening' of sexual mores and sexual availability of non-prostitute women. It was also suggested, that if law enforcement moves prostitution to another area, some men will travel considerable distances to find a prostitute, sometimes combining a visit to a prostitute with a business trip (Winick and Kinsie 1971). This position was supported by the findings of Gagnon and Simon (1973) who also suggested that a large number of men visit prostitutes when they are away from home, so that only when other social controls are loosened do these men visit prostitutes.

Further understanding of men who pay for sex was provided by Prieur and Taksdal (1989) in a study undertaken by Norway's leading survey institution. A group of 1,001 randomly chosen men were asked in a questionnaire if they had 'paid for sexual contact/ intercourse with a prostitute' once or more. Thirteen per cent of these men said they had paid for sex. This group of men, however, had limited individual experiences of prostitution, with a quarter having paid for sex once, a further quarter two to three times, nearly a third had bought sex four to ten times. The number of men dropped drastically to 4 per cent of men who bought sex eleven to twenty times, 3 per cent bought sex twenty one to fifty times, and for the remaining men the figure was 50+ times, or unknown. It would seem, therefore, that a small number of habitual clients were responsible for a considerable volume of prostitution. A number of sailors for example with many experiences of purchasing sex raised the overall average in the Prieur and Taksdal (1989) study. The vast majority of these men (80 per cent) had only bought sex abroad. The researchers concluded that customers were likely to be men who travel more, and those who have more money. It was also concluded that although large, quantitative studies answer questions about proportions, the method is unsuited to illuminate the *meaning* of a social phenomenon for the participants and so a further study by Høigard and Finstad (1992) was developed to do this.

In the same year (1989), the National Health and Social Life Survey in the US, found that although 16 per cent of men had ever paid for sex, only 0.6 per cent pay for sex each year (Michael *et al.* 1992). There was also a decline in the percentage of young men in the 1990s whose first sexual experience was with a prostitute (1.5 per cent) compared to men of the same age in the 1950s (7 per cent). In a sexual behaviour survey carried out shortly afterwards in Britain, nearly 7 per cent (N=82) of the 1,200 male respondents had bought sexual services (Knox, MacArther and Simons 1993). There were differences, however, within the various age groups, and younger men (under 26 years) for example, were less likely to say they had been clients (5 per cent). Ten per cent of the men over 27 years of age said they had paid for sex, and the number of men over the age of 45 years rose to 12 per cent. This suggests a cohort effect of age with older men most likely to report being clients. Across all age groups, men who had been clients were nearly three times more likely to have had a sexual relationship with another man than those who had not used sex workers (Knox, MacArther and Simons 1993: 83).[3] These findings were followed by one of the most significant studies on sexual behaviour in Britain by Wellings, Field, Johnson and Wadsworth (1994), who found that almost 7 per cent (6.8 per cent)[4] of the 8,384 men surveyed said they had paid for sex at least once. Less than a third of these men (1.8 per cent) had purchased sex within the previous year, which indicates that the experience of paying for sex was a past rather than a recent experience. This was especially marked in the older age group. It appeared that single (that is, never married) men were least likely to pay for sex (4.1 per cent), and widowed, separated or divorced men (14.5 per cent) were most likely to do so. Paying for sex rose significantly with increased age, working away from home, the higher social classes (I and II); and the experience of a same-sex relationship for these men. Wellings *et al.* (1994) assert that there has been a genuine decline in payment for sex, which they maintain is due to increased availability of non-commercial sex.[5] In a later study, the same patterns emerged (Johnson *et al.* (2001)) and it was argued that paying for sex is therefore associated with increasing age, previous marriage or current cohabitation (outside marriage), a history of working away from home, and a history of having a homosexual partner. It can be seen from the summary table below that not only does prostitute use differ between the early American studies and the more recent European ones, with twice as many American men paying for sex as men in the UK, but also that, over time, there is a more downward trend of the number of commercial sex clients in the general population, on both sides of the Atlantic. Alongside this decline is the reduction in the number of men having their first sexual experience in a commercial setting. Clients are less likely to be younger men, and are men who travel away from home.

The purchase of sex is not related to age alone, however, but also to other life experiences such as being separated, divorced, and having same-sex relationships with other men. A theme that is consistent across all three countries and the different types of survey is that the commercial sex market is supported by a small number of habitual purchasers of sex. Importantly, while these findings from surveys tell us about incidence and prevalence for some groups of men, they do not tell us *why* it should be that some men pay for sex when they travel and others do not. It is useful therefore to explore some of the explanations that have been made to account for why the client population pays for sex.

Table 3.1 Prevalence and Features of Male Clients in Sex Surveys

Study	Place	Prevalence	Main findings	Conclusions drawn
Kinsey, Pomeroy and Martin (1948)	US	66 per cent ever, 15–20 per cent regularly	Main motivation – sex without complications. Provides a 'certainty' of gaining sexual outlet. Encounters devoid of obligation, with no worry about pregnancy.	Despite high proportion of men paying for sex, there has been a decline over time.
Little Kinsey (1949)	UK	25 per cent	Prostitution regarded by respondents as 'gross immorality'.	[–]
Winick and Kinsie (1971)	US		Average client married man in 30s, 40s, and 50s. Men travel long distances to buy sex. Client numbers have declined over time.	Law enforcement creates displacement. Loosening of 'sexual mores' led to decline.
Simon and Gagnon (1973)	US		Many men only buy sex when away from home.	Loosening of social controls necessary for some men to buy sex.
Prieur and Taksdal (1989)	Norway	>13 per cent	Vast majority of men (80 per cent) only bought sex abroad.	Researchers went on to follow up clients in more depth to

Study	Country	Prevalence	Findings	
Michael *et al.* (1992)	US	16 per cent ever, 0.6 per cent past year	More single men amongst the clients. Amongst married men, more dissatisfaction of cohabitation and sex life. Customers more likely to be men who travel a lot, and men with more money.	find out 'meaning of being a client' for the client.
Knox, MacArthur and Simons (1993)	UK	6.4 per cent ever	7 per cent of men reaching majority in 1950s had first sexual experience with a prostitute. This figure dropped to 1.5 per cent by 1990s.	Decline in initiation. Older men more likely to be clients.
			Younger men less likely to be clients. Older men more likely to be clients. Clients three times more likely to have sex with men than non-clients.	Clients have more variable/ risky sexual experiences overall.
Wellings, *et al.* (1994)	UK	6.8 per cent ever, 1.8 per cent past five years	Younger, and single (never married) men least likely to be clients. Older, widowed/ separated/divorced men more likely to be clients. Clients more likely to have had	Marital status, raised age and/or working away from home significantly related to purchase of sex.

Table 3.1 continues on page 86

Table 3.1 continued

Study	Place	Prevalence	Main findings	Conclusions drawn
			a relationship with another man. Social classes I and II more likely.	Prostitutes have dis-proportionate number of bisexual male clients. Decline in paid sex due to availabilty of non-commercial sex.
Johnson *et al.* (2001)	UK	4.3 per cent[6]	Commerical sexual contact strongly associated with increasing numbers of partners. 17 per cent of those with 10 or more partners in their life-time reported a history of commercial sex contact. Paying for sex was associated with increasing age, previous marriage or current cohabitation (outside marriage), a history of working away from home, and a history of having homosexual partners.	The increased reporting of risky sexual behaviours is consistent with changing cohabitation patterns.

Why do men pay for sex?

One of the first investigations of commercial sex clients *as clients* was done by psychologist Charles Winick (1962) who surveyed 732 men, and who claimed that these men were 'disturbed' in some way. Such explanations found favour in other early studies of client populations by Gibbens and Silberman (1960) and Janus, Bess and Saltus (1977), who used psychoanalytical interpretations, including the role of fantasy, to argue that such men were suffering from some degree of psychopathology. It was suggested that the elements of 'sadism, masochism, and voyeurism were frequently present as incomplete perversions' by Gibbens and Silberman (1960: 114) whose work highlighted, but did not explain, such observations. These studies were, however, noteworthy for providing the ground for the later theoretical developments of Stoller (1976, 1979).

Stoller put forward the first explanation for the behaviour of men who purchase sex, which he suggested was a perversion and as such could be considered to be an erotic form of hatred which is 'a habitual, preferred aberration necessary for one's full satisfaction, primarily motivated by hostility' (1976: 4). The purchase of sex is a perversion (as opposed to a sexual variation or an aberration)[7] because underlying the behaviour is a fantasised act of revenge, in which the subject's sexual life history (including his memories; fantasies; traumas; frustrations; and joys) is condensed. Stoller suggests that this first occurs in 'oedipal development and in those anxieties that derive from the anatomical differences' (1976: 98). Anxiety and mystery, therefore, emerge from childhood and the way our society obscures the discovery of the anatomical differences between the sexes. The end to the mystery comes with the creation of a full-blown, conscious, perverse act (or fantasy of the act). Each episode of sexual excitement draws to the surface the questions and fantasies that are the mystery, and the resultant anxiety can then be reduced only by the perverse act (whether in its performance or in its fantasised state). In the perverse act, one endlessly relives the traumatic or frustrating situation that started the process, but the outcome is marvellous, not awful, for not only does one escape the threat, but finally, immense sensual gratification is attached to the consummation. It was argued that the whole story, precisely constructed by each person to fit exactly his own painful experiences, lies hidden in the sexual fantasy of the perversion (Stoller 1976: 105).

In this theoretical explanation, such fantasy and subsequent sexual excitement is most likely to be set off at the moment when adult reality resembles the childhood trauma or frustration. From clinical data on male exhibitionists in therapy, Stoller (1976: 129) suggests that the perverse act usually occurs following a humiliation, most often at work or from a man's wife. He is then driven into the street by a tension he does not sense as erotic, to search an unfamiliar neighbourhood for a woman or girl to whom he displays his penis. This implies that more anxiety is felt during the perverse sexual act than is usually present otherwise. This anxiety, or the anticipation of danger, he contends, is experienced as 'excitement'.[8] The perversion (that is, the newly created fantasy), therefore does more than solve the mystery. The central theme that permits this advance to pleasure is revenge. It reverses the positions of the actors in the drama and so also reverses their affects. One moves from victim to victor, from passive object of others' hostility and power to the director or ruler. One's tormentors in turn will become one's victims. With this mechanism, the child imagines himself as parent, the impotent as potent, suggests Stoller (1976: 105).

Risk is also an essential part of the perverse act, and Stoller's theory suggests that risk is inherent in the dynamic of revenge. Although, for pleasure to be possible, this risk cannot be too great, the odds cannot be so high that one will experience the same trauma again. Nonetheless, the perversion must simulate the original danger, and this is what gives it excitement. So long as one keeps control, which is possible if it is one's own fantasy, then it is a foregone conclusion that the risk will be surmounted (Stoller 1976: 115). Safety factors must therefore be built into the fantasy to reduce anxiety so that the odds are loaded in favour of triumph. Using a variety of perversions, Stoller illustrates how this risk is contained; for example, the fetish is absolutely passive and so 'cannot threaten, interfere, witness, or accuse; it can be attacked, dirtied, hated, destroyed, and yet it is infinitely renewable ... the obscene telephone caller does not confront his victim and have to suffer the knowledge that she is only human; the prostitute is paid to be agreeable and indulge in acts she might otherwise spurn' (1976: 122). It is through the fetishes such as these that Stoller provides an explanation for prostitute use. Indeed, he follows the work of Bak (1968) to suggest that fetishism is the model for all perversions and that one who cannot bear another's totality will fragment (that is split and dehumanise) that object in keeping with past traumas and escapes. The relationship between customer and prostitute ends instantly after the customer has been gratified, and whatever hostility was held in abeyance during the sexual act is released after it is over. The power equation shifts and the customer who no longer lets himself be humiliated, returns the prostitute to the street (Stoller 1976). The thesis, then, is that sexual excitement and the need to harm one's objects are closely related to the domain of personal dynamics and also other fetishistic behaviours.

Exploring Stoller's theory

Support for Stoller's theory has been found by Holzman and Pines (1982) who attempted to explore the phenomenology of being a client. Thirty clients were interviewed and the findings support the premise that the process of paying for sex would begin with fantasies long before the actual encounter happens. This process occurred in four phases: the conception of intent; the pursuit of the encounter; the encounter; and the aftermath. In the conception of the event, men had high expectations of a positive experience, and in more than half the cases, men said the desire for sex was coupled with the desire for companionship. It was not unusual for clients to shave, bathe, dress fashionably and use cologne before an encounter. In other cases there were expectations of the 'mystery and excitement' that might accompany the payment for sex (Holzman and Pines 1982: 104). A sexual fantasy tinged with elements of fear and adventure was created and nurtured by these men. Such excitement was also tied to the myth of the sexual prowess of the prostitute, and the expectation of an amazing sexual experience. Some men said that the pursuit of the encounter was made exciting by the element of risk and fear for their safety, not from the legal dangers of paying for sex, but the possibility of their own criminal victimisation, such as 'a knife at your throat', or the 'unknown quality of what actually happens' (1982: 109). Clients attempted to manipulate the sex worker psychologically by plying her with alcohol and trying to suppress the business end of the encounter and structure it into a romantic or social one. They stressed a belief that they could seduce the prostitute into becoming an active as opposed to passive paid participant in their sexual fantasy. After the encounter, however, the majority of clients had feelings of disappointment. This was due to the lack of communication with the sex worker, and recognition that the meanings these men had given the encounters had been of their own making and not shared. Many clients just wanted to get away, relieved it was all over. One respondent said: 'I just found it to be a very debasing, humiliating experience for me' (1982: 109), and many others 'felt appalled' at what they had done. Whilst not drawing explicitly on Stoller's work, the main themes of a fantasy build-up, risk, trauma and humiliation are all present in these findings within a discrete four-phase process.

Whilst Stoller's theory is regarded by many scholars such as Weeks (1985) as being the most comprehensive account of *why* men might pay for sex, the focus on hostility, control, triumph, rage, revenge, fear, anxiety, and risk that Western men use in encounters with prostitutes, is somewhat limited by its refusal to address broader power structures within which individuals live out their sexualities. These structures have been explored by feminist researchers, and a common feature of many clients' motivation to pay for sex was found to be the opportunity it provides to escape the conventional male heterosexual role with its heavy emphasis on masculine prowess and dominance (McLeod 1982).

Escaping the conventional male heterosexual role

Following interviews with clients in Birmingham, McLeod (1982) suggested that men went to prostitutes because their marriage could not cater for their emotional and sexual needs, and that these men were too frightened to reveal the truth of the experience of marriage. Instead, she argued, 'men want to hang on to what emotional, social and material security it does provide, while seeking compensation – not always guaranteed – by visiting prostitutes in conditions of secrecy' (1982: 59). She also argued that the form taken by the act of going to a prostitute shows how the sexual urges in question and their moment of relief are highly disciplined. It is not the case that men are electing to have intercourse with the nearest woman in the next minute (which would support a theory of more casual prostitute use). Rather, these men are limiting it to specific time of day, in particular locations with selected women, at certain frequencies and with a strictly-prescribed code of behaviour based on what prostitutes will agree to. This is 'hardly an uncontrollable urge at work' suggests McLeod (1982: 66). Nearly all the men interviewed in McLeod's (1982) study complained about the emotional coldness and mercenary approach of many prostitutes they saw, and those trying to compensate for lack of sex fused with emotional warmth in marriage ended up in the same situation with a prostitute as the one from which they were trying to escape. McLeod's (1982) study therefore supports the findings of Holzman and Pines (1982) by suggesting that the act of purchasing sex is a much-planned event by the client, who hopes for some exquisite release, but instead often finds an empty and disappointing experience.

In a later study, Campbell (1997) found that men said their dislike of and difficulty with 'dating rituals' such as clubbing and chatting up was the reason they entered into commercial sex contracts. This 'difficulty' may also indicate the pressure put upon men in conventional roles that McLeod (1982) and theorists such as Segal (1999) argue are as damaging to men as to women. Men with partners said they wanted only sex with prostitutes – and that they got other things like commitment, intimacy and love from wives (Campbell 1997).

After carrying out 13 in-depth interviews with off-street clients, Jordan (1997) found that most men were seeking sexual solutions for emotional problems, and these men argued that going to a prostitute relieved feelings of despair and intense loneliness. Few men expressed any strong guilt feelings or sense of betrayal towards others in their lives for doing this, and Jordan (1997) concluded that the internalisation of masculine stereotypes legitimated men's roles as sexual consumers. Similarly, this cultural construction of male sexuality was examined by Campbell (1997), who proposed that these men see the encounter as one with no emotional involvement or commitment beyond the 'contractual' arrangement. This dichotomous approach to sex, however, is possibly not confined to men who pay for sex, and Seidler (1992) points out the danger of this conflict to men's psychological health.

Clients in a study by Kinnell gave more than one reason for seeking commercial sex. The most common reason was: 'I do not want emotional involvement' (1989: 4). Almost half the clients who had non-paid sexual partners cited: 'Not enough sex with wife/girlfriend'. Others bought services – usually oral sex – that they said they could not get from their non-paid sex partners. Some clients said they chose commercial sex because they felt 'prostitutes are expert'. Other reasons were: 'Variety/Turn-on/Sex is boring with wife', shyness, or enjoyment of sex workers' company. Single men stressed a need to escape from solitary masturbation, whilst loneliness and old age were reasons given by older men. Kinnell's (1989) study provides some useful insights into these men's motivations for seeking commercial sex, although some of the categories tend to be rather arbitrary, serving to cloud rather than clarify the issue being explored. For example, in the 'variety' category it is not clear if the men mean variety of women, or of services. Also, the phenomenological meaning of 'turn-on' for some of these men could have more to do with the fetishistic representation of the prostitute body[9] in Western culture (see Brooks-Gordon 1997) than the monotony of the same partner and/or sexual position. Alternatively, the term 'turn-on' could be the term these men use for the extensive fantasy build-up seen in the studies of McLeod (1982) and Holzman and Pines (1982).[10] All the same, generalised motivations found by Kinnell (1989) were later supported by the findings of Høigard and Finstad (1992); McKeganey and Barnard (1996);[11] Campbell (1997), and Monto (2000). McKeganey and Barnard (1996) also produced two additional client motives for paying for sex: dressing in womens' lingerie was added to the sexual services men did not feel able to ask their regular partners for, as were sex acts such as being urinated or defecated upon by the sex worker. The second additional motivation was the attraction of the 'illicit' nature of paid sex. These not only support the relationship of client behaviour to fetishism that Stoller (1976) suggests, but also the level of 'risk' inherent in his theory.

McSex as a possible motivation?

Monto (2000) suggests that the men's answers to the desire for 'variety', 'control' and 'immediate satisfaction when aroused' – point to a self-focused and commodified approach sexuality called 'McSex' and which 'reflects a conception of sex as a commodity rather than as part of a intimate relationship' (Blanchard 1994, cited in Monto 2000: 80). Men who want instant gratification, and then shop for a partner with specific bodily attributes, physical body type, or hair colour, were first noted by McKeganey and Barnard (1996). The McDonaldisation thesis which aligns many services to the purchase of fast food (Ritzer 1995) and is clearly one worthy of further exploration in this context.

Client needs and the targeting of interventions

In order to be able to explore the theoretical issues and whether they are supported by empirical investigation, it is necessary and important to examine *who* the men are demographically. This is especially important for targeting interventions for clients in the area of mental and sexual health. Not only are the majority of sex-working women unable to deal with the psychological disturbance these men may exhibit, but also evidence of continuing requests from clients for unsafe sex, strongly suggests the need for campaigns targeted at clients, supported by services aimed at contacting clients (Faugier and Sargent 1997: 136). Vanwesenbeeck and colleagues (1993) believe a client's attitude to going to sex workers and paid sex is related to his protection-style with regard to condom use. The experiences, inhibitions, priorities are linked to self-image and perception of commercial sex, and that information needs to be tailored to these individual beliefs if protective behaviour is to be influenced.

More positive responses about the prostitute's ability to control an encounter, and more client good experiences emerge from research in Holland than that in the UK (see, for example, McKeganey and Barnard).[12] A self-selected sample of 87 male clients, whose mean age was 45 years, was interviewed by Vanwesenbeeck et al. (1993) in the Netherlands, and categorised according to condom use. There were eight categories which comprised: (i) convinced users, whose motive was 'a pleasant hour's relaxation'; (ii) guilty-conscience users, who had guilt about prostitute use due to their religious beliefs, the money spent, and their regular partner; (iii) angst-ridden users, who described their client activities as an addiction over which they have little control; (iv) defaulting users, who see themselves as victims of temptation; (v) maximum selective users, who find one particular sex worker they can be happy (and develop a degree of trust and closeness) with; (vi) minimum selective users, whose motive was to be 'absolutely uninhibited'; (vii) indifferent users, who were widowed and handicapped men who wanted to hold and be held, and (viii) recalcitrant users, who are characterised by desire for power and who describe their prostitute use as an uncontrollable urge or necessary evil, and often feel deceived by prostitutes. The influence of protective behaviour is important because: 'male clients are potential carriers not only of HIV but of many other sexually transmitted diseases to both sex workers and their other partners as they wield considerable power in the decision-making process in relation to safer sex' (Leonard 1990, cited in Faugier and Sargent 1997: 136). It is thus necessary to explore just who these clients are.

Demographic findings from within-client populations

Some basic categorisation of a commercial sex-client population was made by Stein (1974). A total of 1,230 clients of 64 American call-girls were observed and audio taped through one-way mirrors, peep-holes, and wardrobes. The clients were categorised as opportunists, fraternisers, promoters, adventurers, lovers, friends, guardians, juveniles, or slaves. The 'opportunists' treated sex workers as sexual repositories and had minimal contact with them. The 'fraternisers' visited in pairs or groups. The 'promoters' sought personal satisfaction and peer prestige by encouraging other men to visit prostitutes they knew, and wanted social support or non-sexual relationships from the women in return. The 'adventurers' were younger men visiting for sexual experimentation. The 'lovers' sought romantic attachments and were older men wishing to save the women from lives of corruption. The 'friends' were middle-aged, married men wanting companions or 'second wives' supplying sex on demand. The 'guardians' were the oldest category, and saw themselves as protectors of young prostitutes. The 'juveniles' were single, of any age and seeking older sex workers as mother figures. The 'slaves' wanted domination, humiliation or to express homosexual, infantile, transvestite or exhibitionist fantasies. Percentages in these categories varied from 4 per cent for 'juveniles' to 17 per cent for 'adventurers' (Stein 1974). Whilst some of these studies have produced large sample sizes of data (indeed Høigard and Finstad 1992: 25, argue that the data set of Stein 1974; and Janus *et al.*, is 'so sizable that they are on the boundary of the believable'), it has been at the expense of ethical considerations because of the surreptitious way the clients were observed and subsequent lack of consent regarding the interview. Such an exploration shows that client behaviour is variable and whilst further exploration is necessary, it is arguable that more ethical methods are needed to collect data.

The difficulty of reaching commercial sex clients by other means however, was acknowledged by Cunnington (1979) who managed to interview only two clients whilst carrying out her research with the Vagrancy Squad in London.[13] During court observations, however, she noticed that the majority client tourists were Arab, Japanese, German and American, but these men refused to be interviewed. By contrast, street ethnography was found by Cohen (1980) to be an ethical and useful alternative way of studying these men. In 56 hours of observation, 32 clients were openly observed by Cohen, who provided detailed description of men's characteristics as they hired sex-working women working the streets in New York. The mean age of these men was 35 years[14] although a client's age varied with location, with slightly older men patronising higher-status locations and younger men patronising lower-status ones on the city's Lower East Side. Seventy-five per cent of the men were white, 12.5 per cent were black and 12.5 per cent Hispanic.[15]

Client socio-economic status

Inferences were made about the socio-economic status of these men based on their appearance, and those who were 'clean-shaven and wore business suits and neckties' were categorised as 'executives'. Many of the men 'cruised' in expensive new cars such as cadillacs, some of whom were considered to be tourists, foreign business-men or diplomats because of their 'foreign accents'. Clients on the Lower East Side were dressed in working-class clothes such as 'dungarees' and 'cheap soiled open shirts' and tended to drive older cars in the lower price-range. Many men arrived in trucks and vans that served as 'surrogate hotels' and the majority of these men (72 per cent) were white (Cohen 1980: 102). It was also noted, in what are now abhorrently racist terms that 44 per cent of men 'crossed racial lines' in their choice of sex worker with black/white clients choosing white/black sex workers.

This small study also contains some rich description of the persistence of these men:

> Johns in cars usually formed a queue and cruised around and around the corners where prostitutes were located … typically a john circled the area for ten to thirty minutes before selecting a woman or before he was selected by a prostitute. Cruising johns not satisfied with a location's prostitutes visited other street locations along the circuit until a desirable woman was found. Oftentimes a cruising john blocked traffic when he stopped to talk to a prostitute. (Cohen 1980: 63)

Once an agreement was reached, the transaction (usually fellatio)[16] was conducted in the car a few 'blocks' away in a secluded parking 'lot' or side-street (Cohen 1980: 65). The clients without cars, however, usually conducted business in a hotel or used darkened hallways or alleys. Cohen (1980) also noticed other, non-client men during his observations. These men stood around in groups of 2–10 watching street activity, and were rated as 'lower class' or 'unemployed'. It was also found that most clients had a regular prostitute whom they picked up. Such patronage Cohen (1980) attributed to trust, danger, habit, and the personal nature of the service. From his observations, Cohen constructed a model of the client/prostitute market and provided a picture of how this street sex market functions in a heavily policed urban city. The study also illustrates the importance of street ethnography as a method for exploring other factors that may relate to buying sex, such as geography and opportunity.

With sex worker health needs and client condom-use as the central point of her enquiry,[17] Kinnell (1989) provided the first comprehensive dataset of the demographic characteristics and motivations of these men. This study, carried out in Birmingham, found that the mean age at which men became a client for the first time was 30 years. At the time of the data collection, the mean age of these men was 41 years and so the average client had been buying sex for 10 years. The majority of these men were local to the West Midlands (80–95 per cent) with over half (60 per cent) local to the City of Birmingham. Over a quarter (28 per cent) of these men were in professional or 'white collar' occupations; 13 per cent ran small businesses; 45 per cent were in 'blue collar' occupations; 6 per cent were unemployed; and 6 per cent were retired men. The most commonly purchased service was 'straight' (that is, vaginal penetrative) sex by 56 per cent of the men; oral sex was paid for by 20 per cent, and hand relief 12 per cent. These men, two-thirds of whom had non-prostitute sexual partners, also tended to buy sex elsewhere in England, Belgium, Netherlands, France, West Germany, Spain and Portugal. Kinnell (1989) supports the findings from the general population studies with regard to men who travel from home, and their age, but also provides data on a clear majority of local clients, the type of sex clients were buying, and both a broader and a clearer demarcation of social class.

Class, ethnicity, gender, and a pyramid model of prostitution

Street prostitutes have more clients on average than women working off-street. Indeed, the higher up the social scale a sex worker is, the fewer clients she will see (McIntosh 1996). Whilst every model is a simplification, a 'pyramid' model has been useful to describe the status of women within prostitution with the women working from escort agencies through expensive hotels or flats at the top of the pyramid, down to saunas and massage-parlour brothels to the street women at the bottom of the pyramid (see, for example, Perkins 1991). This model also says something about the customer, and according to Høigard and Finstad (1992: 131) the higher up the pyramid he buys from, the higher his own social status. A large number of male clients in other studies, however (see, for example, O'Connell Davidson 1998), came from a much higher social class, were more advantaged socially and economically than the women from whom they bought sex. It has been argued, therefore, that the statistics which confirm that prostitutes and clients come from different social classes (with the prostitute from lower classes and clients from middle-classes) should make us aware that prostitution is a class as well as a gender issue (James 1976).

From the 'impressions' of sex workers, Perkins (1991) estimated that the class backgrounds of 128 clients were: 2 per cent strictly working class; mostly working class 11 per cent; equal working/middle class 28 per cent; mostly middle class 8 per cent; strictly middle class 3 per cent; middle/upper class only 9 per cent; indeterminate mix 38 per cent. One Australian brothel-worker in the study reported: 'most of them are married, working-class guys, between 40 and 60' (Perkins 1991: 332). Another street worker said 'the majority are middle-aged, half would be married, a lot of Italians, Greeks, Lebanese'. Martine, a 26-year-old bondage mistress, said 'Very poor men cannot come to see us very often because our sessions are very expensive. We don't get Asians, Australian Aboriginal men, nor black men from different countries. Basically we get mostly Anglo men' (1991: 332). Such findings, support the pyramid model, but illustrate that there are unexplored issues around class and ethnicity bound up with the commercial sex market and men who patronise it, and what they can afford to pay. Whilst some countries, such as Norway, have shown a lot of overlap between different forms of prostitution, many customers from higher social status groups with higher incomes have been found to prefer indoor prostitution to street prostitution, but the tendency was very weak (Høigard and Finstad 1992).

The mean age of the 143 men in McKeganey and Barnard's (1996) study was 36 years. The majority of the men interviewed were employed, and whilst no economic classes were given, only 16 of the men were unemployed; half of them were either married or living with their partner. Nearly a third of the men had been HIV tested. Most of the men reported having paid for vaginal sex; 89 had paid for masturbation or other non-penetrative sex and 87 men had paid for oral sex. Eleven men said they had paid for anal sex. Despite initial access difficulties, Faugier (1995) managed to interview 120 male clients in Manchester to explore the (sexual and drug-related) behaviour of these participants. These clients were mainly, like Holzman and Pines' (1982) participants, white, married, and self-employed or in professional and managerial positions. They also were mainly British with an average age of 39 years. Ethnicity has been linked by sex workers with 'genuineness' when assessing whether a man will honour the sex work contract and sex workers generally refuse younger men in favour of middle-aged men (Sanders 2004).

The 'rational well-resourced man'

In Streatham, South London, Matthews (1993) constructed a profile of clients out of police records and found that the kerb-crawlers tended to come from locations four to six[18] miles away, with some living over 15 miles away. The ages of these clients ranged from 20 to 59 years, but the majority were in their 20s and early 30s (Matthews 1993). A later study of police data on 280 men reported for kerb-crawling and interviews with 38 clients who visited massage parlours and saunas found slightly wider age ranges – from 19 to 71 years – and also explored social class (Benson and Matthews 1995a). Approximately 50 per cent of these men came from the 20–29 year old age group, with a further 30 per cent in the 30–39 year age group.[19] Social class was measured on Standard Occupational Classifications (SOC) using the job title entered on police records for categorisation. It was found that almost one-third of kerb-crawlers belonged to social class I and II, and that slightly fewer than three-quarters fell into the top three social classes of professional, managerial, and skilled non-manual workers.

From street observation and the analysis of police records, limited outlines of clients were sketched by Benson and Matthews (1995a), and in a recent study in the north of England by Sharpe (1998). These UK studies have shown that although clients come from across the social spectrum, the average street client lives locally to the suburban red-light district, is employed and in his 30s.[20] They construct the male kerb-crawler as a non-violent, presumably white (ethnicity is not explored) 'everyman', an otherwise stable character who goes home to his family after buying street sex. This notional harmlessness permeates the limited literature on commercial sex clients and is apparent in studies by Campbell (1997) and Jordan (1997), as well as in media reports (see, for example, O'Sullivan 1998). Yet residents living in red-light districts do sometimes complain about being harassed by kerb-crawlers and the focus of policing turned further towards kerb-crawling men. A survey carried on the records of 883 street clients who came to police attention for prostitution-related matters by Birmingham's vice squad found that nearly half these men (44 per cent) were between the ages 18 and 30 years; 20 per cent were in their 30s; 16 per cent were in 40s; and only 5 per cent were over 50 years of age (Boyle 1994: 51).[21] Forty-three per cent of these men were in 'blue-collar' occupations, 33 per cent in white-collar occupations and 23 per cent unknown. Nearly half of all these men (45 per cent) came from the Birmingham area itself, 26 per cent from the surrounding Midlands and 28 per cent further afield in the UK. A similar pattern is reported for Avon and Somerset police with clients living along the M5 corridor, between Cheltenham and Exeter – within one hour of Bristol's red-light area (Boyle 1994: 51). One vice officer is quoted as saying 'they are all "Mr Average Collar and Tie", not the creepy-crawlies people expect' (1994: 53). It is argued by Boyle (1994) that half the kerb-crawlers caught in London are from the city, with mid-week being their peak time for 'touring a beat', and suggests that kerb-crawlers were often a greater nuisance than the prostitutes, to point out that the police policy of targeting the women was in error. This is because residents apparently complain more to the researchers about being harassed by kerb-crawlers than by the women. This is a problem, claims Boyle because the kerb-crawlers are infinite and prostitutes are not (1994). The research reported by Boyle is hard to evaluate because it is not made explicit how the data were gathered, but the research she describes seems influenced by the work of Matthews (1993), both in characteristics and motivations.

In a study based in the north of England, Sharpe (1998) constructed a profile of 122 clients from police records, prostitute and police interviews. She found that the clients' mean age to be 37.9 years (with a range of 18–67 years), that a great many of these men came from within the county (84 per cent), and only 10 per cent from neighbouring counties, while a small number (7.3 per cent) came from outside the region altogether. The majority of these men (60 per cent) lived within 10 miles of the city, with 41 per cent living within 3 miles of the city centre and red light district and 18 per cent lived between 4–10 miles of the city.

Using the Registrar General's classification of socio-economic class, it was found that 7 per cent of men are from social class I, 23 per cent from social class II, 47 per cent from class III (of which 28 per cent were manual, 18 per cent non-manual), 6 per cent from class IV, 3 per cent from class V, the remainder (14 per cent) was made of students, unemployed, and retired men. The majority, therefore are in social class III (Sharpe 1998). From the men's comments when stopped by police, it was concluded that 90 per cent of these clients were married. However, Monto (2000) gathered data on 700 street clients at the start of one 'Johns' school, in San Francisco, and he found that clients were significantly less likely to be married and more likely to never have been married than the national sample.[22] These married clients reported less marital happiness than the national sample. In contrast to findings of British sex surveys, almost all the clients reported having exclusively female partners. For over a quarter (27 per cent) of these men, the circumstances of their first commercial sex encounter was set up by a family member or 'buddie', a third (31 per cent) of the men said the context of their first encounter was following an approach by a prostitute, a further third (31 per cent) went to the prostitute without any others knowing. Demographically, the majority of these clients were white, 18 per cent were Hispanic,

13 per cent Asian, 4 per cent African-American. These men were generally well-educated, 42 per cent completed a university degree, 35 per cent a college course, 41 per cent currently married, 36 per cent never married, 16 per cent divorced, 5 per cent separated, 2 per cent widowed. The majority of these men worked full time, a quarter had served in the military.

The act of buying commercial sex, Monto (2000) suggests, is a product of both practical and motivational factors. Motivational factors include social learning – for example, that one has sexual urges needing an outlet, that women in prostitution can be used for that outlet (Gagnon and Simon 1974, cited in Jeffreys 1997: 214). The practical issues include the availability of commercial sex; knowledge of where to find it; money to pay for it; the risk of being caught; disease;[23] and ease of getting the type of service wanted. The motivational factors are more varied and the assumption of merely wanting 'sex' is not reason enough to explain the phenomenon of paid sex, given that many men who want sex choose not to have commercial sex. Not only does Monto (2000) miss the complexity of culture, and the psychological build-up to going to a sex worker, but more importantly, the study is placed within a context that paradoxically argues for a victim stance of sex worker and purports to understand her economic need, but supports a system that takes her clients, often the sole means of support, away from her.

In prostitute interviews, older clients were regarded as less trouble because they were less likely to try and trick the women or be rough. Three sex workers cited ethnicity as a reason for refusing to do business with a client, one saying that black men 'treat us like dirt', offering practical concerns for this racial comment such as if the condom burst and she ended up pregnant then explaining the child's skin colour to her partner and other children would be difficult (Sharpe 1998). Client ethnicity is not the only issue that may lead to tensions within commercial street sex markets, and the commercial interests of other workers on the street may interact or conflict with those of the sex worker and her client. Few studies have studied these relationships which O'Connell Davidson (1998) argues are essentially parasitical in nature.

Tensions and parasitical relationships on the street

The relationship between cab drivers and prostitutes for example is regarded as highly parasitical in nature by O'Connell Davidson (1998):

Taxi drivers are usually a reliable source of information for prostitute-using men arriving in unfamiliar cities about where to find street prostitutes, as well as the bars, discos and night-clubs where prostitutes solicit. Many taxi drivers are willing to do more than simply provide information, and actively solicit custom for specific massage parlours, hostess clubs or entrepreneurial prostitutes in exchange for a 'finders fee' and/or procure prostitutes on behalf of clients in exchange for a 'tip' (O'Connell Davidson 1998: 83).

Whilst O'Connell Davidson (1998) carried out research in the developing world, it is also argued that this is equally the case in Western countries (Jarvinen 1993: 131, cited in O'Connell Davidson 1998) yet few other empirical studies provide evidence of this. Such a parasitical relationship would constitute a drain on any surplus created by prostitutes. This is because any cut that is taken as a 'fee' comes out of the prostitute's takings (whether paid directly to her or her/his employer) and acts as pressure on sex workers to enter into more transactions than are necessary to their own subsistence. It leads O'Connell Davidson (1998) to argue that sex tourism as a social practice is embedded in both structural inequalities and broader ideologies and interests. Some of the sex workers who contributed to a study by Butcher and Chapple (1996) cite taxis, alongside babysitters, as their main expense: 'I've only got £400 in my bank account now and I'm trying to save up for a car. That will save me £200 a week in taxis ... £40 a day on taxis' (1996: 24). Many prostitutes present taxis as a must because they cannot use public transport from appointment to appointment (Boyle 1994). One of the clients, 'Peter', in McLeod's (1982) study, supports this and also indicates an additional tension that the taxi can cause in the prostitution contract: 'I opt for it about twice a week ... They leave the taxi waiting outside, I hate being hurried' (1982: 90). It is also possible to see how other tensions and relationships interact with these. A sex worker in Butcher and Chapple's study suggests that,

> restaurants in the area tend to look after prostitutes, taxi drivers tend to look after prostitutes. At first when the new taxi offices opened, they told us to move, we said 'No, we were here first'. Now, nine out of ten of their drivers, if a girl gets into trouble, will back that girl up. They get so used to seeing them there, if they're not there, 'Why aren't they there?' Also they get a lot of trade from us. (Butcher and Chapple 1996: 44)

This quotation also illustrates the use of cab-drivers to the well-being of the sex-working woman when the trouble comes from her client. Indeed, client violence is a major and much-feared aspect of many sex working women's lives. Segal (1997) suggests that a central aspect of men's use of violence against women lies in social assumptions of men's right to dominate women and expect servicing from them. This has allowed men to express anger and use physical force to get what they want, and get away with it – at least in a society that treats sex working women the way ours does. Yet not all clients are dangerous, and it is an important issue to determine who the dangerous clients might be as Vanwesenbeeck *et al.* point outs because 'interventions on the demand side of the market for unsafe sex are more promising than interventions on the supply side. As long as there are clients who are willing to pay for risky sex, there will be women, who, forced by circumstances, mangled by traumatic experience, and weakened or undermined by their consequences, may be induced to answer the demand' (1995: 514).

One thing emerging clearly from the literature is that there is a continuum of male street behaviour. At one extreme this constitutes the person who cruises without ever soliciting for sex, while the other extreme is represented by the violent attacker. In the intermediate stages there are regular and irregular paying clients. What has not been explored are any links between cruising, kerb-crawling and other offences such as public indecency and violence. Whilst these previous studies have been valuable then, they remain sketchy and sporadic attempts to explore what is of enormous concern for many women on the streets at night. Kinnell (1999) argues that in a humane and just society the greatest concern should be for the most vulnerable women on the street at night. Before we can begin to explore and identify the men of most risk to women, it is necessary to make a detailed study of the men who do approach women on the streets at night.

Methodological shortcomings of previous studies

There are a number of conceptual and methodological shortcomings regarding many of these previous studies. It remains unclear in Holzman and Pines' (1982) study which clients bought sex on the streets or in off-street locations, for these would have different legal implications (and thus the client's 'excitement' motivation). The difficulty of accessing clients meant that the researchers relied on a snowball sample of men known to them. The resulting sample was professional, white middle class and therefore not representative of all men paying for sex, so that whilst criminal victimisation (or 'viccing') is more probable for this group (Maher 1997), the social status of these men may have insulated them from some of the legal dangers of being caught in an illegal sexual contract, as they could afford good legal advice to avoid ending up in court (Humphreys 1970).

Two methods of data collection were used by Kinnell (1989). The first involved interviews with 126 clients by either project workers or sex workers. The second involved observation by eight sex workers keeping a diary of every client they had for four months, up to a total of 50 clients. This is one of many attempts to gather data on prostitution clients that have been flawed because researchers have presented their findings on the client predominantly *through* the interviews gathered from sex workers (for example, McCleod 1982; Faugier and Sargeant 1997). Whilst it is acknowledged that sex workers are in a position to gather data unavailable to non-sex working women, the reliability and validity of data from studies that depend on interviews by sex workers or from diary notes made by them, will suffer from the twin problems of veracity and recall (for example, Kinnell 1993).[24] Holzman and Pines (1982) indicate further problems in such methods when collecting data about off-street clients. They found that clients consciously attempted to influence the behaviour of the sex worker, working to create a rapport with her, and plying her with compliments and sometimes with alcohol. As they suggest, 'given the johns' efforts to psychologically manipulate prostitutes during the encounter phase, characterisations of johns drawn from practitioner-centred research must be evaluated very carefully' (1982: 112).

The inherent defeasibility of previous studies is that none of them take account of the situational context in which these men's motivations were extrapolated. It would also seem naïve to assume that sex workers are the only people whom clients attempt to psychologically manipulate when interviewed, and no account was made of the way people continually construct versions and re-describe events. Given that such construction depends on a person's social perception, self-representation in different social contexts, or to achieve an effect, it is possible that 'participants will in any case orient their accounts, explicitly and implicitly, argumentatively to what others may think' (Edwards and Potter 1993: 35). This is especially likely when a person is talking about a stigmatised activity, and any future studies should take this into account.

Problems inherent in self-selection studies

Despite much media coverage in newspapers, radio, and male magazines, Høigard and Finstad (1992) managed to conduct only 74 interviews, of which 46 were on the telephone and only 28 were face-to-face. These men were not a wide selection of clients, but were reportedly the habitual buyers of sex (Høigard and Finstad 1992: 28). Street contact between the drivers and prostitutes was also observed by McKeganey and Barnard (1996). Trying to interview male street clients in Glasgow proved similarly difficult for the researchers, and only nine of the men reached through street contact agreed to be interviewed. The remaining men declined to be interviewed or gave reasons that were considered 'plainly spurious' for being in the area.[25] A further 68 clients were reached by advertising in the tabloid press, and 66 men through genito-urinary clinics.

Male clients have been contacted directly in studies, but the resulting analysis is nevertheless undermined by possibly inherent biases in self-selected samples of men who responded to advertisements, the national and regional press (Vanwesenbeeck *et al.* 1993; de Graaf *et al.* 1995)[26] and tabloid press (Høigard and Finstad 1992; McKeganey and Barnard 1996). The more recent studies with apparently larger sample groups, by Høigard and Finstad (1992) in Norway, and McKeganey and Barnard (1996) in Scotland, produced only five and nine interviews respectively from *bone fide* street clients. The remainder of the clients in these studies (74 clients and 134 clients respectively) had responded to media advertisements, and the resulting analysis is therefore undermined by the self-selected nature of the sample groups. These studies suffer not only from selection bias, but also the possibility of social desirability bias in responses.

It is possible to argue that this field of study has become methodologically stagnant. Whilst various methods of data collection have been used, such as observation, interviews and police records, these have been used uncritically, and the data gathered have largely been left at the level of description. Moreover, researchers (for example, Monto 2000) have seemingly colluded with unethical and dangerous practices that have been shown to cause displacement, and vulnerability for sex workers. The plethora of results has yielded three different forms of literature, which need to be explored empirically, and the area is ripe for new approaches. Whilst O'Connell Davidson has tested Stoller's ideas, these have not been explored in British street context, the area where theoretically informed policy is urgently required on prostitution.

From previous research, a variety of motivations and concerns have been found for the purchasers of paid sex. Although these previous studies provide *some* insight into the motives for paid sex, for us to understand how far the motivations given in previous studies represent the *underlying* motivations of men seeking commercial sex, they should be compared to those gained in another situational context. The street would appear to be the most promising context for a comparison with these previous studies for two reasons: firstly, given the difficulty of accessing *bone fide* clients, it is one of the few places they can be observed ethically. In the next section of this chapter I describe the activities of the clients of commercial sex workers, and analyse their demographic profiles. The aim is to explore street behaviour of those involved in prostitution from a variety of perspectives that have not previously been used.

Part II: Studies on clients

In this section of the chapter I will examine the prevalence, nature and extent of clients in the UK with an emphasis on kerb-crawling. I will draw on over 500 cases of men who were stopped for prostitution-related 'offences' and behaviours and provide a demographic profile of exactly who buys sexual services, where the men come from, and what they actually pay for.

There were 518 records of men stopped in London for street sex offences in the two years under study, and it is on these records that I now focus attention. The main themes explored in these records were: the age of the men; their occupation; their apparent ethnicity; the type and value of vehicles they were driving; who the vehicle was registered to; the distances travelled; the number of men kerb-crawling in the company of other men; the offence circumstances including the man's state of dress and sexual activity, and the police action taken towards the offence; and finally, the distribution of kerb-crawling offences throughout the week.

Age distribution

There was a broad distribution of age amongst the men, and as figure 3.1 indicates, this ranged from 17 to 77 years of age. The mean age of these men was 39 years. The distribution in figure 1 shows that the greater proportion of men were between 26 and 45 years of age. There were fewer clients between the ages of 46 and 60 years of age.

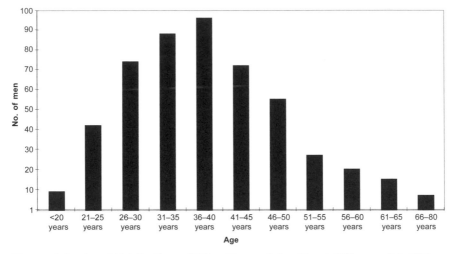

Figure 3.1 Age Distribution of Men Stopped for Street Offences (N=505)

The age categories of the street clients were re-categorised into cumulative frequency for meaningful comparison with previous studies (such as Boyle 1994), which had much smaller sample sizes, and this is illustrated in figure 3.2 below.

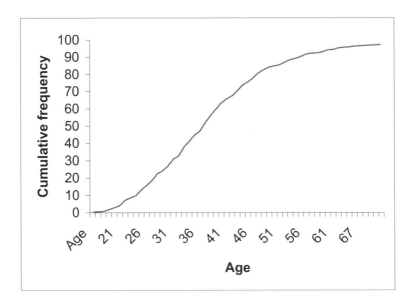

Figure 3.2 Cumulative Frequency by Kerb-Crawler Age

In figure 3.2 above, it can be seen that there is a fairly steep rise in kerb-crawler age from 26 years to 40 years. This increase begins to plateau from age 55 years onwards.

Occupational status

The occupations of the men were coded according to the Registrar General's classificatory system. I refined this classificatory system further when it became apparent that specific patterns were emerging within the data. It can be seen in figure 3.3, that the largest occupational group of men was those in skilled manual jobs who made up 23 per cent of the records (n=121). The three largest groups of men in this category were in the building, driving and catering trades.

These groups included plumbers, joiners and decorators as well as mini-cab drivers, hackney-cab drivers and chauffeurs, in addition to chefs, waiters and a butler. The second largest group comprised men in socio-economic class A, who made up 22 per cent of the data (n=117). This socio-economic group was sub-divided into Professional A and B when it became apparent that there was one particular occupational group who formed a large majority within the traditional classificatory system. This was made up of men in financial professions, and included accountants, bankers and insurance

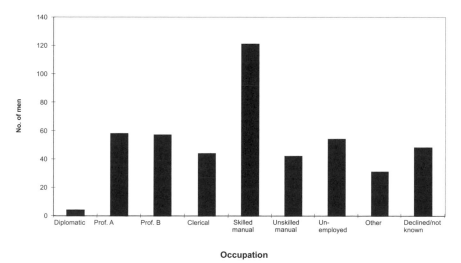

Figure 3.3 Occupational Status of Men Stopped for Street Offences (N=459)

brokers. This group of men are displayed in figure 3.3 as 'Professional A', and made up over half this socio-economic class. The remaining men in this socio-economic group are displayed as 'Professional B' and were either in traditional occupations, which included teachers, a university lecturer, a dentist, and a doctor, or they were in media occupations, and included producers, writers, and an editor. Ten per cent of the men said they were unemployed (n=54).

Eight per cent of men were in jobs that could be classified as unskilled manual or casual work, such as 'building labour' or work in late night restaurants and clubs. White-collar clerical workers made up 8.5 per cent of the occupational classes (n=44). This category included accounts' clerks, hotel clerks, and also salesmen. Six per cent of men were either students or pensioners and these are classed as 'other' in figure 3.3 (n=31), and 9 per cent declined to give their occupational status (n=59).

A small proportion of the kerb-crawlers claimed to be diplomats, and thus immune from prosecution, but only 1 per cent were found to be in such positions (n=4). Examples of men who claimed diplomatic immunity were prevalent in the fieldwork observations. The extract below indicates one such example:

'A car was followed for 15 minutes, slowing, stopping, leaning and peering at any lone women. It has diplomatic licence plates. He picked up a woman who was not regular to the area …

WPC2: 'Do you understand what kerb-crawling is?'
[He spoke quickly and kept raising his voice and talking over the officers, he was waving and pointing. The officers began to speak more softly.]
WPC2: 'Listen, we saw you, you watched her, you followed her.'
Client: 'This was first time, I'm sorry, please, please, I am very sorry, I don't know how this happen. This was first and last …'
WPC2: 'And what diplomatic immunity do you have?'
Client: 'Please, please, I have my wife, my house, this was first time. Please I don't want to lose my family please, please, please?'
WPC3: 'Sir, you've said please many times but you should have thought of this before you followed and picked up a prostitute.'

Client: 'Please? Oh my God, this was first time, believe me.'
WPC2: 'What address was the vehicle registered to?'
Client: 'The Embassy.'
WPC2: 'Have you got any children?'
Client: 'Yes, nine children. I just passed this way and she said she wanted to help. Please, you are going to kill me if you do this. IF YOU ARE GOING TO KILL, DO IT NOW.'
WPC1: 'Sir, as you have diplomatic immunity, I actually have to fill in a load of paperwork and you will be dealt with by your Embassy, and they will decide if you are to appear in court or not.' (Fieldnotes 98/65)

Cases in which men claimed immunity, had to be checked and, if the men were found to have diplomatic immunity from prosecution, the cases were handed over to the Embassy to deal with.

Apparent ethnicity

Using the police categorisation based on appearance, ethnicity was examined from the records. Men of light-skinned European appearance made up 42 per cent of cases (n=221). This can be seen in figure 3.4 below. It can also be seen that the second largest group were men of south Asian appearance who constituted 20 per cent of cases (n=103). Men categorised as having an Arabian or Egyptian appearance accounted for 15 per cent of the cases (n=78). Men of dark-skinned European appearance made up just over 10 per cent of the recorded incidents (n=54). Men of African Caribbean appearance comprised 6 per cent (n=32) of the incidents. Men of south-east Asian or Oriental appearance were a small minority of 3 per cent (n=16).

Type of vehicle

The type of vehicle was recorded in 360 kerb-crawling cases. Figure 3.5 below shows that out of 360 vehicles, 55 per cent were cars (n=288), 10 per cent were recorded as taxi-cabs (n=48), 4 per cent were small commercial vehicles such as vans (n=20), and less than 1 per cent of men solicited from motorbikes or cycles (n=4). There was no vehicle recorded in 30 per cent of the cases, owing to the number of men who solicited on foot (n=148).

Street observation indicated that the number of cars being used as mini cabs was double the figure in the records.

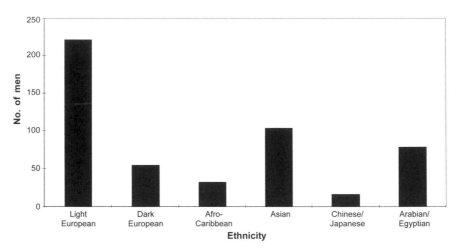

Figure 3.4 Perceived Ethnicity of Men Stopped for Street Offences (N=504)

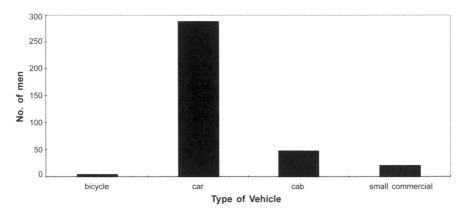

Figure 3.5 The Type of Vehicle (N= 360)

Distance from home address

On the basis of previous research, the distance between where men were stopped and the address they provided was categorised in five-mile intervals.

It can be seen in figure 3.6 below that the first five-mile interval was also subdivided; this was because London has a greater population density than cities used in previous studies. More men provided an address less than one mile from home than any other location, and this amounted to 15 per cent of the records (n=80). A further 6 per

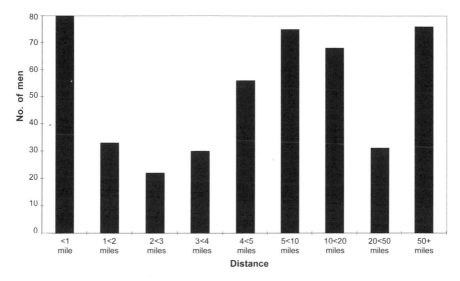

Figure 3.6 Distance from Home Address of Men Stopped for Street Sex Offences (N=442)

cent of men lived between one and two miles away from where they were stopped (n=33), and 4 per cent of men lived between two and three miles away, 6 per cent lived between three and four miles away, and 11 per cent lived between four and five miles away. It was apparent therefore that nearly half the men who were stopped (43 per cent) provided an address less than five miles away from where they were soliciting (n=221). Fourteen per cent of men lived between five and ten miles away (n=75), 13 per cent lived between ten and twenty miles away (n=68), 6 per cent lived between twenty to fifty miles away (n=31), and 9 per cent provided a home address that was over fifty miles away from where they were stopped (n=47).

Providing a non-permanent address

Some of the addresses above were non-residential. Nearly 10 per cent of all the men stopped for kerb-crawling provided a non-permanent or hotel address when asked to give their details (n=56), and figure 3.7 shows the explanations offered for this.

Over two-thirds of the men were tourists or overseas businessmen (n=36); others were working away from home in the UK (n=16); two men provided reasons that I categorised as 'other' (such as social services bed and breakfast accommodation), and one man was a UK expatriate back in England on holiday.

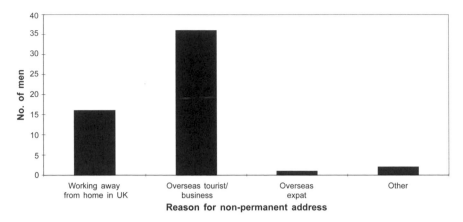

Figure 3.7 Reasons for Giving a Non-permanent Address (N=56)

Vehicle value

Vehicle value was explored on the basis of previous research, and it was possible to code the value of 301 cars. This can be seen in figure 3.8 below.

A third of the cars in the records could be regarded as 'very cheap', for example a 15 year-old Honda Civic (n=100). Over 10 per cent were 'cheap', for example a six-year-old Vauxhall Astra Merit (n=37), 28 per cent were 'mid-range' cars, such as a two-year-old Ford Escort, (n=81). Twelve per cent of vehicles could be coded as 'expensive', for example a two-year-old Range Rover (n=40), and over 14 per cent

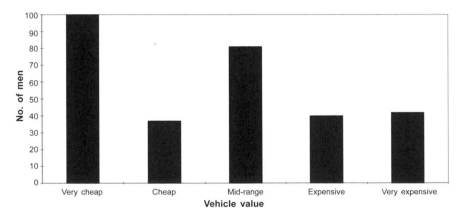

Figure 3.8 Vehicle Value of Cars Stopped for Kerb-crawling Offences (N=301)

were 'very expensive' (n=42). Examples in this category included top-of-the-range, recent-model Porsches and BMWs, and two cases were observed of very rare and valuable sports cars driven by well-known media figures. Indeed, one of these cars was one of only seventeen of its type manufactured in the world. In the cheaper ranges, there were cars with spoilers and other such 'masculinised' modifications.

Registration of vehicle

The majority of cars stopped were registered in the name of the man who was driving. This amounted over two-thirds of the vehicles (n=215). It can be seen in figure 3.9, however, that the remaining third of the men kerb-crawling were doing so in someone else's car. This included company cars, which occurred in 11 per cent of cases (n=34). This was followed by a category in which 9 per cent of cases were coded as 'other' and these included using the car of a brother or cousin (n=28), 7 per cent were registered in the name of a female partner (n=19), and in 4 per cent of incidents a car-hire firm was the registered owner of the vehicle (n=12).

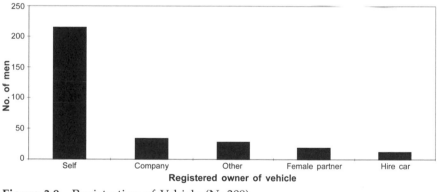

Figure 3.9 Registration of Vehicle (N=309)

Soliciting in the company of other men

While the majority of men solicited alone, there were 35 cases of men who solicited in the company of other men. It can be seen in figure 3.10 below that in 28 cases men solicited in the company of just one other man. In four cases, the men solicited in a group of three, and in three cases, a group of four men solicited together. There was also one incident where six men stopped were travelling in a 'people carrier' vehicle.

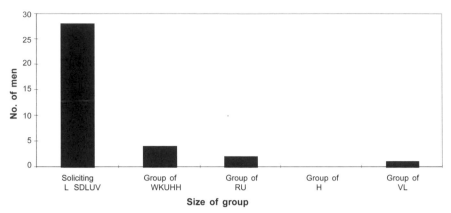

Figure 3.10 Soliciting in Company of other Men (N=35)

From the fieldwork observation it was clear that kerb-crawling in groups creates a higher level of fear amongst the women they solicit, one of whom flagged down a vice car because she was afraid and wanted to move away from a group of punters.

Offence circumstances

Figure 3.11 below depicts the offence circumstances that the men were charged with committing under the Sexual Offences Act 1985. The largest category concerned men who were stopped for 'causing annoyance by soliciting from or near a motor vehicle'. This is the

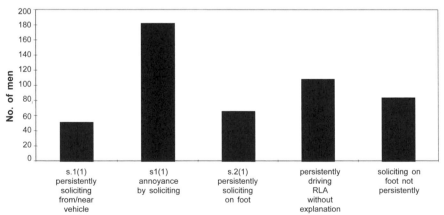

Figure 3.11 Circumstances of Offence (N=489)

second most serious offence under the 1985 Act; these cases comprised 35 per cent of the cases (n=182). This was followed by men who were 'persistently driving around a red-light area (RLA) and unable to provide a reasonable explanation'. These men, described as 'cruisers' accounted for just over a fifth (21 per cent) of the men stopped in the records (n=108).

Offences breached under Sexual Offences Act 1985 (except driving around RLA)

A charge of soliciting on foot (but not persistently), was levelled at 16 per cent of the men in the records (n=83). Men who were stopped for 'persistently soliciting on foot in a manner likely to cause nuisance or annoyance' under section 2(1) of the 1985 Act comprised 12.5 per cent of the records (n=65). Fewer men were stopped for the most serious offence of 'persistently soliciting from or near a vehicle while it was in a street or public place', under section 1(1) for which 10 per cent of men were stopped (n=51). The cumulative distribution of the offence circumstances can be seen in table 3.2.

Table 3.2 Distribution of Offence Circumstances

Circumstances	Frequency	Percentage	Valid percentage	Cumulative percentage
section 1(1) Persistently soliciting from/near a vehicle	51	10	10	10
section 1(1) Causing annoyance by soliciting	182	35	37	48
section 2(1) Persistently soliciting on foot	65	12	13	61
Persistently driving round RLA without good explanation	108	21	22	83
Soliciting a woman on foot (not persistently)	83	16	17	100
Total	489	94	100	

There were no specific circumstances for soliciting children or juveniles at risk. Men who did this were categorised according to the circumstances above.

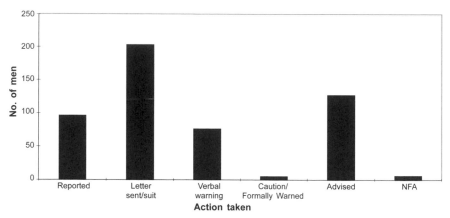

Figure 3.12 Police Action Taken Against Men Stopped (N=513)

Police action taken

As figure 3.12 shows, the most common police action taken involved a letter being sent to the man at his address. This occurred in 40 per cent of cases (n=203).

The majority of letters were sent shortly after the offence, but there were a few exceptions where, because of administrative delays, the letters did not go out at all to these men. In 25 per cent of cases (n=127), the men were advised about their actions, the legal implications, and physical danger to themselves of frequenting red-light areas. In 18 per cent of cases (n=96), the most serious action that the police take in kerb-crawling cases occurred, whereby a man was reported for the offence. In 14 per cent of cases, men were given a verbal warning (n=76). Only 1 per cent of men were cautioned or formally warned (n=5). A further 1 per cent of cases received no further action (NFA) (n=6). These 6 cases were from 1997, thereafter every case was actioned. There was no specific police action, either in the records or observed during fieldwork, taken towards men who were observed soliciting children. These men were treated practically and in documentation in the same way if they solicited an adult.

State of dress and sexual activity

Nearly 10 per cent of the 518 records referred to the clients' state of dress and sexual activity (n=51). In 24 of these records, the clients' state of dress was recorded. In over half of these, the client was described as 'partly undressed' (n=14), in seven cases the client was 'fastening up his trouser fly', and in three cases a client was recorded as being 'fully clothed' and in one case the kerb-crawler was wearing 'women's clothes'. In a further 21 cases, the level of sexual activity in which the client was engaged, when approached by the police, was recorded. Six men were described as having fellatio performed on them when approached; five men were being manually masturbated by the sex worker; four clients were described as being reclined in the car with a sex-working woman; three clients were being touched or touching a sex worker; two men were engaged in penetrative sex with a sex worker; and one client is described as masturbating himself through his trousers when stopped by police. My observation and interviews suggest that these records under-represented the amount of overt masturbation the men engage in; it was not uncommon for a man to park on the side of a road to argue the price down with a sex worker while masturbating himself through his trousers at the same time (Fieldnotes 97/35, 97/48, 98/15). Alternatively, many men would park their cars and then either masturbate as they walked towards the sex worker, or remain in their cars masturbating while they watched her negotiate with another man.

The price and type of sex

In 62 cases, the type of business and price was recorded. The most commonly cited sexual act was 'sex' in two-thirds of these cases (n=43). In the majority of cases, the price agreed was also recorded, such as 'sex at £40'. The next most common service was fellatio – nine cases, and masturbation ('hand relief') five cases. One client was recorded as being overheard to offer payment to 'talk to' the sex worker and another man paid to 'tie up and beat' the sex worker.

Association with alcohol

Three men were on record as being charged under section 5 of the Road Traffic Act 1988, and one man was charged under section 4 of the Road Traffic Act 1988 for being under the influence of intoxicants whilst in charge of a vehicle. My observations suggest that the records under-represent the number that had been drinking, however. Men were seen to be under the influence of intoxicants, and 15 men soliciting on foot were heard to say that they had been drinking, or they smelled strongly of intoxicating liquor.

Weekly distribution of kerb-crawling

Figure 3.13 shows how the kerb-crawling incidents were distributed throughout the week. The number of men stopped for kerb-crawling

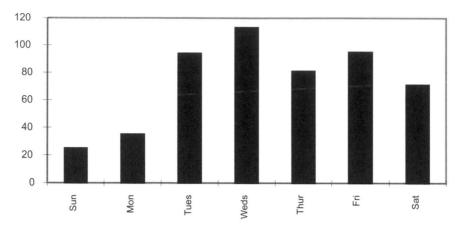

Figure 3.13   Weekly Distribution of Men Stopped for Kerb-crawling

reached a peak on Wednesdays with 113 stops made. The second most frequent day was Friday, when 96 men were stopped. This was followed by Tuesday, when 94 of the men were stopped. Eighty stops were made on Thursdays and only 71 stops occurred on Saturdays.

Days of the week

Sunday appeared to be the quietest day for street client activity in London's West End, with only 25 men coming to notice on this day of the week. Whilst there was some seasonal variation in the actual numbers, the same weekly distribution occurred.

Further analysis: Relationships between variables

Exploratory analysis was carried out on the data described above, and a number of the relationships tested for did not reach statistical significance. These included (but not exclusively) testing the data for relationships between, for example whether the age of the client was related to the circumstances in which he was stopped (to understand whether older men were committing the most serious offences (Spearman's r = −.056, n = 479, p >.22)). Here the classification of offence was ranked in natural order of the degree of seriousness of the offence. This was, however, not significant. The data was also explored to find out whether the action taken by police officers was related to the age of the kerb-crawler (Spearman's r = -.080, n = 501, p > .07) to discover whether older men were more or less likely to receive a more punitive sanction than younger ones. This order was naturally ranked into the level of action the police used of the options available to them. This was, however, also non-significant. The relationship between a man's age and his vehicle value was tested, to explore for example whether the older men had more expensive cars or whether young men were driving the red-light areas in more smart cars. This was, however, non-significant (Spearman's r = 0.46, n = 295, p > .434). The value of the vehicle was tested for a relationship with the distance travelled, to explore for example whether men in more expensive cars were travelling longer or shorter distances than their impoverished brethren. This was non-significant (Spearman's r = .124, n = 230, p > .061). It would have been interesting to explore where, for example men from long distances actually travelled from, but as post code information had only been used to in order to calculate the distance in the first instance, and as actual location was not coded as a variable itself, this was not possible. Future research might usefully code individual postcodes as variables to explore any links between the working site and the direction of men's homes. Also it might possibly provide further insight into the direction the men travel, and more information on the spatial movement of these men.

Some statistical patterns were significant that might have been predicted on common-sense assumptions. For example, men who provided a hotel address were more likely to come from a home address a long distance away (Spearman's r = .55, n = 25[27], p < .01). Further exploration using analysis of variance between groups (ANOVA) of the difference in the variable 'distance to home' by whether men said they were in a hotel or not was carried out, there was a significant effect of whether men were in a hotel to the distance of the incident from their home (F (1, 372) = 27.736, p < 0.0005). It was also found that men of higher occupational status drove higher value vehicles (Spearman's r = −.34, n = 275, p < .000).

Interesting patterns in the data did, however emerge that were significant, both theoretically and statistically. The following section outlines those findings and patterns which achieved statistical significance as well as some non-significant findings of theoretical or political interest.

Ages of men soliciting in the company of other men

It can be seen in table 3.3 that a cross-tabulation of the men's age groups with the incidents of men who solicited with other men

Table 3.3 Cross-tabulation of Age with Group Size

Median age group	Two men	Three men	Four men	Six men	Total
29 years	11	2			13
34 years	13	1	2	1	17
41 years	2				2
53 years	2	1			3
Total	28	4	2	1	35

shows these men to be clustered in the two younger age groups. Although this frequency with such small numbers did not achieve significance in a chi squared test, it shows a tendency of younger men soliciting in groups.

Age of men and type of area

On the basis of past research (see, for example, Cohen 1980) that found a relationship between the type of area and the age of men, Pearson's chi squared test of expected and observed frequencies was carried out on age and distance, but this was non significant. Hence there was no apparent significant relationship between the age of men and type of area (for example, Notting Hill, Sussex Gardens, or Mayfair).

Distance from home address and ethnicity

Men of light-skinned European appearance and Arab/Egyptian appearance were significantly more likely to live within one mile of where they were stopped than any of the other ethnic groups (Pearson's chi square value 18, df1, $p < 0.001$).

Type of vehicle and ethnicity

A cross-tabulation of ethnicity and vehicle in table 3.4 shows that most of the mini-cabs stopped were significantly more likely to be driven by the Asian men (Pearson's chi square value 25, df20, $p < 0.001$). Findings from fieldwork observation indicated the number of mini-cabs driven by Asian men to be an under-estimation because officers would enter the vehicle by manufacturers make (for example, a 'blue VW') in the records. This meant it became coded as a car instead of a cab in these statistics, yet it was frequently observed during the fieldwork that the majority of cars that were stopped were found to be private or hire cars trading as mini-cabs on the informal economy. This was indicated by bundles of business cards printed with cab firms' names on the dashboards, as well as the presence of a two-way radio.

Indeed many of the unskilled occupations entered in the records were observed to be what have been considered ethnically stereotypical jobs (for example, Irish builders or Italian waiters), but the level of

Table 3.4 Cross-tabulation of Perceived Ethnicity and Vehicle Use (N=351)

	Light European	Dark European	Afro-Caribbean	South Asian	Chinese/ Japanese	Arabian/ Egyptian
Bicycle	2			2		
Car	128	28	17	59	10	37
Mini-cab	9	6	2	20		6
Hackney cab	4					1
Small commercial	9	3	1	5		2

ethnicity coded on police records was not detailed enough to explore this further. It was possible, however to classify age by ethnicity, and this can be seen in table 3.5 below.

One way ANOVA shows there is a significant link between age and ethnicity (F (5, 488) = 15.904, p < 0.0005) is the contrast that occurs between men of light European appearance and all the remaining groups of men, i.e. there is a significant difference between the age of men of light European appearance and the rest, but not between groups of men other than those of light European appearance. These

Table 3.5 Classification of Age by Ethnicity

Ethnicity	Mean age years	Number	Standard deviation
Light European	43	218	11
Dark European	38	51	11
Afro-Caribbean	33	32	10
South Asian	34	100	9
Chinese/Japanese	34	15	8
Arabian/Egyptian	36	78	9
Total	39	494	11

Table 3.6   Age Differences Between Perceived Ethnicities

	Number	Subset for alpha = .05	
		1	2
Afro-Caribbean	32	33	
South Asian	100	34	
Chinese/Japanese	15	34	
Arabian/Egyptian	78	36	
Dark European	51	38	
Light European	218		43
Significance		.126	1.000

men of light European appearance were older than the remaining groups of men.

Value of car

On the basis of past research (see, for example, Cohen 1980) Pearson's chi squared test of expected and observed frequencies was carried out on the value of the car and type of area, but the result was non significant. There was thus no apparent relationship between the value (or type) of the car and the type of area.

Relationship between offence and police action

There was a highly significant positive correlation between the seriousness of circumstances in which a man offended and the level of police action taken against him, (Spearman's r = .49, p<0.001, one-tailed). The majority of men were thus penalised according to the seriousness level of their offence under the Sexual Offences Act 1985. Notwithstanding this, and the child protection duties of the squad, it was interesting to note during the observation that the action taken towards men who were soliciting juveniles was identical to that of men who solicited adult sex workers.[28] The treatment of men who were not UK residents did not follow this pattern, however. An interesting exception to the relationship between the offence and the police action taken emerged statistically in the relationship between non-permanent address and ethnicity as described below.

Provision of a non-permanent address and ethnicity

Most men providing a hotel address were light-skinned European men (n=32). These men were overseas tourists or business visitors, and were significantly less likely to go to court, and they were significantly more likely to receive a verbal warning or no further action than any other type of censure (Pearson's chi sq. value 14, df 2, p<0.01). This occurred even when they had committed a more serious level of offence. This attitude towards tourists and foreign business visitors is described by one officer in the following way:

> WPC: 'They see nothing wrong. Quite often, well, whenever you stop a foreign guy generally for kerb-crawling or whatever, you know they're quite amazed how seriously we take it. You then, sort of, try and explain to them that we're doing it as much for their own good as well, because the pimps know that they're a tourist as well, they [pimps] know who they can have the wallet off, who they can have, you know, the nice jacket off or whatever, then tourists are putting themselves at risk as much as anything else'. (Female officer, age 26, A Team/2)

The quotation above indicates the general approach towards tourists and foreign men. My observations indicated that many officers accepted that foreign men did not know the law, and they were less critical of these men. There was thus a difference in attitudes of officers towards these men and others, such as cab drivers. It was apparent during fieldwork observation that if men could prove that they would soon leave England, either by presenting a return air ticket, or a passport with a visa stamp on it, then the officers accepted this, and did not take matters further.

Discussion of findings

Men of all ages buy sex

My findings have shown that men of all ages solicited to buy sex. The mean age of these men was 39 years, and this was consistent with previous studies. Indeed the finding was identical to the age found by Faugier (1995) in her Manchester sample of men, although it is slightly older than that found by Cohen (1980), Benson and Matthews (1995a), McKeganey and Barnard (1996), Sharpe (1998) or Monto (2000), and slightly younger than that found by Van Wesenbeeck et al. (1993) and Kinnell (1989). Banding the age categories for meaningful comparison with other studies such as Boyle (1994) showed that the age distribution is broader in this London sample than in her study, there were twice as many clients in upper age groups as found by Boyle (1994). I did not however, find the evenly spread age distribution found by Plumridge (1996). More specifically, my figures support the findings of Matthews (1993) who argued that the majority were in their 20s and 30s, and Benson and Matthews (1995a) who found 30 per cent of men in their 30s. Further analysis did not find any evidence to support Cohen's (1980) finding of the older men in more expensive locations such as Mayfair, with men of all ages frequenting each of the three main areas policed. A significant difference was found between the ages of men of light European appearance and the ages of each of the other ethnic groupings.

Occupational status

My findings reveal that the occupations of the men were not evenly represented; the largest group of men stopped were those in skilled manual jobs. The majority of these men were in construction or catering trades. The construction of the Heathrow Express fast train service to Heathrow Airport and the redevelopment of the Paddington Basin area had increased the number of male construction workers in the area at the time of the research, and one linked factor between these groups of men may be that both the waiting staff working nights and builders working away from home have free time in these areas, cash payments and a fluctuating income, so that they are not financially accountable to their regular partners (for the money given to a prostitute). The skilled manual work category also included a number of cab drivers, and it is possible that because some of these men have jobs that entail travelling through a red light district at times when the sex workers are working, that these men build up sexual relationships with the women.

The next largest occupational group involved men in the highest socio-economic class and over half of those recorded in this category were accountants and men in financial business. There is no geographical reason why this was the case, given that the majority of financial institutions are in the city rather than in the West End of London. When I explored the home distances of these men, there was no pattern of travelling home from work to explain their presence. Indeed many of them had gone out of their way home in the early evening, or were stopped in the early hours of the morning, so another explanation is required. The professions were not equally represented in this socio-economic class, for example, there were no lawyers in the sample.

Overall these findings support Perkins (1991) who found all social classes represented, but more strongly support the findings of Kinnell (1989) who found very similar percentages of 'white collar' and 'blue collar' workers, and a similar number of unemployed men in London to McKeganey and Barnard (1996). My findings provide a far wider variety of socio-economic groups than Holzman and Pines (1982) or Faugier (1995), whose studies concern off-street client groups. Such narrow occupational groups may be a function of the type of data collection methods, which focus upon different types of client group.

Given the large number of men in the three highest occupational classes, there is no evidence for the pyramidal model of prostitution (Perkins 1991) in which men solicit women of a similar standing in prostitution hierarchy. The number of men in managerial and professional classes suggests that there may be a motive for buying street sex as opposed to off-street options. It is likely that these men could afford to buy sex off-street, and thus there is a question about the attraction of street sex, and the value of its sordidness in providing them with particular thrill and excitement. It is possible that this group of men may eroticise the perceived 'sordidness and dirt' like clients in Faugier and Cranfield (1995) and Campbell (1997). One particular finding concerning those who claimed diplomatic immunity seemed to be a function of researching in the capital.

Diplomatic immunity

The claiming of diplomatic immunity presented an interesting practical policing issue in this context. This is because grades of immunity vary. Principals and attachés have grade one immunity, which covers everything they do, but ancillary staff such as cleaners, and chauffeurs have limited immunity restricted to their hours of work while at the Embassy, for example. The police procedure in instances where diplomatic immunity was claimed, was to check the man's claimed level of immunity on the Central Index of Privileged Persons. Men who have diplomatic immunity according to the Vienna Convention (s. 22) cannot be reported for the offence and the officer in the case has to bring it to the attention of the Foreign and Commonwealth Office. Thereafter, the Embassy decided on any penalty. Attitudes vary, however, amongst the different embassies towards this type of offence. The Russian Embassy, for example, has transported employees out of this country within 24 hours. Other embassies view such offences more leniently, but I was told by officers that most embassies are displeased in the first instance that an employee has come to the notice of the authorities for any offence in the host country.

Ethnicity

Whilst data based on appearance are notoriously problematic, my findings (drawn from police records) indicate that men of light-skinned European appearance made up nearly half the sample. This was followed by men of Asian appearance, and men of Arab or Eygptian appearance. Men of African Caribbean appearance and men of Oriental appearance constituted a small proportion of the records. O'Connell Davidson and Layder (1994: 72) suggest that people are not randomly observed or stopped by the police, and it was interesting to note that the combination of the men who were non-WASP (non-white Anglo Saxon Protestant) in appearance amounted to more than half the sample (55 per cent), whereas the WASP men comprised less than half the cases (42 per cent). The proportion of Arab/Egyptian men was reportedly representative of the large local Arab community in these areas. Indeed, these men, along with light-skinned European men, were significantly more likely to live within a mile of where they were stopped than any of the other ethnic groups. Both these categories of men therefore were soliciting within their home communities.

Men of Afro-Caribbean appearance were represented in only small numbers in the kerb-crawling records, given that the black population in Britain is urban-based, living in predominantly larger cities in the UK: in 1991, according to the census, no less than half of all non-white people lived in Greater London (McDowell 1998) and the research site encompassed Notting Hill, where there is a large Afro-Caribbean residential population. The findings may refute racist fantasies of black sexuality and of these men paying for sex (Segal 1994), but perhaps also represent the racism of sex-working white women who reject black clients (Sharpe 1998). There were very few Oriental men in the records, as Cohen (1980) found. This suggests, that despite the absence of a cultural bar to buying sex (cf. Allison 1994) it would appear that Oriental men do not solicit for sex on the street. Asian men constituted a fifth of the men in the incidents, and the number of Asian men is higher even than the number of men found by Knox *et al.* (1993) who concluded that these men have little access to women outside marriage, and were therefore more likely to pay for sex with women. Whilst that might account for some of the men who pay for sex, it does not account for why all the men pay for sex with women, rather than go to places where they could meet sexually-available women, for example.

My study reflects a very different spread of ethnic groupings compared with previous work (including Cohen 1980; Holzman and Pines 1982; Van Wesenbeeck *et al.* 1993; Campbell 1997; O'Connell Davidson 1998; Monto 2000) all of whom found the overwhelming majority of clients to be white. This latter finding may suggest that the self-selected samples utilised by researchers under-represent men of colour. The street-sample studies were in the US (that is Monto 2000, and Cohen 1980), so it may signal a difference in police practices between Europe and the US with regard to who gets stopped for street offences. The observation and analysis of further records in this study were invaluable in indicating a possibly more complex reason for this – as I discuss below.

Relationship between type of vehicle and ethnicity

Pure discrimination is said to be an 'elusive chimera' that no method can conclusively pin down (Reiner 1993: 5). Cultural explanations may include the understanding that the 'culture of criminal justice system can not be seen as a free-floating and independent source of its practices' (1993: 15). It is possible that suggestions of institutional racism in the Metropolitan Police Force leads to over-representation of Asian men in the figures. It is also possible that whilst some of these men were kerb-crawling, many of them may have been touting for mini-cab business. While I watched these men being questioned by vice officers, they exhibited many cues that were interpreted as guilt, including nervousness, minimal eye contact, and evasion under police questioning. In their attempt to avoid censure for working on the illegal economy, it is possible that some men ended up charged with kerb-crawling, a sexual offence when they were actually touting for cab business. It highlights the issue first mentioned by O'Connell Davidson (1998) about the parasitical relationships that emerge in the sex economy over and above those concerning the pimp. It is not possible from these findings to ascertain what the relationships were between cab drivers and sex working women in this study. It is possible in the case of drivers and others working in the locale of the red-light district that they are more likely to get to know the women and that meetings are more relational than parasitical. An alternative perspective is that these men have chosen their job because of the proximity it affords them to sex working women at different hours of the night. However, it is relevant in this respect to note that cab drivers are not only legally prosecutable in this respect as clients, but are also prosecutable under section 30 of the Street Offences Act 1959 – directed at a male person who is kept wholly or partly by a prostitute.[29] There are also wider social questions that these findings raise.

A structural account of these findings would necessarily have to explore the position of Asian men which involves proximity to sex workers at busy trading times. One reason for the preponderance of Asian men driving mini-cabs has been suggested by Hubbard (1997), who argues that deliberate recruitment policies pursued by mill and factory owners in the 1950s and 1960s targeted migrants from Mirpur, Campbellpur and Peshawar, because they were stereotypically regarded by employers as a source of cheap, hardworking labour prepared to work long hours and night shifts in England's clothing industry. The recession of the late 1980s and decline in the textile trade left many men looking for alternative employment. Mini-cabbing, along with working in Asian restaurants, were the main forms of (self) employment thereafter. Cultural expectations of providing for large extended families lead these men to work long hours where they know there will be business, and sex workers typically spend a lot of money on cabs. It is thus possible that cab drivers also build up working relationships with the women, as the work of O'Connell Davidson (1998) indicates, or more social relationships develop between Asian cab drivers and sex workers, as illustrated in the literature of Kureishi (1997).

It is also possible that numbers of Asian cab drivers have increased in the area owing to racist attacks. Attacks on Asian cab drivers have meant that it has become commonplace for drivers to 'cover each others' backs' whereby a cab carrying fare of two or more young white men will be followed by another driver (Ahktar 2000). This is a strategy that white cab drivers have not needed to consider, and one that has resulted in twice the number of Asian drivers in any one area at a given time. It is a strategy that may also account for the high number of Asian men driving cabs on the streets. It is possible that these men then become the 'sacrificial' men of the law, who, like other economically and culturally marginalised 'subordinated' masculinities, become the primary object of the criminological gaze.

Records in my study reveal that licensed hackney cabs were driven in all except one case by white men, and interestingly, in interviews, many of the female police officers said they particularly disliked hackney cab drivers kerb-crawling.

Distance from home address

With regard to the distance between where a man is stopped for kerb-crawling and his home address, the findings show that there was a high concentration of men living very locally. This concentration of men living locally is higher than previous research has shown, and there is also a higher concentration living further than 50 miles away. This bimodal distribution is different from the findings reported in Matthews (1993) and may be a function of the higher travelling distances generally experienced amongst those working in the metropolis and those in the suburbs, and the number of men in construction trades mentioned earlier, who live in the area from Monday to Friday each week.

Giving a non-permanent address

The men providing a hotel address were light-skinned European men, and many were tourists. The high number of tourists supports Cunnington (1979) who found that the majority of men she observed in court said they were tourists. In this study, however, men in the records (and observed on fieldwork) who said they were tourists were less likely than others to go to court. Evidence from my observation indicated that this seemed to be due to organisational expediency on the part of officers. The actions of these men lend support to the suggestion of Simon and Gagnon (1973) that when social controls are loosened some men pay for sex, and that of Prieur and Taksdal (1989) that access and opportunity play an important part in men choosing to pay for sex.

Vehicle value

Whilst the largest group of cars were those in the 'very cheap' range, there was no pattern of the most expensive cars in the more expensive areas, or cheaper cars in cheaper areas, as found in previous research by Cohen (1980). During the fieldwork observation, however, it was apparent that the men driving the more expensive cars were also those who provided occupational details of higher socio-economic status. With regard to the use of cars as social symbols and their role as external indicators of masculine sexuality as suggested by Høigard and Finstad (1992), there were many cars that had been individually customised with spoilers and paint work. It is arguable that not only does this play a role as an external indicator of masculinity, but it also makes the owners more identifiable when a car is individually customised in this way. This heightens the risk for the owner of being recognised by somebody who is familiar with the car. Such risk was exemplified in the two rare sports cars that were so unusual and 'dramatic' in appearance that the risk of being recognised was very high for their owners. The risk of discovery was also apparent for the men who kerb-crawled in cars registered in the name of someone else because letters would be sent to the person in whose name the car was registered. Although the majority of cars were registered to the driver, a third were registered as company cars, or in the name of a female partner (especially for men who provided details of being self-employed).

Soliciting in company of other men

While the majority of men solicited on their own, there were cases where there was soliciting in the company of other men. In the majority of these cases this was carried in the company of just one other man, but incidences were found of up to six men soliciting together. In one incident, a sex worker flagged down a police car to escape from a group of men. This raises complex questions about masculinity and motivation.

While previous studies such as Høigard and Finstad (1992) and Monto (2000) suggest that initiation occurs via one member of a cultural group towards another member, it is unclear whether that is the case here. Indeed, the question of how masculinity was accomplished remains open. Further, were there other interplays, such as competition and hierarchies amongst men regarding who goes first with a woman? Do they watch each other (as Boyle (1994) mentions) – to become a 'bodily performance' in the way sport does (Connell 1995: 54) and with the homoerotic tendencies that encompasses? Although it is not possible to address such questions within the confines of this thesis, the questions are nevertheless important in directing attention to the complexity of the situation.

All the incidents where men solicited with other men disproportionately represented younger men, and the findings support those of Boyle (1994) whose interviews with punters revealed some of the reasons why these men said they did so, 'I always go with my mates, usually after we've had a few beers or if we're away on a weekend rugby trip if one of the lads mentions it. It's a laugh. I suppose I feel a mixture of guilt and a buzz from the excitement of it all' (Boyle 1994: 53). 'I don't think I'd ever visit a prostitute on my own. When it's happened it's always been a spur-of-the-moment suggestion ... it's more being one of the lads' (1994: 58). It is possible that for men certain types of public behaviour like visiting a prostitute is only possible in groups. Do these men, therefore, need the support and gain courage from the company of another man to carry out a socially deviant act? Brooks Gardner has argued that 'teams can help men to depoliticise their offense' (1995: 106). Such findings certainly raise questions as to whether or not the law should attempt to place some control over men soliciting in groups.

Offence circumstances and police action taken

The most common offence circumstances under the Sexual Offences Act 1985 were men stopped for 'causing annoyance by soliciting from or near a motor vehicle', which is one of the most serious offences in the Act. This was followed by the men who were stopped for persistently driving round a red-light area without a good explanation, that is 'cruising', which is not an offence at all. My research finding relating to 'cruisers' support the findings of McKeganey and Barnard (1996), and Høigard and Finstad, (1992) concerning recorded and observed behaviour of these men. Their presence may also support the theory of perversion by Stoller (1979) who suggests that voyeurism and prostitute-use are closely related. Such a relationship raises theoretical questions with regard to whether this is the start, on a continuum of behaviour that would build up to prostitute use, which has been suggested by Hanson and Harris (1998). Such a possibility might extend the 'slow-build' theory put forward by Holzman and Pines (1982).

The finding of men who admitted that they were 'looking' is theoretically interesting. This is because although voyeurism is classified as a paraphilia (DSM-IV-R), research into voyeurism *per se* has not been applied to men who observe the commercial sexual arena, apart from Høigard and Finstad's (1992) finding that 'looking' for red-light district voyeurs, had a sexual value of its own. Voyeurism has, however, been linked to prostitution in the theoretical literature by Hanson and Harris (1997) who suggested that voyeurism was preferable to paying for sex for many men because it had the advantage of being cheaper and had low involvement with the law. My findings dispute this last suggestion, given the number of men in this study who were stopped by the police for driving around the red-light area. Indeed, I would suggest that my findings exemplify the elements of both risk and control mentioned in Stoller's (1979) theory, as the chance of being caught was high for many of these men. This risk is thus part of what makes 'looking' so exciting for these men. Some men said they were 'looking', but that prostitutes were 'too dirty' to consider doing anything further and there was an element of hostility in their words. O'Connell Davidson (1998) has suggested that men who construct prostitutes as 'dirty' eroticise an image of the 'dirty whore'. Future research might explore this notion further. Future research might usefully explore the notion of voyeurism and prostitution at a street-based level, especially in relation to other 'perversions'.

Relationship between offence and actions

The most common action taken by the police was to send a letter to the man's home address. Whenever possible the police gained a home address, although many officers would accept a business address or a hotel address. Other men were 'advised' against kerb-crawling, or given a verbal warning, a minority of men were charged or cautioned for the offence. There was a highly significant positive correlation between the seriousness of circumstances in which a man offended and the level of police action taken against him.

Men were thus penalised according to the perceived seriousness of their offence under the extant legislation. The police were thus prosecuting only the most serious cases. Notwithstanding this, and the child protection duties of the squad, it was disturbing to note during the fieldwork observation that the action taken towards men who were soliciting juveniles was identical to that of men who solicited adult sex workers.[30] This remained the case, even when the juvenile solicited was obviously very young. The children's ages ranged from 12 to 17 years, with the most common age being 15 years. Whilst the child was taken into police protection, the client would receive only the penalty pertinent to their soliciting action. Arguably, in these cases, the letter of the (kerb-crawling) law was applied rather than the spirit of the law in which child protection issues are by all accounts meant to take precedence. It is a policy that perhaps leaves these men at liberty to attempt to purchase children at a later date with relative impunity. This finding of men who solicit sex children has not been apparent in previous research on kerb-crawling behaviour.

State of dress and sexual activity

Examination of the records revealed the state of dress for some of the kerb-crawlers in London, the type of sex commonly being requested, and the prices offered for different forms of sex. Some men were partly undressed, or doing up their trousers when stopped. The type of sex requested was most commonly recorded as penetrative sex, followed by fellatio, and manual masturbation. Interestingly the records indicate that when men were actually 'caught in the act' this was more commonly fellatio than anything else. During the fieldwork interviews it was apparent that the records possibly under-represented the number of men who were in the middle of some form of sexual activity when spoken to by officers. Being confronted by such activity led to officers gaining greater insight into the vulnerability of the adult female sex worker than had hitherto been the case.

Weekly distribution of kerb-crawlers who were stopped

The number of men who were stopped rose to a peak in mid-week. The second most frequent day was Friday, which is when many men get paid. Street business slowed down again on Saturday, Saturdays, however, were regarded as a quiet evenings by most of the police officers, a day when most men were expected to be at home with their families. Sunday appeared to be the quietest day for street-client activity in London's West End. On Sundays, officers spent a large proportion of their time dealing with paperwork, owing to the perceived lack of activity on the streets. The number of men stopped increased during the beginning of the week, and on Tuesdays a 'warrant list' came out – this was a list of the names of sex workers who were wanted for the non-payment of fines. Police activity tended to be directed at the street more on Tuesday and Wednesdays. This distribution is similar to that described by Høigard and Finstad (1992), who reported that street sex activity peaks midweek in Norway as well.

Chapter summary

In this chapter, I have provided an outline of the demographic characteristics from the records of over 500 kerb-crawlers stopped in London. The findings support previous work in the area with regard to the occupational status and age of the men stopped for kerb-crawling. New patterns were found in the data, however, and some of these, such as those concerning hackney cab drivers and diplomats, may be a function of research in a metropolitan area. A significant relationship between ethnicity and vehicle use was found which might be embedded in broader inequalities and interests with regard to Asian men. Men were found to travel much shorter distances than in previous research, which may also be due to a metropolitan sample. Male tourists or business visitors who provided a non-residential address were treated more leniently (that is, more likely to avoid a court appearance) than UK residents. A large number of men were found to be voyeuristically cruising the area, and some largely younger men were found to be soliciting in pairs or groups. Men were found in a variety of states of undress and sexual positions, although the records possibly under-represented these. Finally the weekly distribution of kerb-crawling was found to peak in mid-week. Chapter 4 explores the policing of the men and women in sex work to explore the tensions in implementing policy.

Notes

1 Criticisms of Kinsey's (1948) methods have been advanced on axiomatic grounds. The quality of the reports has been criticised because all interviewers were males; this may affect the statistical results by as much as 10 percentage points. Also, data concerning such intimate personal experiences are unlikely, when collected by direct question and answer procedure in a short interview, to be accurate. Although reliability was high when measured in re-interviews, Kinsey had not accounted for memory errors in the way he processed and analysed his data as he lumped retrospective and current reports together (Terman, cited by Lieberman 1982).

2 This survey was the first national random survey of sex to be carried out and avoided the complaints and controversy of the original Kinsey (1948) study. 'Little Kinsey' involved three related surveys (The Mass Observation Unit 1949). The first was a randomised 'street sample' of over 2,000 people, the second was a postal survey of 1,000 of three groups of 'opinion leaders', the third was a set of 'directive' questions with responses from 450 members (Stanley 1995: 211). This survey, Stanley (1995) counts as one of the most important pieces of British sex research when looked at with a scrutinising eye for its insistence on the equal validity and importance of coupling the quantitative results with qualitative data.

3 The percentage of men who said they had also had a sexual relationship with a man was 13.4 per cent compared with 4.9 per cent of those who had not used female prostitutes.

4 Because Wellings et al. (1994) recognise that paying for sex is a stigmatised activity they suggest that prevalence estimates should be regarded as minima.

5 This is suggested by the rising proportion of women with 10 or more

partners in a lifetime found in the parallel survey on women (Wellings *et al.* 1994).

6 There is improved accuracy for reporting sensitive behaviours since NATSAL 1990 (Copas *et al.* 2002).

7 An aberration is an erotic technique that differs from one's culture's traditional definition of normality. These would include such behaviours as those set off by a brain tumour or drug; or sexual experiments initiated through curiosity, but that one does not find exciting enough to repeat.

8 A word used not to describe voluptuous sensation so much as a rapid alternation between fear of trauma and hope of triumph (Stoller 1976: 105).

9 Indeed, O'Neill (1997) argues that the 'aestheticization of the whore' (1997: 8) in contemporary culture needs to be explored along with masculinity(ies), to analyse fully and understand prostitution today.

10 Despite these flaws, the studies of McLeod (1982) and Kinnell (1989) were both vital starting points for research on clients, and the first studies that had the concerns of sex working women as a pivotal aim.

11 The main five reasons found by McKeganey and Barnard (1996) were: the chance to buy particular sex acts; opportunity to approach a large number of women; chance to have women with specific characteristics; contact with sex workers can be minimal; and the element of thrill involved in paying for sex.

12 These may be a reflection of the different legislative and social climate in the Netherlands (see Outshoorn 2001; Brandt 1998; Golding 1986), which has a long history of greater toleration and openness regarding sex work.

13 This was the forerunner of the Street Offences Squad, the main unit for policing street prostitution in London.

14 This was 36 years for the white clients, 34 years for black clients.

15 Although one Oriental man and one Indian man were observed, these were included respectively in the white and black categories.

16 Fellatio was the service of choice because, Cohen (1980) concluded, it does not require the same security measures as intercourse because both partners need not undress.

17 Both health needs and condom use include violence. Kinnell (1989) was the first researcher to expressly connect the violence meted out to sex working women with a need to research the clients.

18 Matthews' (1993) graph however, illustrates that the majority come from less than five miles away.

19 There may be a slight discrepancy here, as the description Benson and Matthews (1995a) provide of their data is different to the actual graph they present, nor do they give the total number. It is therefore, not clear whether they have included the sauna clients' details in this.

20 The average age in studies from the Netherlands is higher at 45 years of age.

21 The remaining 15 per cent were of unknown age (Boyle 1994).

22 Many of the demographic questions were identical to a General Social Survey allowing for comparison with a 'general' population.

23 Monto (2000) does not take account of the HIV literature that conclusively points to the client as the person who presses for unsafe sex.

24 Although it must be noted that this situation occurs because working women cannot keep questionnaires/diaries on site because it might be used as evidence that they are working.

25 It is unfortunate that McKeganey and Barnard (1996) were dismissive of the clients 'plainly spurious' reasons for being in the area. Had the authors' methodological toolbox been larger they might have been able to provide useful data on the manner of excuses and argumentation of these men.

26 This study acknowledges that the self-report method under-represented the Turkish and Moroccan men who form a substantial number of clients of Latin American window sex workers in the Netherlands.

27 The n size here relates to the number of men who provided an address for which the 'land' mileage could be calculated. It therefore excludes men who are overseas tourists or business visitors.

28 This accords with the Sexual Offences Act 1985 which, although drafted to cater for men soliciting women, guidelines suggest that 'any provision of this Act of the word "man" without the addition of the word "boy" shall not prevent the provision applying to any person to whom it would have applied if both words had been used, and similarly with the words "woman" and "girl"' (Blackstone 1997: 212).

29 In *R v Farrugia, Borg, Agius, and Gauchi* (1979) 69 Cr. App. R. 108 Agius set up an escort agency, and two mini-cab drivers, Farrugia and Gauchi, would take women on an assignment. On arrival the driver would introduce the girl to her assignment and collect the agency's fee, usually £17.50 and his fare. There was no evidence that the fare was excessive. Nearly all the activities were late at night. The defence submitted that this did not prove the defendants 'knowingly lived wholly or in part on the earnings of prostitution'. They may well have made part of the living out of prostitution, but that was not the same as living on the earnings of prostitution. All four were convicted. Their appeal to the Court of Appeal was dismissed on the basis that all four knew what the girls intended to do. What they received came from intended prostitution as earnings. No direct payment had to be proved (Jerrard 1995).

   Those in driving jobs are over-represented within the standard range of (police) ethnic categorisations. This supports Humphrey's (1970: 43) findings on men seeking impersonal sex, who found the largest single occupational class in the sample were truck drivers.

30 This is in accordance with the Sexual Offences Act 1985 which, although drafted to cater for men soliciting women, actually concerns juveniles

too. The interpretation guidelines suggest that 'any provision of this Act of the word "man" without the addition of the word "boy" shall not prevent the provision applying to any person to whom it would have applied if both words had been used, and similarly with the words "woman" and "girl"' (Blackstone 1997: 212).

Chapter 4

Policing street prostitution

This chapter will illustrate the practical problems in contemporary policy on prostitution by exploring the difficulties and complexities involved for those policing and enforcing the law as it is presently drafted. An understanding of policing responses will be presented through the use of a case study of the vice unit response in a large metropolitan city. The chapter will examine the competing demands and pressures on police officers, which include the demands made by residents to rid their neighbourhoods of 'vice', the vulnerability of street prostitutes and juveniles at risk (JARS). Police views on clients and sex workers will provide insight into the perceived legitimacy of the law as it is currently framed and interpreted and will illuminate how policy is enacted on the ground. The chapter will also explore contemporary police responses to violence against women using data from the case study, the actions of voyeurs who circle the district, and how the police deal with the competing accounts that male sex clients provide when questioned by the police. This interaction will be explored in depth to show specific behavioural patterns and develop a unique theoretical model of the interaction, which also aids understanding of the motivations to buy sex and also has implications for the practice of policing street sex offences.

The rules of engagement

There are regular calls from the police for police powers to be increased (Brain *et al.* 2004) yet the way that prostitution is regulated by the police in England and Wales has been subject to much criticism (e.g. Lopes-Jones 1990; Sagar 2005). Karen Sharpe (1998) shows how police tactics and strategies for policing 'vice' differ across space, based on a number of factors including staffing levels; financial constraints and the discretion of senior officers; specific understandings; unwritten 'rules of engagement' between police, prostitutes and punters and rules which differ markedly across time and space. She argues that the policing of prostitutes and kerb-crawlers is uncoordinated and ineffectual. Expanding on this, Hubbard (1999) suggests that overwhelmingly, it appears that the policing of prostitution takes a complex and spatially variable form where the morality of individual officers coalesces with wider understandings of vice laws. By contrast, Westmarland (2001) illustrates the significance of the gendered status of policing, contending that certain policing roles are given/adopted by 'gendered specialists'.

Both Matthews (1993) and Sharpe (1998) illustrate the scope of the interaction between police and clients of commercial sex as a useful context for the further understanding of the client/prostitute relationship. From sketches culled from observation, the following responses to police officers were considered representative of the clients, suggests Matthews (1993):

'Not that. I am a married man. I have got a small kid.'
'Look, I'm a married man with two children, sir. I don't want this trouble, sir. Can I speak to you about this?'
'Does my work have to find out?'
'Oh, come on, officer. You are a young bloke, you'll understand.'
'Does this have to go anywhere? This is the first time I've done this.' (Matthews 1993: 14)

From these extracts Matthews argues that it is possible to see the concerns, embarrassment, and fear of wider censure in the accounts of these men. Sharpe (1998) used her observations of police and street client interaction, also, to argue that there was much confusion in the minds of men arrested regarding the actual laws of kerb-crawling:

Almost without exception men arrested for the offence would protest their 'innocence'
or they: '... didn't realise it was an offence to drive round a red light district to look at the women'
or they: ... had not actually had sex with a prostitute'

or that they were '... just driving round the area because curiosity had got the better of them and they were just driving round to have a look' (Sharpe 1998: 131).

This study also found that many men expressed horror, bordering on indignant outrage that it could be thought that they were '... *the kind of man who needed to go to prostitutes*' (Sharpe 1998: 131). Neither study, however, analysed the excuses of these men to explore street clients' justifications in any detail, nor explored the legitimacy of policing prostitution.

Street interaction in Norway

The observations of police and punters in red light districts has furthered our understanding of why men buy sex. Høigard and Finstad (1992) support the idea that propositioning a prostitute is an activity on a continuum of behaviour that builds up from the decision to go to the red light district, and culminates in the contract with the sex worker. They suggested that:

> 'the experience of being a customer becomes a project that unfolds: from a thought that crossed the mind like a possibility and a temptation, to a determination that slowly solidifies ... to the drive down to a district, titillating rounds where the fantasy can play freely with living pictures' (1992: 89).

Their conclusions are based on the work by Prieur and Taksdal (1986)[1] who observed contact between male clients and prostitutes. During five summer days 2,834 cars were observed. These included a number of smart expensive cars and cars with features that contribute to a 'masculinised' image such as tinted windows, louvres or spoilers. It was found that the majority of Oslo's street prostitution takes place in the middle of the week between 6 p.m. and midnight, and they analysed the details of 332 men who circled the red light district. These men were categorised into three groups: peepers, negotiators and customers. Peepers were men who drove round the red light district, and four possible motives were suggested for the behaviour of these men. One was that peeping or voyeurism has its own sexual value which results in some men masturbating as they drive around, as one woman explained: 'They're not all johns, you know – all they do is drive around and around here while they jerk off' (Høigard and Finstad 1992: 88). A second was that some peepers said they felt a sense of powerlessness and dare not approach the women. A third was where the men said they felt powerful just knowing they *could* have sex with the women. For the final group, driving and watching was part of their solitary mental foreplay as they built up to the act of going to a prostitute. The 103 men who made contact with the prostitutes were called 'negotiators'. The majority of negotiations, however, did not end in prostitution, and some of these were peepers who pushed a bit further – proving to themselves that they *could* have the sex worker – then retreated. The majority of negotiators, however, were would-be clients who did not agree a price, act or location with the sex worker. Men drove around an average of four to five times before being observed as customers. Some men picked a woman up right away; the average took half an hour to pick up a woman.

In order to explore how the experience of the encounter and aftermath of the encounter compared, Prieur and Taksdal then interviewed 74 habitual buyers of sex. The majority of these men had specific reasons why they chose to pay for sex, and Høigard and Finstad (1992) found similar motives to Kinnell (1989) for buying sex. These motives were:

- 'sexual acts';
- 'new women';
- 'a different and exciting experience';
- 'easy and non-committal';
- 'one-sidedness'; and
- 'availability'.

The motive of 'sexual acts' encompassed acts many people see as common elements in a varied sex life, for example, oral or anal sex, but were acts that these men did not feel able to ask their regular partner for. Men for whom 'new women' was a motivation presented a picture of masculinity where sexual experience with many women was central. The clients who wanted 'a different and exciting experience' said they were curious as to what prostitution entailed. Many men said prostitution was an easy, non-committal solution to their needs, and married men did not feel as unfaithful as if they had an affair – and it was easier to hide from their wives. Those who stated that 'one-sidedness' was the attraction wanted to escape aspects of more mutual sexuality such as technique, or intimacy and emotions. For those who stated 'availability' to be the attraction, the authors argued that the red light district was a symbolic arena where the men could obtain confirmation that women exist for men. Attraction to prostitutes as the embodiment of availability elicits a feeling of power in these men (Høigard and Finstad 1992: 97).

Different categories of client also emerged: sailors, singles and married men. Many sailors, for example, stated that their initial encounter was a form of manhood ceremony, and one client recounted: 'they told the woman to make sure I was not a virgin when I came out again ... afterwards the guys were standing there clapping, what I really wanted to do was throw up' (Høigard and Finstad 1992: 29). This later became a leisure activity 'with the guys' rather than with the woman. Older sailors visited the same woman in each port, who represented the security and closeness of a 'reserve marriage'; one man said: 'women restore order out of chaos' (1992: 30). It was proposed by Høigard and Finstad (1992) that sex is not the primary desire, but that other longing is resolved through sex, and it is because these men lack words for this longing that their needs are thus sexualised.

The single customers were found to have high anxiety, distance and helplessness with women. These men were 'outsiders' to mainstream society in that they had difficulty managing finances, a job, or a social network. Buying sex is a flight from performance expectations and their own inadequacies. These men have such low self-esteem that they do not feel able to approach a non-prostitute woman, and the company they pay for is primary, the sexual is secondary. Høigard and Finstad (1992) suggest that these men see their single status as deviant in a culture with strong expectation of pair-forming bonds, and that commercial sex is damaging for these men as their distance from non-prostitute women increases further with each string of new defeats, and their self-esteem sinks lower. The responses of married men, however, differed according to their age. Younger customers had fundamentally different requirements from the older men. The younger customers said their sex life at home was satisfying; they were purchasing complementary, well-defined sexual actions in addition to what they had at home. Older married men were generally searching for some semblance of mutuality in their paid sexual experiences, for if it was too blatant a one-sided release, it affected their desire and ability. The majority said they would prefer a close sexual relationship with their wives, but as sex had declined or was now non-existent with their wives, they sought a new, close and stable relationship. These men wanted sensitivity, closeness and intimacy. It is reported that 'he comes to the prostitutes with all his pent-up longing for closeness, physical contact and sex. And often as not, he is deeply disappointed with what he obtains' (Os Stolan 1995: 72).

Any theory to explain these men's experience must be gender-specific, argue Høigard and Finstad (1992: 101), and they find Object Relations theory (Klein 1928; Dinnerstein 1976; Chodorow 1978) persuasive to explain and understand these customer experiences. This is because Object Relations theory suggests answers to the different experiences men and women have, and how men, through their early upbringing, develop a vulnerable sexual identity, and have difficulties acknowledging feelings of dependence and intimacy. Intimacy that is not linked to their sexuality becomes a threat to their fragile sexual identity, and boys are thus socialised to translate feelings of intimacy into sexuality. They suggest the typical conflict between 'lack of desire' that clients say their wives have, and their own 'inability to talk about the relationship' finds much psychological resonance in this explanation. Høigard and Finstad (1992) suggest that men solve this by becoming commercial sex clients.

Voyeurism

In the past observational studies of street interaction the police not only deal with men who solicit women for sex but also voyeurs. Voyeurism has been defined as:

'a paraphilia of the solicitational allurative type in which sexual/erotic arousal and facilitation or attainment of orgasm are responsive to, and dependent upon, the risk of being discovered while covertly watching a stranger disrobing or engaging in sexual activities' (Money 1996: 273).

It is the extreme expression of impersonal sex, distant without any emotional vulnerability, and because the victim is unaware of being observed, the voyeur may feel in complete control over the relationship and feel no risk of rejection. Indeed, the 'onlookers' (Cohen 1980); 'peepers' (Høigard and Finstad 1992); 'carloads' (McKeganey and Barnard 1996); 'hooligans' (Perkins and Bennet 1995) found in a variety of studies on street sex work conform to the profile of the classical voyeur who neither wants nor tries to create a relationship with his or her victims, and while some voyeurs masturbate while watching their victims, others masturbate later, while remembering the events (American Psychiatric Association 1980). In a review, Hanson and Harris (1997: 317) point out the advantages to the voyeur of this behaviour in comparison to engaging a prostitute. Voyeurism is inexpensive, with relatively low involvement with the police, and even though the prostitute–client relationship requires little emotional involvement, the voyeur's relationship requires even less.

According to Money, voyeurism is a displacement paraphilia that 'involves a segment of the preparatory phase of an erotic and sexual activity before genital intercourse begins' (Money 1984, cited in Kaplan and Krueger 1997: 304). Pure voyeuristic behaviour used to be generally viewed as a nuisance offence by the law, as a pathetic attempt to steal sexual pleasure from others. In the Sexual Offences Act 2003 it became a sexual offence. From their observations McKeganey and Barnard (1996) comment upon the phenomenon of non-client voyeurs driving around in their cars. The presence of these men was obviously felt strongly by McKeganey and Barnard, who suggest that 'the red-light district exerts a magnetism for some people whose interest is perhaps best described as voyeuristic. So there are often carloads of people who come to look and perhaps also to shout (mostly pejorative) comments at the women' (1996: 18). These findings add another dimension – a layer of aggression – to the behaviour cited by Hanson and Harris (1997). Aggressive voyeur/exhibitionist behaviour was also noted by Perkins and Bennet who found that:

> 'carloads of young hooligans … made their obnoxious presence felt by driving past with their genitals hanging out of the windows and screaming obscenities. But they also proved to be dangerous, for in 1982 six sex workers were hit by cars apparently aimed at them by these men' (1995: 240).

McKeganey and Barnard found it to be:

> 'a salutary experience to stand on a street alongside a prostitute and observe the reactions of people in the cars cruising by, the faces of solitary drivers, or the groups of young men, and sometimes women, who drive round the red-light area intrigued by the sight of the women' (1996: 71).

This study also found that a central issue of concern to these men was that of power and control, and whilst men talked of buying 'dominance' over the prostitute, it could also be an unsatisfactory experience and one man said 'on unknown territory with your trousers down, you can't really say, that wasn't good enough once it's over, you can't really demand your money back, can you?' (1996: 53). These men have difficulty coming to terms with what turns into a paradoxically emasculating encounter for them, after the high expectations they have of commercial sex. The authors suggest that this male expectation of dominance contributes to the potential volatility of the client-sex encounter.

Theoretical integration

The accounts of twenty-four men who paid for sex were analysed by Plumridge *et al.* (1997) in New Zealand to examine how they explained and justified their pleasure in it. Two sets of competing interpretations emerged. Firstly, men claimed the commercial exchange was a 'mutual emotional and sexual relationship', but also asserted that payment of money discharged any other obligations associated with relationships. The authors describe this as a 'profoundly self-serving interpretative schema' in which sex workers are given an identity to place the client in a 'benign light' (1997: 165). The rhetoric about freedom from obligation contradicts the rhetoric of mutuality even though, for some men, it is their primary emotional relationship.

Building upon these findings, O'Connell Davidson (1998) attempts to integrate social, structural and psychodynamic explanations for the purchase of sex in order to account for such expectations of dominance. In her study of men who take part in sex tourism, she uses a Marxist definition of power to point out that the men who feed off the economic misfortune of local women and children in poor countries delude themselves by seeing their power as individualised, instead seeing themselves bearers of neo-colonial power. She argues that there is an erotic charge in the passivity of the woman or child who has had to submit to sexual acts they do not want in return for money, and clients are thus able to also eroticise vulnerability and powerlessness, from the 'toothless vagrant who will agree to unprotected anal penetration for a paltry sum' to the hungry child of the third world (1998: 144). These contradictions, she explains, are why sex tourists and 'sexpatriates' do not appear to be happy (for examples, see Seabrook 1996) as the affliction results from their confusion of power with honour (1998: 88). Such self-delusion reaches its apotheosis, however, in the sex-tourist manuals and web-page noticeboards where men attribute 'honour' to themselves by saving women from being abused worse by another client (from a distant culture).

O'Connell Davidson (1998) also investigated the different ways clients construe prostitutes as therapeutic objects and/or dirty objects. Using Stoller's (1979) theoretical construction, she argues that here the sexual narratives of vengeance and control are as powerful as any enacted by other clients. For example, clients who state their motives as sex therapy construct a narrative in which they privilege their loneliness or *need* of care, and in which they see the prostitute as having power to withhold the care and mothering these men feel they need. The *control* of their own safety is what carries the erotic charge for these clients; they can *command* access, which they see women as having the power to withhold. Prostitute use for this group of men can be understood as a straightforward way of gaining access to female bodies which would otherwise be denied or restricted. Through prostitution or sex tourism, these men can claim membership of a dominant masculine community that otherwise eludes them.[2] On the other hand, clients who construct prostitutes as 'dirty' eroticise both the public availability of the prostitute woman and her impersonal attitude to sex. The image of the 'dirty whore' is thus exciting, and hostility to the 'bad woman' has sexual value. It is arousing because it conjures images of other men. Other penises, other semen, and the 'image of objectified cunt' becomes all the more arousing when constructed and visualised in relation to other men's cocks as disembodied sexual organs (O'Connell Davidson 1998: 140). Added to this eroticisation and 'fucking dirty whores', is the ability of the man to command, as a result of economic power, a woman or child to submit to sexual acts for payment. Prostitution is valued, therefore, because it strips women of that autonomy and contact with the 'debased whore' becomes an act of vengeance against a 'good woman's demands of monogamy and sexual restraint' (1998: 158). Although clients eroticise their prostitute use in a number ways, these are all arguably a defence against 'anxieties around gender, subjectivity and selfhood' (1998: 160), and men who are ambivalent about relationships with non-prostitute women typically fear being engulfed, infantilised, out of control, open to rejection and humiliation.

However a client views the sex worker (as therapist or dirty whore) the real or imagined risks (of discovery, robbery or disease) are eroticised. This is why men pay far more for sex without condoms in an 'internal game of risk with fantasized dangers' (O'Connell Davidson 1998: 155).

What is it about the street?

The notion of risk, argues O'Connell Davidson, accounts for the famous and wealthy who kerb-crawl 'to experience excitement and a subsequent sense of triumph and mastery' (1998: 155). The secret transgression of going to sex workers is underpinned by the same dynamic that makes telling lies pleasurable for children; it creates an illusion of power by being able to manipulate other people's perceptions – and is arguably an effective medium of control as well as a source of exhibitionist pleasure in itself – giving the man a sense of invincibility, inner 'triumph' and mastery. The illicit nature of street prostitution makes it more exciting than off-street prostitution for men who have tried buying sex both on and off-street, according to Faugier and Cranfield's (1995) findings. Men who responded to a media advertisement to be interviewed said they needed a 'sordid' environment, or needed the risk of arrest, disgrace or physical violence. In a study addressing similar issues, Campbell (1997) also found that although the majority of men in her study did not want to be caught, for some men the illicit nature of street sex gave it a particular thrill and excitement. The conceptualisation these men make of risk is not yet understood, but suggestions are that these will not be simple neutral information interpretations, but rather very active contexts of argumentation and justification (Plumridge *et al.* 1996). Many of the motivations found in studies by Høigard and Finstad (1992) and McKeganey and Barnard (1996) support those of Kinnell (1989), and the categorisation of peepers, negotiators and customers lends weight to the 'slow build-up thesis' described in Holzman and Pines (1982).

This section has illustrated how previous studies have shown the street to be a useful site for understanding the regulation of prostitution as the censure of the law is what creates the 'illicit' context that men report to be part of the excitement and therefore the motivation to pay for sex. It is fruitful to explore the interaction of these men in conjunction with the law, and as the officers see them. In the next section I employ a theoretical perspective which takes language as embedded in its situational context, what might be described as a 'discursive action model' (Edwards and Potter 1993), to examine the techniques men use to explain their actions to the police. This is because men's use of language and description when seeking to escape legal sanction might indicate something about their motives. In this way I aim to fill gaps left by previous studies in our understanding about clients. Using a large metropolitan 'vice unit' as a case study I will explore the cost of contemporary policing response in terms of the effects of displacement of prostitution-related activity, the vulnerability of women and children, and the civil liberties of men who are stopped by police for prostitution-related behaviours.

Case study – police targeting practices

The sample of people who were stopped, and on which much of the study is based, depends upon search and patrol practices of the officers. It became clear during the fieldwork that the police officers used a variety of methods to seek out and define kerb-crawlers. The officers would operationalise kerb-crawling in a variety of ways. First, methods used to seek out the men would range from officers parking in streets 'just to see what happens', and patrols which began in one area moved on to a different area if there was little or no kerb-crawling activity to be found. The decision upon where to start patrolling could depend upon previous experience. If, for example, an officer had worked on the territorial support group (TSG)[3] they would use a working knowledge of an area's crack houses to park nearby and watch the women from the crack house plying their trade. The customers of these women would then be targeted. Knowledge of an area played a large part in the officer's decision to patrol an area and in determining subsequent targeting practices once there. A good working knowledge of side streets and one-way alleys made for a greater choice of unobtrusive observation posts, and lack of familiarity with an area could mean that individual officers would give the area a wide berth. The wider reputation of an area within the force influenced decisions on whether to police it or not. It was felt, for example, that despite the 'rebirth' of Soho as a bohemian and fashionable place to dine and stroll in early evening, some officers regarded Soho as a 'no go' area after dark. Such officers did not consider it safe to patrol Soho in pairs on a night shift because of the level of drug activity and gang involvement there – it was considered 'best left for the TSG'. Thus, Paddington and Mayfair were patrolled more at night than either Soho or Notting Hill. Alternatively, areas (even including these) might be chosen for patrol on a given evening because they had not been covered for a while, or because of their proximity to a station (for example Harrow Road Station) the officers had to attend on police business.

Patrolling practices did not always rely on police business, however, and the decision to keep a watch on one area as opposed to another might rely upon the proximity of an area to the fast food outlet from which a police team had chosen to get their main meal (known as 'stopping for refs') on a shift. The decision on where to patrol was frequently dependent upon the police vehicle used; for example if officers patrolled in the so-called 'brothel-wagon', its noisy diesel engine could be heard by kerb-crawlers and sex workers alike from afar. On the basis that this vehicle sounded very like a hackney cab, decisions were made to patrol in territory used by hackney cabs, such as near cab shelters and popular cab-turning points.

The decision as to which vehicle to use was in its turn dependent upon the availability of vehicles and, if extra vehicles were needed by the Organized Vice Squad for a specific covert observation operation, then the Street Offences had to manage with what was left. The areas patrolled were also related to the previous events on the shift. For example, if a juvenile at risk was returned home to an outer urban area, then officers would patrol the route through which they travelled back to the centre of the metropolis.

Several well-known street corners were popularly targeted by all the police teams. These street corners were where prostitutes known to the police regularly worked. The speed at which sex-working women and their regular clients met and transacted a deal was very fast. A known sex worker would be spotted working one minute, have disappeared the next minute, only to reappear on her corner within ten or fifteen minutes. It is possible, therefore, that regular clients of particular workers would be under-represented in this study because they would need less crawling to make a choice and start the transaction. Male and female officers tended to differ in their targeting practices, with female officers more likely to target kerb-crawlers (and express more satisfaction from stopping them) than male officers. This issue is returned to later and discussed in more detail.

Policing styles and their implications for the sample of kerb-crawlers

Even when the prior decision was made to target the kerb-crawler rather than the sex worker, there were conventions that determined which charge was levelled at him. These were dependent upon broad interpretations by individual officers of what constituted acceptable levels of both 'persistence' and 'nuisance'. The nuisance level included (although not exclusively) the following:

149

- the mileage a man travelled whilst being followed;
- the number of circuits he made of a particular red-light area;
- the length of time he tried to pursue women; and
- the speed at which he drove (for example some men drove so slowly that cars behind them had to overtake to make any progress).

How many times a man slowed was also a factor, and for some men it would depend on *how* they slowed down. For example, these men would maintain a steady pace until they saw a sex-working woman and then suddenly halt. Headlight flashing was also interpreted as part of kerb-crawler behaviour, as men would use this to attract the attention of a working woman or to determine whether she was working or not.

Persistence was judged more by a man's body language than by that of his driving behaviour. One determining factor was whether a man was staring at females in a very obvious manner; whether a man beckoned to females, and if so how many times he did so. If he was talking to female pedestrians from a car, this too was factored into the decision on whether to stop him or not. If a man left his vehicle to talk to females he incriminated himself and the officers logged how many females he approached. Shouting at or co-ercing lone females was also held to be part of soliciting practice that resulted in men being targeted. These were police targeting practices which would certainly generate distinctive samples of kerb-crawlers, and the subsequent analysis is the product of such practices.

Policing, gender, and power

Data collection began in the wake of the Macpherson Inquiry, and the research of Brown, Cambell and Fife-Shaw (1995), and Horn (1997). I expected harassment of all types to be a 'ubiquitous phenomenon' (Brown 1999) in this police force. There was much debate at the time about institutionalised sexism and racism in the Metropolitan Police and I had taken gendered patterns of power, domination and disadvantage amongst police officers as a given, yet an analysis of the interaction produced some surprising results, because the culture in this squad appeared to be different. There was a necessary awareness of gender. Indeed, gender sometimes determined how jobs were allocated between officer pairs – for example, if it was necessary to body-search a sex worker. Also, women were, as in other forces, in the minority at senior level. There were no women at Inspector level or above although one had worked there previously. The dynamic was nonetheless different to that described in previous research with regard to women, race, and other bigotry. One of the reasons was because the female officers' critical mass and personalities reversed the usual power dynamic found in police forces at ground level. Many of the women were sitting their sergeants' boards and using this squad as either a career move up the ranks, or as a way to do more interesting policing at the same level and escape being marginalised (doing 'hand-holding' work) in other policing squads. Three of the women had done their sergeants' boards; two of the women were black. Another reason was the demographic characteristics and biographies of the male officers: two men were married to social workers; many of the men had degrees and had experienced different cultures such as university culture before policing; many of the male officers had female partners or daughters whose experience of harassment in the police force these men understood more deeply than any policy document they would read. It was interesting that these men would mention harassment issues first with comments such as 'if you want to look at harassment too, my girlfriend, she's in a uniformed branch at station, she's had a terrible time of it'. Thus they showed an insight and awareness into the structural conditions in which policewomen generally work and reflected their difference by comparison.

There were, however, a few isolated men who made the occasional politically incorrect comment about (but not to) women in general. These comments got squashed very quickly in peer communication. By using particular forms of speech such as 'old sweat' and 'seventies cop' for men who held sexist notions, these policewomen constructed these men as passive objects of the past, turning sexist attitudes into out-of-date relics of previous decades. The women's use of banter and humour constructed the men who held such notions into objects of a distinctly female gaze. The result was that on an unofficial level the women had a clear hold on the ridiculousness of such posturing to a degree that the rare man who tried it, was soon pre-empted and crushed. Female officers thus negotiated and maintained power by their use of language.

Policing patterns of street sex offences

There were 518 records of men involved in kerb-crawler incidents during the fieldwork period. A record was made of each man involved in a soliciting incident even if he shared a car with one other man (or more). Any shortfall in the analysis (for example with regard to the number of vehicles) is therefore against this baseline. Table 2 below shows that the police records comprised 313 men in 1997, and 205 men in 1998 (up to November). During this time, there

Table 4.1   Incidents Recorded by Street Offences
Squad for 1997–1998

Incident	1997	1998	1997–1998
Kerb-crawling	313	205	518
Prostitution	2000	1160	3160
Juvenile at risk	37	100	137
Total incidents	2350	1465	3815

was a concomitant drop in the charging of prostitutes, which went
from 2000 in 1997 to 1,160 incidents in 1998. Alongside this, there
was evidence of an increase in the number of juveniles found to be
'at risk' on the streets who were taken into safe custody. In 1997
there were 37 incidents of juveniles at risk being taken into police
custody. By 1998 this had increased to more than 100 incidents, a 150
per cent increase.

One factor to note about this pattern of incidents is that while
the 518 incidents of kerb-crawling related to 518 individual men,
the prostitution incidents – which were prostitution charges brought
against women – related to no more than approximately 60 individual
women[4] and the total number of cases of juveniles at risk comprised
no more than 30 names.

Whilst kerb-crawling-related incidents were a high priority for
the Street Offences Squad, helping a 'juvenile at risk' (JAR) had the
highest priority of all, and these figures, in common with offence
statistics more generally, were a reflection of resource allocation and
police activity. In this case, the figures reflect the activities of a squad
whose duties were divided between policing prostitution and child
protection. Taking a child into safe custody entailed liaison with
social services to develop a framework of support. This was arguably
a more time-consuming task than charging a young person for a
prostitution-related offence (which is what the police did in previous
years). Attention given to child safety issues in this way therefore
appears to have had a reductive effect on the kerb-crawling figures.
Whilst causality cannot be inferred from a correlational relationship,
it was apparent during the fieldwork observation that when a kerb-
crawler solicited a juvenile at risk, he would be dealt with in the
same way as if he had solicited an adult woman, but the juvenile at
risk would be taken into police protection.

It was also apparent in interviews with officers that liaising with
social services and developing a network of support for juveniles

at risk was not only time-consuming but a sometimes frustrating process. In the words of a female officer:

> Sometimes you've a juvenile in and I don't care what they're in for or what they've done, but that social worker is supposed to be there for them. Some social workers take three or four hours to turn up. I appreciate that in inner city areas they can have huge case loads but that is their job, and even if they said they'd be there as soon as they can, it would mean at least they were making an effort. (Female police constable, age 31 years, Fieldnotes 98/38)

The very task of engaging young people at risk and developing relationships with them in order to gain enough information to help them was itself a time-consuming process. These cases were often a major source of concern for officers. As one experienced officer commented:

> The thing that gets to me in this job is the juveniles ... the children upset me. I'd been on the Unit a short time and there were two juveniles, one fourteen, one fifteen, and they'd been in care all their lives. All they wanted was someone to love them. We brought them in – when both of them were together, they were dead mouthy. But I spent three or four hours with one of them, while I questioned her, we had a sandwich and a coke, and when alone she opened up to me, and it was so sad, all she wanted was someone to love her and these blokes [pimps] latch on to that very quickly – saying things like 'I love you' and buying them things, and then put them to work on the streets. They get them to bring so much money home every night. When we brought this one in she had a great big bruise on the side of her face, the whole side of her face was swollen. I handed her over to Social Services and they put her on a train up North and she's probably on the streets somewhere else now. That really upsets me. It makes you feel very helpless really. (Female police sergeant, age 34, Fieldnotes 98/37)

In interviews, it was not unusual for the officers to draw on such case studies and make predictions about the life chances of juveniles without specific multi-agency frameworks or strategies in place to support them after leaving police protection.

Police-recorded incidents of prostitution

Over the period under study, there were 3160 incidents of prostitution recorded by the police. While the majority of these were soliciting charges, others were cases where sex-working women had either not turned up in court to face soliciting charges, or had not paid fines, and were thus 'wanted on warrant'. In such cases, women were held in police cells overnight and taken to court the following day to be charged. As mentioned above, there were approximately 60 women named in the records as being 'active' in central London during the research, which creates an average of 61 charges per woman over this period. Nevertheless, police officers expressed ambivalence about imposing these charges. Only two of the older officers felt that charging sex workers had a deterrent effect. Others were cynical about the high level of so-called 'clear ups' it created, and the majority (17 out of 23 officers who were asked about this or who raised it in conversation) referred to the 'blatant unfairness' of charging the same woman again and again under the 'revolving door' policy that 'makes a mockery of the whole system' and within which they were expected to work (Fieldnotes 97/22). This difference in attitudes between officers, even on the same team, was exemplified by one officer who said:

> I have an attitude that my sarge doesn't really agree with, that I think these prostitutes are not criminals. I mean they're not like drug-dealers, or burglars or anything like that. At end of the day, they're breaking the law but you don't have to treat them as such. I mean they're not breaking into old people's houses and robbing old people, and most of them are quite reasonable people. (Male police constable, age 28, Fieldnotes 97/37)

A more mutual and understanding attitude towards sex-working women, however, had to be balanced with demands from residents that police remove women from the streets. In focus groups, it seemed as though officers recognised pressures sex-working women may have been under. The relationship with prostitutes on the one hand and residents on the other appeared to make officers question how reasonable the residents' demands were that officers enforce 'the law':

> WPC: We're not going to *solve* the problems of toms. We're just *here*. We just have to patrol Paddington because the

residents would be up in arms if we didn't do it and because it's against the law, they get arrested. Like we're not going to stop those girls doing it, so best to build up a reasonably pleasant relationship with them so that they don't give you any trouble. In that way I think everyone's happy then, aren't they?

MPC: Some have got a problem with drugs and that's the only way they're going to get it. I'm not saying that's a reason why. Or somebody's getting pressured by their man which is the person who should be taken out, but because people pay £450k or half a million pounds to go and live in Paddington and suddenly realise there's prostitutes. They know that, they go there, so they just like to go and complain about it all the time, which amazes me. Somebody lives in Westbourne Park Road and there's prostitutes, its like buying a million pound house off All Saints Road and saying 'Oh no, there's drugs and prostitutes. What are the police doing about it?' Some people should open their eyes and look. (Focus group/D Team/15)

In over 50 per cent of the police cases (n=276) a sex-working woman was specifically mentioned by name in the kerb-crawler records in relation to the kerb-crawling charge. In 251 of these records, the sex worker was not only mentioned by name, but also with the abbreviation 'KCP' for 'known common prostitute', or 'KBVC' meaning 'known by virtue of cautions'. In 10 per cent of these cases two women were present (n=22), and in one case a juvenile at risk was mentioned by name. In 31 cases, police action was taken against the sex-working woman. In two thirds of loitering cases the sex worker was cautioned (n=21), and arrested in a third of these cases (n=10). The extract below shows how police officers suggested that this figure was not as high as it might have been if they had carried the law out to the letter:

I think they realise as well that basically we don't prosecute them as much as we could, but as soon as they're arrested, they're straight back on the beat again. Officially we could go straight back and say right, you're nicked, get in. But the policy basically is to let them off the next time unless there are a lot of them working. We say it doesn't work that you know, you *could* get arrested for every [soliciting] offence. A lot of them think if they get charged once, they won't get charged again that night, but it doesn't work that way you know, you're always telling them, but they seem to think if they run up to you with a bit of paper, and that annoys me. I mean it's not your warrant to work, don't push it. Obviously they get charged now and again, don't they? (Male officer, age 26, Focus group, B team 97/68)

These attitudes contrasted with the attitudes held towards kerb-crawlers. Female officers, in particular, found it hard not to find many of the male street clients ridiculous, and found the job of policing vice changed their attitude to men in this respect. One female officer explained how she felt towards kerb-crawlers and how it affected how she now saw people:

I've been doing this for a year now, and it was only four weeks ago I caught somebody actually having sex, and it brought it home [to me]. You know, you're talking to some gentleman who's just been in the sexual act and he's been reported – and he's a boner – and you're trying to keep a straight face and he's still got an erection in his joggers, and you're trying not to look down, and the prostitute is like giggling across the road ... We *do* look at people (men) in a different light, you know. (Female police officer, age 24, Fieldnotes 98/9)

It was not uncommon for officers to relate in interview that they only understood the vulnerability of the sex-working women's lives after they saw them actually engaged in sex with a client. It was not unusual for officers to witness this occurrence, and one officer related such an event:

We caught Tina in the [client's] car, with her leg going. She was in the middle of full shag or whatever. Some bloke was on top of her and all I could see was her leg going like that, and you don't actually think of them doing the act. You know that they do it and they're prostitutes and must deal with them [the clients] all the time, but when you think of them doing it, actually catch them doing it, which happens a lot, it's really weird. To think that every bloke they take off with in their car, that's what they're going off to do. (Female police constable, age 26, fieldnotes 98/62)

In interviews with female officer pairs, it was apparent that they held views about certain types of kerb-crawlers. In the extract below, they explained the reasons for these views:

B: Do you stop [men in] any occupations more than others?

WPC1:   Taxi-drivers are bad, aren't they? Ooh like to get 'em.

B: Black-cab or mini-cab?

WPC2:   Black-cab.

B: Black-cab drivers?

WPC1:   There's one, he often works, you know, Mayfair and when he's kerbie-ing, he'll light up a fag and wait in the corner and then circle a couple of times watching the girls, but there's loads of 'em slow down. The worst ones for it are taxi drivers.

B: Really?

WPC1:   You can never prosecute a taxi driver because he's got an excuse looking for a fare. Never get a taxi driver, they're the worst ones aren't they? There's been a couple of reports through info [intelligence] that taxi drivers are picking up the girls. One guy, a guy after one and a half hours trawling around after him and he's working every single one of the [red-light] areas, all three of them, one and a half hours, he's one that's gone Sussex to Cleveland over to Westbourne Park. I do hate cabbies kerbie-ing.

B: Why?

WPC2:   Because they're in a position of public trust. It undermines that trust. Anyway, you wouldn't want to sit in a cab where he's shagged a tom, would you?

(Interview female officer pair, B team 1998/8)

Thus there was an element of frustration in the officers' views about hackney cab drivers who kerb-crawled. These men appeared to elude prosecution because of their hackney cab status which allowed them to pick up anyone. The frustration for the female officers appeared to be linked also to what these officers saw as an abuse of trust as well as public hygiene concerns.

Many of the cars that the police stopped seemed to be working as minicabs although these were not licensed as such. This is illustrated in the following excerpt from the recorded interaction between the driver of one such car and a female police officer:

WPC: Do you know why we've stopped you, sir?
DRIVER: I've been driving round too many times. I've been taking a person back. I keep driving.
WPC: That's the reason we've stopped you ...
DRIVER: I've only got £1 on me.
WPC: Am I right or am I wrong?
DRIVER: You're right, but I am looking for a good place to work. I can tell you now that I didn't go for the women.
WPC: Who's at your home now, sir?
DRIVER: My mother.
WPC: Is the car registered to you?
DRIVER: No, it's a rental car.
WPC: How can I verify that you are who you say you are?
DRIVER: I don't have a home number but I can give you my brother's mobile number.
WPC: Do you work at all?
DRIVER: Yeah, in a petrol station.
WPC: Who are you hiring the car from?
DRIVER: My mate, who's just started doing it.
WPC: Have you got your documents or insurance?
DRIVER: Yeah, yeah, [provides details of friend car hired from.]
WPC: What insurance do you have for mini-cabbing?
DRIVER: I'm not mini-cabbing, I'm finding a place to work.
(fieldnotes 98/90)

This interaction interview between police and driver shows that the initial stop was for kerb-crawling activity and it turned to unlicensed cabbing, although the hired vehicle in this transcript was later recorded as a car rather than a cab, the police officer felt sure the driver was using it as a cab.

Police interaction with kerb-crawlers: 'catching kerbies'

When police officers stopped a man suspected of kerb-crawling to interview him, the notes they made of the interaction were written in free text and appended to the official pro forma. The interview and interaction with the police was recorded verbatim, as far as possible, by police officers, for evidentiary purposes. These records were, therefore, of exceptionally good quality as records of events. From the police records and my observations of police interaction, I use grounded theory to construct a model of the interaction of officers and men stopped for soliciting and kerb-crawling, and then subject these responses to a second level analysis by using discourse analytic techniques to examine the various strategies men use to neutralise their actions.

Interaction of police and kerb-crawlers

The attitude of men stopped by police can be placed on a continuum of compliance and remorse immediately following an event. This is illustrated in figure 4.1 below. Over 50 per cent of the men in the police records who were stopped for kerb-crawling were recorded as being 'co-operative' when stopped (n=178). Nearly a quarter of the men (23 per cent) were recorded as initially being 'reluctant' to give their details (n=82), although these men provided the information after the police observations of their actions were described to them, 14 per cent of men were seen to be 'remorseful' about their actions (n=49). A further 7 per cent showed 'extreme remorse' when men were observed to burst into tears (n=24). A small number of men (n=18, 5 per cent) declined to provide their details.

Parallel sub-categories of response

Alongside the display of such attitudes, the kerb-crawler responses in the police records appeared to contain four sub-categories of response. These can be seen in figure 4.1. The sub-categories were:

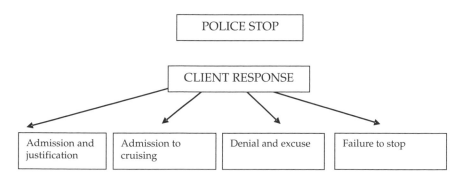

Figure 4.1 Sub-categories of Street Client Response Following Police Stop

- the admission of kerb-crawling;
- the admission to cruising but a denial of kerb-crawling;
- the denial of kerb-crawling;
- a complete failure to stop for the police.

These positions can be placed on a continuum of remorse and of co-operation with the police whereby the admissions were at the extremely compliant end and failures to stop at the least compliant end. These four categories of response will now be explained further.

Admission and justification

Admissions were present in 161 of the records, and appeared to be more likely to come from men who were discovered in the act of receiving straight, oral, or manual sex from a sex worker, or who were in varying degrees of undress (or in women's clothes in one case) when stopped by the police. In 52 per cent of the cases of admission (n=83), men provided a *full and open admission* that they were looking for a prostitute and full details of who they were and where they were from, were offered. Examples of this from the records included: 'admitted he'd arranged sex at £40' (record 97219) and 'admitted he'd asked for hand relief for £30' (record 97296). A *straight admission* came from 35 per cent of the men (n=56), whereby men were less open but nonetheless admitted the offence. Some men provided justification for what they were doing without direct or overt admission, for example 'I wanted someone to talk to' (record 98065).

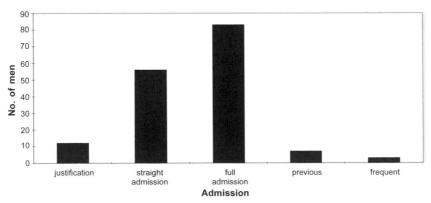

Figure 4.2 Admissions – Level of Behaviour (N=161)

Admission therefore seemed to be implied by this justification in the records. This occurred in 2 per cent of cases (n=12). At the extreme end of the admission scale was a full admission of soliciting and that of previous similar conduct. In one such case, it was recorded that the man 'admitted looking for a tom he had used last week' (record 97065). Such admissions occurred in 1 per cent of cases (n=7).

There were also a few cases where men admitted the activity and also that it was a frequent activity. This occurred in 0.5 per cent of cases (n=3) and included for example a man who 'fully admitted, said he had a problem with prostitutes and couldn't help himself' (record 97147). In such cases, the man appeared to offer as his justification a psychological or physical compulsion outside his control.

The men's admissions were usually followed by attempts to justify their actions, by ignorance of the law, for example, which was a more common justification with tourists or overseas business visitors than with British men. A few men made appeal to some sad and mitigating circumstances, such as 'I admit, I was driving around to talk with the girl. I lost my wife two months ago' (record 98013). Another example in this category includes the record of a mini-cab driver who 'admitted his fare is looking for a prostitute' (record 97031) whereby the admission was justified by referring to the higher authority of his customer.

Admissions to 'cruising' but denial of kerb-crawling

The next sub-category to emerge was the admission of 'cruising' but a denial of kerb-crawling. In the last chapter I described that there were a number of cases where men had been stopped for driving round a red-light area without a good explanation (n=108). In 28 of these records, it had been noted that these men admitted to 'cruising' but denied kerb-crawling. Three differing types of explanation emerge from these cases, as can be seen in figure 4.3 below. The reason given by thirteen men was that they were driving around the red-light area because they were 'simply curious' and they would 'admit to being curious' (record 97012). Other men said they were 'looking' but would not buy sex (n=12); examples of their explanations included, 'sorry mate I was just looking at the girls' (record 98052), and 'I like looking at the girls' (record 98005). Men in the 'looking' category were adamant that they would not solicit a street sex worker; one admitted 'to seeing the prostitutes, but said they were too "dirty" for him' (record 98119).

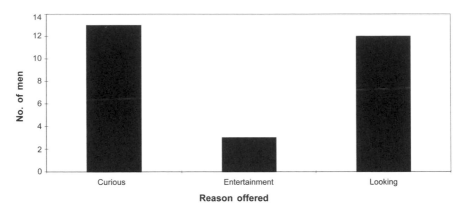

Figure 4.3 Reasons Why Men Said They Were Cruising (N=28)

A small number of men said that driving around the red-light area was a regular form of entertainment for them (n=3). These men explained that they were 'only having a laugh'. In the case where this conduct was a group experience to be shared with other men, there appeared to be an element of voyeurism. This is evident where the man was recorded as saying, 'he knew it was an RLA[5] and was just showing a friend around' (record 97036).

Denials and excuses

The most common response by men stopped for kerb-crawling behaviour was denial. This was recorded in 203 cases. It can be seen in figure 4.4 that in 71 per cent of these cases men denied the activity, and constructed a specific excuse for some otherwise inexplicable actions (n=145). The men's excuses will be explored in detail later.

The next most common response was a straightforward denial by men; this group comprised 17 per cent of the denials (n=36). These men said they were emphatically 'not looking for a prostitute' (record 98037), and offered no excuse for their presence in the red-light area, for example. The behaviour of some men was described in the records as 'mildly confrontational'; this group comprised 7 per cent of the men who denied kerb-crawling (n=15). A small minority, 1 per cent of deniers, were described as 'verbally abusive' (n=2), or 'aggressive' 1.5 per cent (n=3), and in two cases there was a pursuit when the men failed to stop. So far I have described three sub-categories possible of attitudes and responses: admission and justification; admission to cruising (but denial of kerb-crawling); and denial and excuse. I next explore the final sub-category, that of failure to stop.

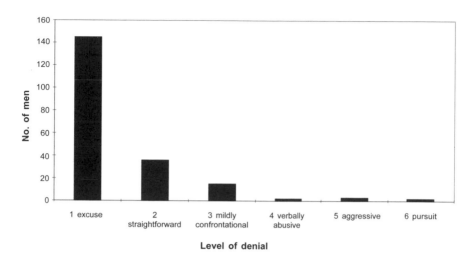

Figure 4.4 Kerb crawler Denials and Recorded Level of Behaviour (N=203)

Failure to stop

Whilst the patterns of interaction between kerb-crawlers and the police so far described in this chapter account for almost all of the data, there were two rare and notable exceptions. In these cases, which I observed during fieldwork, the drivers failed to stop after being asked to do so by police officers. In the first of these cases, a seemingly high-status white male in a high-performance car accelerated off into the night instead of stopping. He had been approached to stop by a black female police officer, who showed her warrant card and asked him to pull over. The police pursued his car through London but were unable to keep up, and the car was later traced and the driver appeared in court charged with kerb-crawling and reckless driving. Later documentary evidence from the court records and my fieldnotes taken in court showed how this man used a fear of 'viccing'[6] that he'd suffered previously as his excuse to escape from the law on this occasion.

> Mr ... denies kerb-crawling and his excuse for reckless driving is the colour of the black female officer's skin – the man told the court that he just remembered seeing a black female face at the window. He said that he had given two black women a lift

in the past and then been robbed, so he had been frightened and sped off. (Fieldnotes 97/23)

The white stipendiary magistrate was not satisfied with the excuse and the man was found guilty of both offences. The second 'fail to stop' case concerned a man in a stolen car. The driver ran over the police officer who attempted to stop him, and the sex worker escaped from the car. The details of this case were as follows:

> The punter sped off, running over a male police officer, who was lying in the road. The sex worker, Carmel, later managed to escape from the car. The sergeant said 'It was a deliberate attempt to run down an officer. Last time it was Sheila they tried to run over.' The ground was searched because Carmel said 'he threw out a spliff but it smelt more like Charlie[7] to me'. Carmel had escaped from the punter's car when he stopped at a junction to avoid hitting another car. She was very badly shaken and glad to see the police. She said she had been suspicious when the punter ignored her directions to a location for sex. The injured officer was taken to hospital. Carmel joined the team for a cup of tea at the station and to relay to an inspector the events leading up to the officer's injury. (Fieldnotes 98/48).

In this incident, the stolen car had been used in an armed robbery in the week prior to the kerb-crawling incident. Although both car and driver were extensively searched for, the car did not turn up until a year later.

I have presented four categories of response, and shown how prevalent each of these were in the records and observations. Interestingly, a series of phases emerged from the fieldwork observations and interviews with officers, which would not have been apparent from the records alone. These phases characterised different reactions these men went through during their interactions with police officers. It is to these phases that I now turn.

Phase order

A distinctive pattern of interaction occurred in 95 per cent of kerb-crawler incidents that I observed with police officers, and also in interviews and focus groups with police officers where officers described the interaction from their own perspective. Further analysis, using the 'discourse action model' of Edwards and Potter (1993),

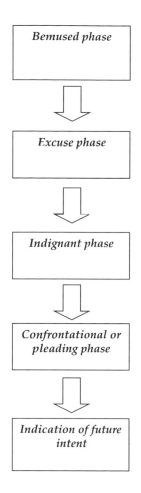

Figure 4.5 Sequence of Interaction between Police and Kerb-crawler

helps explain what kerb-crawlers were possibly trying to do in each of these phases; these are outlined in figure 4.5.

When men denied soliciting, their 'discourse of defence' appeared to be constructed in five possible phases. I have called these: the bemused phase; the excuse phase; the indignant phase; the confrontational or the pleading phase; and in some cases these would be followed by an indication of future intent.

The bemused phase

From the interviews and observations it appeared that drivers were initially bemused that they had been stopped. This was apparent in remarks such as: 'I hope you don't think I'm the sort of man that goes to prostitutes' (Fieldnotes 97/34), or, 'Oh no Officer. Do I look like the kind of man to go to a prostitute?' (Fieldnotes 98/18) in which men constructed the kerb-crawler as a moral 'other' – a 'type' or 'sort' of man from whom they wished to set themselves apart. These remarks were accompanied by head-shaking and broad grins as they complied with the police requests for details and documentation. The men also exhibited nervous laughter, which developed into concern about the offence. Some men then shrugged their shoulders, smiled apologetically and admitted to either 'cruising' or soliciting, and offered some justification. This often resulted in the man receiving a verbal warning from the police officers about the dangers of red-light districts late at night. Alternatively, they were told that they would shortly receive a letter of warning. This phase was described by one young male police officer as getting 'the smiling over with', he explained:

> If you go straight in with the kerb-crawlers and say, 'Listen like you're not going to get reported, you're going to get a letter da-di-da, you're not going to go to court, no-one need know straight away.' No messing. You know, you get it over and done with and he's embarrassed. He'll get the smiling over with and give you his details. (Focus group, B Team 97/22)

The excuse phase
Following the bemused phase, many men admitted to kerb-crawling or cruising, but more commonly, however, men provided some excuse to account for why they were not soliciting. The following extract illustrates the transition from the bemused phase to the excuse phase:

> When the officers pointed out to him what he'd been doing, he laughed 'I hope you don't think I'm the type of bloke that goes with prostitutes. I was just burning oil off. (Fieldnotes 97/8)

Thus the man attempted to provide a reason why he was not soliciting for sex, substantiating this with his reason for driving around the red-light district three times at an unusual hour. The excuse phase also often included the assertion that the man was married, in such phrases as, 'But Officer, I'm a married man'. Interestingly, during my fieldwork observation, I observed that this seemed to have the opposite of the effect these men appeared to be trying to achieve:

The female officer pursed her lips and looked at him with disgust. The male officer replied 'most kerb-crawlers are married, they're looking for something a bit different to what they've got at home'. The man was completely nonplussed and got stroppy. (Fieldnotes 97/12)

As the extract suggests, the disclosure of a man's marital status may have different consequences depending on the gender of the officer questioning him. Male officers commonly constructed a 'discourse of variety' meaning that the majority of the men they stopped were married, and that many of them were looking for a different sexual service, or a different woman to their non-paid partner. The effect on the female officers, however, was markedly different, with many showing visible distaste to the information offered. Their replies to the men reflected an 'HIV discourse' that encompassed discussion of safety and the transmission of disease; using this discourse, the female officers implied that the man should be more responsible and considerate to his family. This discourse assumed the sex worker more liable to infect the client than the other way round. There also appeared to be another discourse evident in the perspectives of female officers which I have called the 'discourse of betrayal', in which notions about transgression of trust, intimacy and fidelity were apparent, though this was used less often than other discourses. Within this discourse, policewomen appeared to take the perspective of the kerb-crawler's partner whom they considered a 'wronged woman'. Such identification with a 'wronged' partner seemed to solidify the female police officers' stance against kerb-crawlers and their feelings that subsequent penalties should be meaningful.

The indignant phase
Having been allowed to provide a brief explanation, it was usual for a street client to be told by the officers what they had observed, how long he had been watched for, his route, and how many times he had been seen doing various circuits around the red-light district. Sometimes this information elicited an admission or a pleading phase, but more commonly the discourse proceeded to the indignant phase. A young male police officer described a typical interaction as follows:

First we say, 'Can you explain your actions?', and the bloke answers 'I've asked her for directions' and then you say, 'Hang on, we've been following you for the last ten minutes you've been down blah, blah, blah streets' and suddenly they'll change they'll say yeah, okay I'm sorry, when they know how much we know about them, their reaction changes immediately doesn't it? Under surveillance for an hour and a half you know, literally tailing him, but he was quite indignant to start with but when we told him his route and everything, and he was calm as anything after that. (Focus group, A team 97/23)

As this extract from the focus group discussion indicates, the indignant phase may be fairly brief. It may, however, escalate into a further phase of confrontation. Whatever its length, the indignant phase is typically characterised by the man saying 'I'm not happy with this at all' and/or 'I want your details/number/name' and so on to the officers concerned. Again drawing on my observational records, this stage was frequently accompanied by the client raising his voice, pointing to the officer, folding his arms or stabbing the air to show how his route was at odds with their observations. This can be seen in the following extract, from fieldnotes recorded at 2.55 a.m. at Sussex Gardens, when two sex workers and a client were watched and the man was subsequently stopped:

Client:	… I just said hello to the lady.
WPC1:	Why did you say that?
Client:	I'm a man, I can say that can't I? I'm a man.
WPC1:	Do you feel you have a right to talk to lone women at night, sir?
Client:	Yes, I am a man, aren't I?
	[The man gives his address, a restaurant in Herts. He has £140 in cash but no ID]
WPC1:	This is a very long way round to Hitchin, sir.
Client:	I KNOW THE ROADS BETTER THAN YOU.
MPC1:	Sir, stop raising your voice please.
WPC1:	You are not allowed to stop women and talk to them.
Client:	I was on my way to see my son.
MPC1:	Is there someone we can check with to verify your address, sir?
Client:	I'm not lying. I've been working at my restaurant in Hitchin.
WPC1:	You've admitted that you've stopped a young lady. We need an address for this summons. If you cannot give us an address, you'll stay in a cell overnight

until you go to court in the morning. What was your phone number, please?

[He starts to raise his voice again.]

Client: It's upstairs. That's why I've got a mobile phone. Tomorrow you can telephone them, no problem. I've got three girlfriends, and in the morning you can phone them.

MPC1:   Sir, how can we verify you are the owner of the vehicle?

Client: I can go to the police station in Hitchin and present my driving licence to them.

(Fieldnotes 98/56).

Not only does this extract illustrate the indignant phase in the man's conduct but also it was possible to see how his indignation escalated throughout the street interview process. In interviews, vice officers explained that the 'indignant' phase was also applicable to other types of police work. One male police officer explained:

A lot of them we've questioned, we've noticed that if someone is caught driving around or they've got their back up, they very often rely on 'I'm going to complain against the police and want your number', that sort of thing. In all sorts of police work that happens, especially plain clothes. The majority of complaints that come in because of that. But because the bloke thinks 'The only way I can get off of this is by complaining against the police' and you've seen it first-hand, know what its like, it's like that all the time isn't it? (Focus group, A Team 97/22)

Confrontational/aggressive phase

Following the indignant phase, men either admitted that they were kerb-crawling and gave their details, or they proceeded to plead. In a very small number of cases, however, the men became argumentative and took down the officers' name(s) and details. These men were observed to be more confrontational in both body language and response speech, saying things such as, 'Do what you like. I've done nothing wrong' (record 97195). The records indicated that in some cases it was recorded that the man 'became abusive and denied taking any of above actions' (record 97221) when told how they had been observed and followed. In 19 out of the 32 cases that I observed, the men would instead move from being indignant to a phase of pleading.

The pleading phase

The pleading phase was characterised by the kerb-crawler begging to be allowed off the charge, citing reasons such as: 'please officer, you'll ruin my life' (record 97284), 'you will break up my marriage' (record 98067), or 'I will lose my job' (record 98119) or family. For some men, there was a duality in this, whereby they would be beseeching and supplicant towards male officers, but, were dismissive of female officers, whilst at the same time imploring the officers to allow them to go. This can be seen very clearly in the Fieldnote extract below:

> A white estate car was followed for 24 minutes. He parked and approached one of the regular sex workers. He talked to her on the corner. She shook her head, then turned her back to him and crossed her arms. He walked away, then turned and shouted a few things at her from the opposite street corner over the traffic, as if to re-open negotiation. He walked twenty yards back to his car masturbating himself through his trousers. When the two officers approached him, he would look only at the male officer, he refused to look at the female officer (or me, about four feet behind them). He shook his head when told he had been watched he said that was not what he was doing. When it was pointed out what an offence it is, he started to beg, 'Please no, you will ruin my family. I am a married man with children. My mother was very ill in the London Hospital in fact, room no. 46. You can check. Please, please, please …' He started to crouch at the knees slightly, bending supplicantly and with outstretched arms, hands upturned and his fingertips meeting … He followed the two officers across the road as they walked away, his body still leaning forward, still pleading behind the police car as it moved away. (Fieldnotes 97/21)

From my observations, the objective of such pleading appeared to be an attempt to diminish charges or mitigate the circumstances. In practice it only appeared to prolong the incident.

Indications of future intent

A final response from the men was to provide an indication of future intent when they stated that they definitely would not turn up in the area again. In 65 cases in the records, men gave an indication of their future behaviour. This ranged from the seven men who said they would not go near the area again, to the eight men who gave some sort of indication that they would solicit again as they visited the area on a regular basis.

Heart attack phase
Whilst discussing the findings with some of the officers in focus groups to test the emerging model of conduct, it became clear that a further phase had been witnessed by some officers with experience in other vice units. This occurred when the pleading phase failed to achieve its objective and the man started to open his shirt neck buttons asserting faintness or feigning a heart attack. As this phase remains to be grounded in evidence by observation or data from the records, it remains an interesting but unsubstantiated possible addition to any model of kerb-crawler behaviour. It was not a phase that I observed directly and so it is not included in the model.

A model of police interaction with kerb-crawlers: 'catching kerbies'

My analysis has shown that there were some clear patterns of conduct and speech at work when police stopped men for soliciting offences. These included four types of response from the men: admission, admission to cruising but not kerb-crawling, denial, and failure to stop. There were also five possible phases of response which characterise the interaction between kerb-crawlers and the police: the bemused phase, the excuse phase, the indignant phase, the pleading phase, and the indication of future intent. From all of these findings it was possible to build a coherent model of this conduct in figure 4.6 below.

Further analysis of the excuses of kerb-crawler denials

In 145 out of 203 cases of denial, excuses were provided by the men (see figure 4.3 above). Excuses (n=145) were much more common than justifications (n=95). The excuses were thematically coded to distinguish types of excuse and the 'techniques of neutralisation' that the men appeared to use to justify or deny their actions. Different types of excuses to emerge included the denial of volition, intent, agency, and excuses that involved an appeal to mitigating circumstances.

Denial of volition
This category included excuses to the police officers in which men attributed their actions to psychological or physical causes. This was

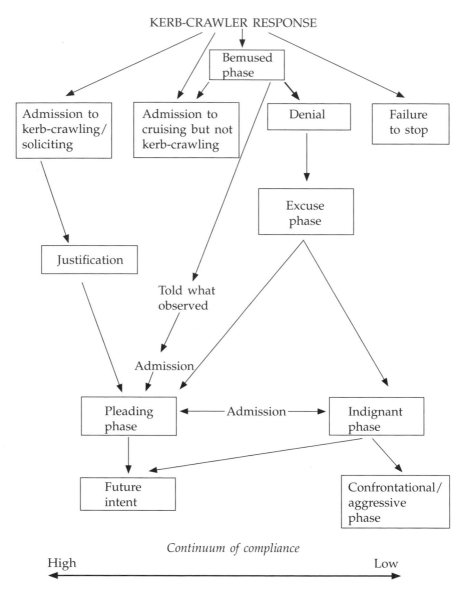

Figure 4.6   Police Stops and Kerb-crawler Responses

seen in the example of a man who said he was 'driving around trying to clear his head' (record 97115), or another man who said he was only stopping women in his car at 3 a.m. because he was 'feeling depressed' (record 97088). An attribution to physical causes was apparent in one man's excuse of illness, in which he was recorded as saying 'he couldn't want a woman as he had cancer of the throat' (record 98106).

Denial of intent

The research also revealed that some men argued to the police that there had been a misinterpretation of their intent. This was apparent in cases where men claimed to be looking for something; various men claimed to be 'looking for a friend' (record 97040), or 'looking for a parking space/off-licence/hotel/night club/toilet/somewhere to urinate'. The denial of intent was also seen in cases where various men claimed to be waiting for something; examples in this category included 'awaiting a phone call' (record 98206) or 'waiting for a cab' (98037). The same denial of intent was also seen in cases where men claimed that their reason for stopping and soliciting a woman belied motives that were essentially charitable. These cases included men who claimed they had stopped because: 'she looked cold' (record 98162); in one particular case a man said that 'his charitable crusade was giving out blankets to prostitutes who looked cold' (record 97256); another man said that he was 'rescuing women' (record 98144).

Denial of intent was also seen in cases where men claimed that they could not find their way, where it was recorded that 'he stated he was lost' (record 97009), or where men claimed there had been a case of mistaken identity. Some men maintained that there had been a mistaken representation of the relationship between themselves and the sex workers, asserting that they were having a non-commercial one. These contained fantasy elements and romantic notions which ranged from 'it was a chance meeting with an unknown female' (record 98167) to 'he invited her back for dinner only' (record 98016), for example.

Denial of agency

Many men denied their agency by attributing their conduct to structural or mechanical concerns about their cars, or to some higher authority. This first category of excuse could be seen in the example of one man who said he was: 'trying to clear vent his engine which was misfiring' (record 97136), or another who was 'warming his car engine up' (record 98076). Attributions in this category also pertained to the internal environment in the car, seen in the excuse by one man who argued he was 'listening to song on the radio' (record 98202) or another who was 'finishing listening to a radio play and couldn't go home as wife would hear the car and run out' (record 97059). Men also denied agency by attributing the kerb-crawling behaviour to some higher authority. This could be seen in the case of a cab driver who was: 'only stopping women because his passenger told him to' (record 98129).

Appeal to mitigating circumstances

It appeared from the police interaction and the records that men appealed to mitigating circumstances in two types of ways; by using sad tales or an arrangement of facts to highlight some aspect of his regular partner's conduct, or, alternatively, to scapegoat the sex worker. Examples in the 'sad tales' category came from men who said they: 'never normally did this but had just split up with their girlfriend' (record 98171) or others who said they were 'having trouble at home' (record 98006). Other men were less specific and gave less information, but nonetheless made comments such as they had just had an 'argument with partner' (record 97296). The men who blamed the sex worker argued that: 'she waved to me' (record 97010), or 'he had parked up and she just asked for a lift' (record 98094) to argue that their conduct was merely a response to hers.

Discussion of findings: Sub-categories of response

My findings have shown that the situational context in which police stop men for kerb-crawling and in which men attempt to account for their behaviour is a complex one. The majority of the men were recorded as being co-operative with the police and their categories of response could be placed at the compliant end of the continuum of responses to the police. Within the patterns of conduct and speech at work when men were stopped for soliciting offences, I found there were four types of response: admission, admission to cruising but not kerb-crawling, denial and excuses, and failure to stop.

Admissions

Admissions were most likely from men who were recorded as being caught in the act of receiving a sexual service from a sex worker, or in varying degrees of undress, and the police recorded specific details of these. In extreme cases, men would admit to kerb-crawling on the recorded occasion and to frequent or previous instances. Unlike previous researchers (Kinnell 1989, Høigard and Finstad 1992, and McKeganey and Barnard 1996), none of this sample of clients gave a positive reason for visiting sex workers. This could be because the research was police focussed, and clients were less likely to cite positive reasons to police officers than to sex workers. Alternatively, the positive reasons noted in other studies could be due to the client's attempts to ingratiate himself with the sex workers. This is possible in the study by Kinnell (1989), or due to the self-selected nature of the samples in the other studies which comprised of clients who visit sex workers frequently. My findings support many of the motivations found by Kinnel (1989), Høigard and Finstad (1992) and McKeganey and Barnard (1996) apparent in the responses by men who admitted and justified their purchase of sex. These included loneliness and sad tales.

Admissions to cruising but not kerb-crawling

A number of cases were found of men who admitted to 'cruising' around the red-light area in their cars but who denied any kerb-crawling activities. There were three types of response from these men: those who said they were 'curious', those who said they were 'looking', and those who said it was a form of 'entertainment' for them. The finding of 'curiosity' as a motive supports the findings of Høigard and Finstad (1992), McKeganey and Barnard (1996), and Sharpe (1998). The men who said that cruising around the red-light district was a form of entertainment added a further dimension to the phenomenon of 'peepers' found by Høigard and Finstad (1992) and alongside the findings of McKegany and Barnard (1996), shows such cruising to be a widespread phenomenon in red-light districts. I did not observe any of the overtly antagonistic or aggressive behaviour found in their study during my own observation or in the records, however. This may be due to a regional difference between Glasgow and London, or due to a methodological difference between the two studies. My observations were predominantly made from a car; I observed from the street only when men were actually being booked, or when I was walking in the company of two officers, whereas McKeganey and Barnard (1996) made their observations entirely standing on the street alongside sex-working women.

It was not possible in this study to find out whether or not cruising led up to the purchase of sex (as a preliminary activity) – though clearly there are suggestions from previous studies (Høigard and Finstad 1992, for example) that the activities are linked. To find out whether or not cruising as a leisure activity leads up to the purchase of sex would require a longer follow-up and the cross-matching of records from other police force areas. This may be a useful avenue for future research to explore.

Denial and excuses

It was common for men to deny the offence, and there were different levels of denials shown in the police records. Using the distinction between justifications and excuses that justifications imply that the act is good, or at least *permissible* in the circumstances, whereas excuses *acknowledge* that the relevant act is *bad* in some way, with an implication that they are due to external agency (Austin 1961), both of these were counted and explored.

Failing to stop

There were two cases of men who failed to stop, and these showed different responses and possibly motivations. These cases demonstrated a non-compliance with police officers, and the rare but real risk to officers in this work, as well as the more frequent risks faced by sex workers. One of these cases also indicated a link to another serious and violent crime – an armed robbery – and the case illustrated a more mutual understanding that has emerged in the current climate policing of paid street sex between the police and sex-working women. These types of cases have not been noted in previous research, but in one case, studied in depth through to its conclusion in court, the kerb-crawler used the excuse of a fear of 'viccing', which Holzman and Pines (1992) found to be part of the 'thrill' for some men.

Phase order

With regard to the phases identified (bemused, excuse, indignant, pleading, and in some cases, the indication of future intent phases) and their sequence, Potter and Wetherall (1987: 33) have argued that the construction of accounts is important for three reasons:

- it reminds us that accounts are built out of extant linguistic resources;
- it implies active selection in what is used and what is missed out; and

- construction also emphasises the potent, consequential nature of accounts.

I would suggest that these men create their version of kerb-crawling and thus display their evaluation of what kerb-crawling is, through their construction of these phases.

The bemused phase
The first phase was one of bemusement, although it is not clear whether the men were bemused because they did not realise kerb-crawling was against the law, or whether it was part of their confusion regarding the law. It was apparent, however, in the bemused phase, that the men's responses supported the comments reported by Sharpe (1998) about the 'sort' of man that goes to prostitutes. These comments arguably exhibited some underlying beliefs about the sort of men who will pay for sex – that is that men who buy sex are less worthy than those who do not.

The excuse phase
In the excuse phase the majority of men used their marital status as a defence. To use their marital status as a defence in this way reflects notions that these men held about marriage, and social expectations about sexual relationships within marriage. The men seemed to disclose their marital status in an attempt to set themselves apart from other men. They attempted to elicit sympathy by arguing that the charge would upset a stable relationship, and clearly hoped to encourage a benign response in order to lessen any penalty that might follow. For the majority of men the aim might have been to indicate that they did not need to *buy* sex as they could have it at home with their non-paid partners. The immediate reference to their married status supports the general findings of Høigard and Finstad (1992). I was unable to discern whether or not the motivational factor for married men was that paid extra-marital paid sex would be easier to hide from their wives than an affair (Høigard and Finstad). The excuse phase also included the type of comments Matthews recorded as representative, although my findings did not find support for Matthews' (1993) claim that kerb-crawling was a 'casual' activity for many men (that is, an opportunistic activity).

The research also revealed a gendered pattern of response by officers towards the marital status of the punter. Specific discourses were constructed: male officers constructed a discourse that encompassed 'sexual variety', that is, male officers believed that men were simply seeking variety. Female officers used either a 'discourse of betrayal' within which they emphasised monogamy and the need for sexual restraint and the need to protect the 'good woman' at home, or they used an 'HIV discourse of health' in which they stressed the need for sexual restraint and protection from the 'debased whore'. Such a gendered pattern of response merits further exploration in future research.

Indignant phase

A further phase was that of indignation, which officers in the focus groups suggested was also applicable to other types of policing. It was similar to a reaction found by Humphreys (1970) in *The Tearoom Trade* where it was argued that men stopped for sex offences in public lavatories wore their indignation like a 'breastplate of righteousness' (Ephesians 6: 14, cited in Humphreys 1970). My findings regarding this phase also show that the men's behaviour appears to be part of an ordered pattern of response that either escalated into confrontation, or dissolved into pleading.

The confrontational phase

Some men went through a further phase where they became confrontational or aggressive. This may have been a response to being found out. Within Stoller's (1979) psychoanalytic framework, it is possible that these men behaved angrily and rather like little boys caught lying, because their secret was found out; thus they sought to lash out at the person who discovered them. Such confrontational conduct has not been shown in previous research. This may be due to the self-selection in studies by McKeganey and Barnard (1996) or Høigard and Finstad (1992), which excluded men who had been found out.

The pleading phase

Some men went through a phase of pleading. This appeared to be an attempt to escape being penalised. My observations indicated, however, that such pleading only prolonged the incident. There was an interesting reaction to officer gender from some of the men who pleaded, who clearly found it difficult that they were dealt with by female officers. A final response from some of the men was to provide an indication of their future intent, *(indication of future intent phase)* when they stated they would not appear in the area again, whilst others stated that they would solicit again as they visited on a regular basis.

Further analysis and of deconstruction of kerb-crawler excuses

Further analysis of the excuses men provided produced a variety of accounts, and many of the client excuses conformed to Sykes and Matza's (1957) classic techniques of neutralisation as well as Semin and Manstead's (1983) typology of accounts. These included the denial of volition, the denial of intent, the denial of agency, and the appeal to mitigating circumstances. The denial of volition was found in cases where men excused their kerb-crawling by attributing it to physical or psychological causes. In these cases, there was an element of compulsion that was not casual; but rather, it seemed that men were drawn to the area to pay for sex because they could not help themselves. These findings thus support an addiction model of kerb-crawling, and lend weight to the suggestion by Stoller (1979) that such behaviours are deeply rooted in the psyche.

In the cases that reflected a denial of 'intent', various men claimed to be looking for something or waiting for something, whilst others claimed there had been a mistaken representation of the relationship between themselves and the sex worker to argue that it was not necessarily a commercial relationship. The latter accounts included an element of fantasy, which supports the finding of Høigard and Finstad (1992) who first noted the fantasy element for men in the visiting of prostitutes. The findings also provide empirical support for the 'rhetoric of mutuality' created by clients, found by Plumridge *et al.* (1996). These findings support those of Holzman and Pines (1982) who found that men created the prostitute as an 'active' rather than as a 'passive' participant in the man's individual sexual fantasy.

Denial of intent was also seen in the cases of men who argued that their intent in kerb-crawling was essentially a charitable crusade because they felt the woman 'looked cold' or 'needed rescuing'. These excuses are suggestive of the interpretation by O'Connell Davidson's (1998) that such men eroticise passivity and vulnerability, in much the same way as the men who solicit toothless vagrants and children: future research might fruitfully explore this. A denial of agency was shown by men who suggested their kerb-crawling behaviour was actually the result of some structural concern about their car, or in response to some higher authority, in the case of cab-drivers.

My findings indicate that men appeal to mitigating circumstances in two main ways:

- they appear to try and turn themselves into the victim of their non-paid partner's behaviour; or

• see themselves as victims of the sex worker's behaviour.

In cases where men said that they were seeking sex because they had just had an argument with their partner, the findings support Stoller's (1979) theory in that men may resort to their chosen perversion following humiliation or rage. It is interesting to speculate on whether or not the kerb-crawling activity became a form of revenge against their regular partner in which the kerb-crawler turned himself into an avenger of such wrong-doing. In cases where men placed themselves as victims of the sex worker's soliciting, and blamed the sex worker by arguing that the sex worker had 'waved' at them or had 'just asked for a lift' it is possible that for some men 'waving' would signify the sex worker's 'availability', as Høigard and Finstad (1992) found. Alternatively, it is possible these men construct their conduct as a mere response to the demands and dominance of the sex-working woman. This supports O'Connell Davidson (1998), who suggested that men eroticise the phallic, dominating woman. This process may not be deliberate or intentional, indeed the men may not be consciously constructing this explanation, but rather construction emerges as they make sense of phenomena or carry out unselfconscious social activities like blaming or justifying (Potter and Wetherall 1987: 34).

Theoretical model of police and kerb-crawler interaction

My analysis has shown that there was evidence of a sequential pattern in the interaction between police officers and kerb-crawlers and from these patterns it was possible to construct a model of kerb-crawler response. There are implications for public order from such a model. It is important in policing to know the complexity of people's possible responses. Also, in the cases of men who failed to stop, the research suggests that risk-assessment within policing strategies should take account of the rare but real possibility of such an occurrence. A theoretical model of this sort is also useful to facilitate the identification of target groups to ensure more effective intervention than normally achieved in blanket approaches. Wider legislative policy has to be grounded in how people actually behave, and my model of kerb-crawler behaviour provides new information in this respect. Such a model, based on empirical findings, also has implications for future research. One such implication is that knowing the breadth of how people account for their behaviour should be reflected in the design or application of any type of self-report instrument. Knowing the complexity of behavioural responses may also help to define research questions more accurately, or help define pre-determined limits to test attitudes psychometrically.

Policing patterns of street prostitution

My findings illustrate that the policing of kerb-crawling was part of a range of duties carried out by the Street Offences Squad that included the protection of juveniles at risk, and the charging of prostitutes. The protection of juveniles took priority over other duties, and the number of protection incidents appeared to have an impact on the number of other incidents that were policed. These included charging of prostitutes and kerb-crawlers. It was also shown that although police attitudes towards charging prostitutes varied, officers felt sex workers were often under various pressures, and considered that charging them was a policing function that lacked legitimacy. Officers, did not, however, like to see sex workers flaunt this policy openly by waving evidence that they had been charged already as a 'warrant to work'. The charging of prostitutes was also a function that had to be balanced with competing demands from residents.

I found that in over half the recorded cases, sex-working women were constructed in a perjorative way and in a way that ran counter to the way in which police officers spoke to them. Despite the apparent sympathy expressed for the women, and the perceived lack of legitimacy for the legislation, officers did impose charges against women for soliciting. The implication of this for the sex worker is that not only are her previous cautions used as evidence against her, but also against her clients; that she is labelled not only in the sex worker records but also in other records serves to reinforce the pejorative nature of 'common prostitute'.

Attitudes to kerb-crawlers also varied, but this varied according to occupation and residential status rather than actions. In interviews, many of the female police officers said they particularly disliked hackney cab drivers kerb-crawling. They felt this was tantamount to breaking the 'public trust' in them. As public servants themselves, they took a dim view of this, and they took particular pleasure in stopping and booking 'cabbies'. This occurs despite some apparent difficulty officers have in gaining firm evidence on hackney cab drivers. Difficulties in gaining evidence include the fact that hackney cab drivers have a wide range of legitimate reasons to be stopping beside women, which includes touting for casual cab fare business. It is easier for the police to charge mini-cabs as they are not supposed to tout for casual business, and procedurally it is the same as ordinary cars. The prosecution of hackney cabs, however, requires extra paperwork and specific documentation.

Chapter summary

The policing of kerb-crawlers was found to be only one part of policing duties. Other duties involved the protection of juveniles at risk, a task which was seemingly more time consuming than catching kerb-crawlers. Whilst sex workers were constructed in the records in a pejorative way, this was inconsistent with the way they were treated in practice, which was with notional acceptance and sympathy. Officers expressed reluctance to charge women with soliciting offences, though in fact did so. I have also explored the ways in which police stop men and women involved in commercial sexual encounters and how they all interpret this behaviour. My findings suggest that kerb-crawler responses occurred on a continuum of compliance with the police. Four sub-categories of response emerge on this continuum, from admissions (which were more likely from a man discovered in the act of receiving some sexual service) and admissions of cruising but a denial of kerb-crawling, through to the denial of kerb-crawling, and a failure to stop. I observed that there is a sequential order of phases in the behaviour of kerb-crawlers when interacting with the police. These are: the bemused phase, indignant phase, confrontational phase or pleading phase. In some cases there followed an indication of future conduct. In the 'bemused phase', men would construct those who paid for sex as 'other'. Following this phase men would go through an 'excuse phase' in which they would use their married status as a badge of immunity. This information elicited differential responses according to the gender of the officer. Male officers responded using a 'discourse of variety', whereas female officers constructed a 'discourse of betrayal' or an 'HIV discourse'. Kerb-crawlers would then continue to an 'indignant phase', a phase officers claimed was common to other aspects of policing. Kerb-crawlers then proceeded to either a 'confrontational phase' or a 'phase of pleading' in which they performed exaggerated verbal and body gestures which appeared to protract the incident. A final response in a small number of cases was to provide an indication of future intent. In focus group discussion, officers stated that they had witnessed a further phase whereby men accused of kerb-crawling pretended to have a heart attack. While previous research had suggested some of these responses, this research has provided new information, both on the men who became confrontational or pleaded, and on the sequential order and construction of these accounts.

From the empirical findings, it was possible to build a coherent model of police interaction and kerb-crawler conduct. Within this model, further analysis of the excuses revealed that excuses were much more common than justifications. By deconstructing the justifications and excuses men made to defend their actions, it was possible to gain insight into the thoughts that may precede and make this act possible. These excuses conformed to techniques of neutralisation found by Sykes and Matza (1957), and included the denial of volition, intent, agency, and the appeal to mitigating circumstances. These findings challenge the views that kerb-crawling is either a casual matter (Benson and Matthews 1995a) or always 'a project that unfolds' (Høigard and Finstad 1992); rather, it is complex and varied in both nature and explanation. In many of the phrases the men used, support for Stoller's (1979) theory of perversion was found. My findings suggest that the accountability of kerb-crawling conduct is not only more sophisticated and rule-governed behaviour than previously thought, but also perhaps more deeply-rooted in the psyche than previously expressed in the literature on kerb-crawling. This has implications for future research and public order policy.

Notes

1 Whilst this study is cited, it is available in full only in Norwegian. Cecilie Høigard was the research director and Høigard and Finstad (1992) report it at length in English. The reader is directed to this text.
2 This is apparently heightened in sex tourism, where the time spent in 'ludicrous drink-sodden posturing with other men telling tales of conquests' outnumbers time spent in sexual congress with their 'dream women' (O'Connell Davidson 1998: 174), with whom the language difficulties preclude even small talk.
3 Formerly known in popular parlance as the 'riot squad'.
4 This figure is not exact because of the aliases women sometimes use.
5 Red-light area.
6 Term used to describe the victimisation of a potential client by a woman sex worker.
7 Cocaine.

Chapter 5

Violence, victimisation and protection

> Usually the last customers of the night were local 'brasses' or prostitutes. The taxi drivers knew them well, often driving them to liaisons. At the end of the girls' shifts, the men would ferry them home, though sometimes the women would join them for a drinking session at the office. Occasionally the drivers would go with the girls. 'A ride in exchange for a ride,' it was called ... Bettina had known Parvez for three years ... Once he had rescued her from a violent client ... (Kureshi 1997: 120)

This chapter will explore a central aspect of life for many women in prostitution: the issue of violence and victimisation. Violence against prostitutes is endemic and there have been a large number of high profile murders of prostitutes. The chapter will examine the victimisation of women by punters and also from pimps to provide an insight into the prevalence, nature and extent of victimisation and violence against women working in the sex industry.

The law has been criticised for contributing to the violence women suffer at the hands of clients, vigilante groups, and pimps and so the chapter will also explore women's victimisation by the law. Legal policy victimises women working in the sex industry by, for example, criminalising certain behaviours related to prostitution as well as health measures prostitutes employ as legal evidence of prostitution-related behaviours and offences including the use of condom possession as legal evidence of prostitution. The current discourses including the 'rhetoric of disposal' and popular conception of 'sex slavery' will be explored; and whether these concepts are helpful to the empowerment of women in the sex industry will be discussed.

This chapter examines sex workers' vulnerability to violence, in the context of current debates outlined in previous chapters and rapidly changing public policy towards commercial sex in England and Wales. Data from the case study site and from a large non-governmental organisation involved in helping prostitute women will be used to further our understanding of those who perpetrate such violence by exploring the criminal histories and subsequent offences of men who are clients. Evidence from analysis of attacks on sex workers, and from reports on the deaths of 73 sex workers murdered or unlawfully killed between January 1990 and December 2002 (Kinnell 2004), suggests that the context of sex work – whether it takes place on the street or indoors – has a strong influence on the vulnerability of the sex worker. Information about attackers suggests that many are serial offenders, with implications for how the criminal justice system deals with such offenders. Further, this chapter seeks to demonstrate that current policing strategies and much public policy towards commercial sex exacerbates sex workers' vulnerability to violence, to the extent that it is possible to conceptualise violence against sex workers as an aspect of public policy which aims to deter but actually punishes for involvement in sex work. The social and human costs of ignoring rights are also discussed alongside the emergence of sex workers' labour rights following the affiliation of the International Sex Workers' Union with Britain's largest trade union in 2002. In doing this the chapter will explore how aspects and side effects of the policy outlined in chapter 2 contributes to the violence suffered by sex workers.[1]

Vulnerability

Many studies which report on sex workers' vulnerability to violence attribute this vulnerability to their personal characteristics, such as criminal histories, family background and drug use. The violence of clients towards sex-working women is a recurrent factor in the extensive literature on prostitution (see, for example, James 1976; Silbert and Pines 1982; Perkins 1991; Høigard and Finstad 1992; Lowman 1993; Barnard 1996; McKeganey and Barnard 1996; Whittaker and Hart 1996; Maher 1997; Miller 1997; Benson 1998). Such violence is not culture-bound: it marks the lives of sex-working women across countries as diverse as South Africa, Thailand, Turkey, USA and Zambia (Farley, Baral, Kiremire, and Sezgin 1998). The one thing *all* sex workers share in common is physical and psychological risk (Edwards 1993), and all forms of violence have been overwhelmingly associated with street work as opposed to off-street prostitution (Kinnell 1993; Boyle 1994). The women who are most vulnerable to begin with are put under greatest pressure. For example, one of the main concerns among drug-using street-sex workers is how drug use increases their risk of physical danger from clients rather than the long-term effects of the drug itself (Cusick 1998).

Kinnell (2004) argues that much less attention has been paid to questions explored by Benson (1998) of who commits such violence, what forms it takes, what strategies sex workers adopt to avoid violence, how police and courts treat crimes against sex workers, the role of the media, policy makers and general public, and why some sex workers experience violence but others do not.

The dearth of literature examining violence against sex workers from this perspective may be a result of the way sex work has been conceptualised in recent years, by commentators who accept the assertion that prostitution is 'in and of itself, violence against women' (Jeffreys 1997). Within this discourse no woman is deemed capable of consenting to commercial sex, and even lapdancers are regarded as victims of violence, 'forced' to commodify their own bodies. Where no qualitative difference is made between the 'violence' of society which 'forces' a woman to become a lap dancer, and the violence that expresses itself in beatings, rape and murder, there is no incentive to understand or reduce the latter sort of violence.

Also worrying is the ease with which these beliefs about prostitution elide with repressive state policies toward sex workers, and with punitive religious views on sexual morality. Proposals to improve sex workers' safety by legitimising their working situations are rejected as legitimising violence against women, since sex work itself is deemed violence. Alternatively, such measures are rejected lest they 'encourage' women to enter or remain in prostitution, by making it safer and therefore more attractive.

The logical corollary of such arguments is that violence against sex workers should not be prevented, because it acts as a control on the numbers of women involved in prostitution. But violence against sex workers is not inevitable and can and should be prevented, whether or not it acts as a deterrent to women being involved in the business. The focus here is on violence against female sex workers,[2] since women are the subject of the discourse referred to above about how violence in the sex industry should be understood. Violence is understood to mean acts which cause physical harm or fear of physical harm, the circumstances in which it happens and does not happen, and the characteristics of those who commit such violence. This necessitates examination of the role of the judiciary, police, policy makers, media and public in reducing or exacerbating violence against sex workers.

The law in England and Wales criminalises trafficking, procuring, controlling, aiding, abetting and living off the earnings of sex workers, thus placing many kinds of relationship between sex workers and others outside the law. Abuse and violence occur within these criminalised relationships – a substantial minority of murders of sex workers are attributed to people in these categories – but the first part of this chapter concentrates on a study of violence committed while the victim is at work, whether engaged in street or indoor work, since it is principally concerned with the interaction between violence and state policies towards public manifestations of sex work, i.e. the location of sex work activity. Information about violence against sex workers has been drawn from a variety of sources:

- newspapers, media, internet;
- reports of attacks collected by agencies working with sex workers; and
- published and unpublished research addressing these issues.

Defining and quantifying violence against sex workers

Defining violence against sex workers presents problems: should all violence against sex workers be included or only violence committed because the victim is a sex worker? Sex workers may be attacked because they are in vulnerable places or situations, typically, on the street, at night, perhaps affected by alcohol or drugs – but these circumstances also apply to victims who are not sex workers. Even the court process may not be able to determine why attacks happened. Offenders may misrepresent their motivations, juries may not convict, and some convictions are later overturned. It is therefore often difficult to decide if a crime against a sex worker relates directly to her occupation. This chapter concerns violence committed against sex workers, rather than violence committed because the victim was a sex worker.

Quantifying violence also poses problems. Sex workers are a hidden population so obtaining representative data is difficult.

However, surveys of sex workers' experiences provide some information, whereas no data is available through the criminal justice system on such experiences. Sex workers frequently do not report attacks to the police, and even when they do, police do not routinely record the occupation of the victim, even when the crime is murder (Brookman and Maguire 2003). Finally, categorising types of violence is problematic. For example, clients frequently take back the money they have paid after sex. Since consent was given on the basis of payment, some women view this as rape, others regard it as robbery. Some incidents defy categorisation: the man who clambers over the sex worker, fully clothed, then defecates in his trousers, may be an unwelcome customer, but has he committed assault? If yes, is it sexual assault? What about the client who tries to kiss the maid?[3] Is he committing an assault? If so, it is not comparable to that committed by a client who 'kicked and punched her for an hour, until her friend came and shouted for an ambulance' (London Ugly Mugs List April 2001).[4] Different analysts will adopt different approaches to defining categories of violence, so some variations between results in different groups of sex workers can be expected.

Context of violence

In the UK there are no locations where sex work can take place legally, although a woman working alone, in premises she owns herself, and who does not advertise, is probably only liable to prosecution under civil planning regulations, i.e. for running a business without planning consent. The Sexual Offences Act 1956 and subsequent legislation criminalises the management of indoor work, making the premises in which sex work occurs, and those deemed responsible for the premises, the focus of criminalisation.

Legislation on kerb-crawling criminalises street work, through criminalising sex workers and clients for their use of public space. Both strands of law lead to covert behaviour by sex workers, their clients, and anyone involved in organisation of the business, or provision of indoor premises for the purposes of sex work, but policing strategies in relation to sex work vary from place to place and from officer to officer. Many towns and cities have areas of street soliciting, and some have brothels which advertise themselves as saunas or massage parlours. There are also numerous private addresses where sex workers operate, attracting custom by word-of-mouth, advertising in coded (but widely understood) language in the personal columns of newspapers or in contact magazines, or on the internet.

This type of work takes place in rural and suburban areas, as well as in towns and cities. There are escort agencies through which sex workers may meet clients in hotels, restaurants, or in the clients' own homes. Sex workers may also work from pubs and clubs, in lorry parks, and at motorway service stations. Whichever work style is adopted, the criminalisation and stigmatisation of sex work leads to covert behaviour by both sex workers and their clients and the avoidance of contact with the police, or others who might report them to the police. In this criminalised, stigmatised and covert world, it is not surprising that violence takes place, but it is clear that some sex work environments are more dangerous than others.

Experience of violence amongst sex worker populations appears variable, but although different methods may account for some variations, most results indicate that street workers are much more vulnerable than indoor workers. Research in Glasgow, Edinburgh and Leeds (Church, Henderson, Barnard 2001) found that 81 per cent of street workers had ever experienced violence from clients, compared to 48 per cent of indoor workers. Similar results were found in Birmingham in 1993 (Kinnell 1993), where 83 per cent of street workers had experienced violence at work, compared to 53 per cent of indoor workers, most of whom were reporting on violence experienced at a time when they did street work.[5] Benson (1998) also found high prevalence amongst mainly street workers in Nottingham, as did May (2001) amongst street workers in London, where 54 per cent had been attacked within the previous 18 months. A multi-centre survey of street workers for the Channel 4 TV programme *Dispatches* in 2001 (Guardian, 16 September 2002), found that 73 per cent had been attacked in the previous year.

The relative safety of indoor work highlighted in Birmingham and Edinburgh has been questioned by London-based researchers and project workers, as escalating levels of violence have been reported at indoor premises in London during the 1990s (da Silva 2000). However, only 17 per cent of sex workers attending a central London service (Azevedo, Ward, Day 2002) had ever experienced violence at work. Analysis of 243 reports to the London Ugly Mugs List from May 2000 to January 2002 (Kinnell 2002) shows that, while indoor workers made many more reports (84 per cent), only half of these involved violence, and under 7 per cent involved sexual assault (see table 5.1). In contrast, despite the small number of reports from street workers, they were much more likely to report sexual or other assault

Table 5.1 London Ugly Mugs Reports, May 2000 to January 2002 (Kinnell 2004)

Incidents reported	Indoor (%)[6]	Street (%)[7]	All
Sexual assault/rape	13 (6)	14 (37)	27
Robbery with violence	64 (31)	7 (18)	71
Assault	15 (7)	10 (26)	25
Theft	16 (8)	2 (5)	18
Other (non-violent)	97 (47)	5 (13)	102
Total	205 (99)	38 (99)	243

not involving robbery than were indoor workers: 82 per cent of street incidents involved violence and 37 per cent of these were sexual assaults.

Indoor workers were more likely than street workers to report robberies, 81 per cent of which involved violence, much of it extreme. Robbers may view sex work premises as 'soft targets', perhaps because they do not expect crimes to be reported to the police. This may be related to rising numbers of foreign women at premises in central London, since the presence of 'illegal status' women may deter the reporting of crimes to the police. Nevertheless, although under 40 per cent of crimes at indoor premises were reported to police, this was double the rate of reporting by street workers in London, and by indoor workers in Leeds and Edinburgh (Church *et al.* 2001).

Many reports from indoor workers described the effectiveness of CCTV and the presence of others in averting or reducing the severity of incidents, such as one of attempted rape where the women present managed to lock the assailant out of the room, and: 'The maid and others in the building kicked the door open when they heard the woman call out. He didn't see the camera and the maid saw him come back in ...'

Escort sex workers, unlike many other indoor workers, are usually alone with clients, in premises they do not control. Only nine reports to the London Ugly Mug List were made by escorts. However, six of these nine incidents involved violence: a much higher proportion relative to the number of reports than amongst other indoor workers, but lower than amongst street workers.

Neither are the presence of others, doors, locks and CCTV available to street workers. Street workers, although they may solicit in sight of other sex workers, are usually alone when they encounter problems. Once they have a client, street workers usually leave the soliciting area, so that sexual encounters take place elsewhere. They may be safest in their own homes, if other people are about to help should clients turn violent. However, most avoid this because they can be evicted from social housing for taking clients to their homes, so other locations are used: alleyways, industrial estates, lorry parks, derelict buildings, country areas, and sometimes hotels or other indoor premises. Once in clients' cars, they have little control over where they are taken, and may be trapped by clients parking their cars against walls, or using central locking devices.

Hostility or indifference to sex workers from the general public may inhibit helpful interventions. One account noted: 'the woman screamed to people in the vicinity but nobody came to help her' (London Ugly Mugs List October 2001). But 'people in the vicinity' can save lives. Noel Dooley, who stabbed a sex worker in Bradford 43 times in October 2000, was confronted by passers-by, leading to his swift arrest and to prompt attention for his victim, who survived; Gary Allen, who attacked sex workers in Plymouth in 2000, was interrupted on two occasions because 'people in the vicinity' intervened.

What kind of people attack sex workers?

Benson (1998) and Pearce and Roach (1997) have described a range of people who attack sex workers: other working women; 'predatory men', 'people on the streets', including vigilantes, and those intent on property crime, as well as clients. The Birmingham survey found that at least 70 per cent of incidents of violence were ascribed to clients in all categories except kidnapping, while other investigators appear to have only measured violence from clients (Kinnell 1993). The high proportion of attacks ascribed to clients has led to assumptions that a high proportion of clients are violent.

Who are the violent clients and how prevalent are they?

When men are stopped by the police, the police national computer (PNC2) is used to find out if a man has a criminal record. This is represented by a Criminal Records Office number (CRO) affixed to the man's name. From the police records examined for this study[8] 63 men were found to have a previous criminal record registration. The records of 22 men could not be traced but each type of conviction was explored for the 41 men in the records, and these convictions (both custodial and non-custodial) can be seen in table 5.2 below. Since the research is concerned with examination of the *range* of previous offences rather than the number of previous offences, each type of offence was counted only once even if the man was convicted several times of an offence in the same category. The offences nevertheless add up to more than the total number of men. The age of these men ranged from 23 years to 66 years. The average age was 40 years, and the mean distance travelled to where they were stopped for the kerb-crawling 15 miles. The majority were in cars, but seven were in small commercial vehicles or mini-cabs, and one was on a bicycle. The most common previous convictions were for violence against the person. These accounted for 21 per cent of kerb-crawlers' previous offences. Convictions for property offences accounted for a further 20 per cent of mens' previous offences. Serious driving offences accounted for 10 per cent of the men's previous convictions. This was followed by an equal number of convictions for: robbery, possession of an offensive weapon, malicious damage, and drug offences, which all accounted for 8 per cent of the previous convictions.[9] Fraud offences accounted for 7 per cent of the previous convictions. Serious sexual offences also accounted for 7 per cent of previous convictions, and these ranged from indecent exposure with intent to assault a female, to convictions for serious sexual offences such as rape.

Definitions of 'violent' offending are contentious so the widely acknowledged definition by Zamble and Quinsey (1997) was used, which defines a violent offence as 'one involving a personal attack or threat, that is, any form of assault, and robbery' (1997: 120). It was

Table 5.2 Previous Convictions of Kerb-crawlers

Type of offence	N	%
Violence against the person	16	21
Theft, handling, shoplifting	15	20
Driving offences (serious)	8	10
Possessing an offensive weapon	6	8
Malicious damage	6	8
Burglary, robbery	6	8
Drug offences	6	8
Frauds and forgery	5	7
Sexual offences	5	7
Taking without owner's consent	2	3
Total	77	100

not always straightforward, however, to discern violence within each of these previous offences. For example, one case that illustrates the difficulty of discerning violence within an offence concerned a man who was arrested by British Transport Police, and later convicted of 'affray' at an underground station. This was recorded as 'a ticket dispute with three women'. Further examination of the records revealed that 'he kicked one of the women who fell to the floor and he continued kicking her' (PNC2/98). Thus it reveals an incident involving violence against a woman, which was coded as one count of 'violence against the person'. In another case there was a 'warning marker' affixed to a man's name on the PNC for violence, and he had multiple previous convictions for criminal damage and burglary.[10]

Subsequent offences of kerb-crawlers

The records were also examined for any convictions the men received that were subsequent to being stopped for kerb-crawling. In a careful follow-up of these cases it was found that 11 of the men with a criminal record prior to their kerb-crawling offence were subsequently re-convicted for a different offence within a short reconviction follow-up period. The records of one case were unavailable because the records had been retrieved by court officials. This meant that although 11 men were re-convicted, the records of only ten men could be explored.[11] The shortest follow-up period was three months. There was thus a differential follow-up for these records. The longest reconviction period was 23 months and the shortest was three months; the actual offences of the men who were re-convicted can be seen in table 5.3.

In the reconviction follow-up period there were six cases of violence against the person, two drug offences, two serious driving offences, one sexual offence and one case of fraud.

Table 5.3 Subsequent Offences of Street Clients

Type of offence	N
Violence against the person	6
Sexual offences	1
Frauds and forgery	1
Drug offences	2
Driving offences (serious)	2
Total	11

Individual cases of subsequent offending were examined in more detail and are shown in table 5.4. This shows individual previous offences, the date of the kerb-crawling offence and any offences committed by these men *following* the kerb-crawling offence. The table perhaps presents a conservative pattern of offences. For example, in the first case the man's actual conviction was for the possession of an offensive weapon – a machete – in 1982. There were also three cases of assault brought against him in 1983; so if his offences had been counted in terms of arrest rates (as in some recidivism studies) rather than actual convictions, then these figures would be higher on the previous offence item in table 5.4.

In Case 2, the man had one previous conviction. This was for common assault in 1991; he was also stopped for driving around a red-light district without an explanation the same year. He was charged with kerb-crawling in 1997, and subsequently stopped for kerb-crawling again in 1998, but this time with five other men in the vehicle, all of whom also had previous criminal records.

In Case 3, the man had two previous convictions for common assault. His kerb-crawling offence was in 1997 and he had a subsequent conviction for the possession of a class B controlled drug. He also had a charge of common assault pending. This man's record contained a number of queries. He was from Nottingham, and there was a query on his record concerning whether he might be a pimp or not, as he was in regular contact with a number of sex-working women who also travelled down from Nottingham regularly. A further query written on his record related to whether he was dealing drugs. His record was also marked as 'DNA confirmed', to illustrate that his DNA was stored on the national database.

Not all the cases involved violence. For example, Case 4 had a previous conviction for handling stolen goods in 1985. Twelve years later, in 1997, he committed a kerb-crawling offence. A year later, his subsequent convictions were for two cases of drink-driving. There was no violence either in the records of Case 5, where the man simply had previous convictions for shoplifting, non-patrial overstaying of leave, driving without a licence, and driving without insurance. Following his kerb-crawling offence, his conviction was for the evasion of customs duty.

There were, however, a number of violent and some grave[13] offences in some of these criminal histories. Case 6, for example, had a list of convictions running to 21 pages, including multiple counts of: assaults on women using violence, actual bodily harm, common assault, threats to kill, using threatening behaviour in the street, possession of a controlled drug, and possession of an offensive weapon (a blade). Following the kerb-crawling offence in 1998, his offences included drink-driving and violent assaults on women. Case 7 was also found to have a series of convictions. These included a first offence of shoplifting in 1978, followed by two convictions for criminal damage, two convictions for using threatening abusive behaviour, and a conviction for burglary. His kerb-crawling offence was followed by a conviction for threatening abusive behaviour the same year.

Interestingly, analysis of the records also revealed that there was a subsequent sexual offence charge pending in relation to a man with no violent history. Case 8 had 18 previous convictions for theft by deception, two for theft, and others for driving while uninsured, handling, and shoplifting. Three months after his kerb-crawling offence, a warrant was issued for his arrest on a charge of rape. Notes attached to his case stated that he was in possession of a controlled drug, and that he 'drove victim to Casterly Lane and raped her' (PNC2/98).

Case 9 had a conviction from 1983 for drink driving (for failing to provide a specimen). His kerb-crawling offence was in 1998. Later that year, he was convicted for violent assaults. He was also convicted of actual bodily harm to a police officer as well as being convicted of drink-driving and driving whilst disqualified.

Finally, Case 10 had a list of 16 convictions for serious offences, the first of which was for robbery in 1993. His conviction history included a range of offences. These included obtaining services by deception ('cab bilking')[14], shoplifting, obtaining property by deception, common assault, assault on a police officer, being in charge of a dangerous dog out of control, obstructing police ('swallowing drugs'). His kerb-crawling offence was in 1998. This was followed by two convictions, one for threatening and abusive behaviour and another for supplying a class B controlled drug.

For the sake of clarity, these data concerning subsequent convictions in table 5.4 do not include cases whose previous offences came to light following the two-year follow-up period, such as the case of the 'fail to stop' kerb-crawler who ran down a police officer in a stolen car. Here the man was later found to be linked to an armed robbery prior to the kerb-crawling offence. Cases such as these were not included because they were processed after the two-year follow-up period.

To summarise these findings, 11 of these men were re-convicted within the follow-up period for each person – up to two years.

Table 5.4 Convictions Prior and Subsequent to Kerb-crawling 1997–1998

Case	Convictions prior to kerb crawling[12]	Kerb crawling	Subsequent convictions
1	1982 Offensive weapon (machete) 1983 Assaults × 3	1997	Pending – Assault against person
2	1991 Common assault	1997	1998 Kerb-crawling (charged with five other men, all with criminal records)
3	1995–1996 Common assault ×2	1997	1998 Possession of class B drug Pending – Common assault
4	1985 Handling	1997	1998 Drink-driving × 2 (RTA 1988, section 4)
5	1979–1982 Shoplifting Non-patrial overstaying leave Driving without licence or insurance	1998	1998 Evasion of customs duty
6	1982–1993 Range of offences including: Actual bodily harm Threats to kill Possession of class B drugs Threatening behaviour in street Common assault Possession of offensive weapon (blade)	1998	1998 Driving while 'unfit' 1998 Dangerous driving 1998 Driving while disqualified × 9 Violent assaults on women
7	Six convictions from 1978–1989 including: Shoplifting Criminal damage Threatening abusive behaviour Criminal damage	1998	1998 Threatening abusive behaviour

Table 5.4 continued

Case	Convictions prior to kerb crawling[12]	Kerb crawling	Subsequent convictions
8	1984–1996 Theft by deception × 18 Theft × 2 Handling, shoplifting Driving without insurance Drink-driving	1998	1998 Theft of mail 1998 Drink-driving 1998 Possession of class B drug (cannabis) Pending – Rape
9	1983 Failure to provide specimen/Drink-driving	1998	1998 Violent assaults on police 1998 Actual bodily harm Drink-driving and disqualified
10	1993–1997 16 convictions Robbery Assault on police Common assault Threatening behaviour Dangerous dog out of control Shoplifting	1998	1998 Threatening abusive behaviour 1998 Supplying class B drug

Bearing in mind that the actual numbers are extremely small, it has been shown that 70 per cent of re-convictions involved criminal violence, 30 per cent of subsequent re-convictions involved drugs, and 30 per cent of subsequent re-convictions involved drink-driving. From the records analysed here, 6.3 per cent of men stopped for kerb-crawling offences had a criminal record number from a previous (non-custodial) conviction. This figure is *lower* than the general population in which one in three men have had a standard list offence by age 40 years (Home Office 1995; Farrington 1994). This low level of official offences has to be set against the certain under-reporting of the high number of injuries that sex-working women were observed to have received from clients throughout the research. The men with the most prior convictions had the most subsequent reconvictions. The re-conviction rate for more serious sexual offenders was 5 per cent. These findings show that, just as the violence within prostitution occurs in a minority of exchanges, there are some serious violent and sexual acts committed by kerb-crawlers that involve a very small number of repeat offenders.[15]

The data in this study is based on re-conviction rates although this has been considered a 'proxy measure of reoffending' as:

> it is estimated that only 2 out of every 100 offences committed result in a criminal conviction ... Therefore, reconviction rates will always underestimate the true level of *reoffending* (Lloyd, Mair and Hough 1994).[16]

Tentative as it is, the research suggests a link between kerb-crawling and more serious crimes committed by only a small number of these men. This is a phenomenon which deserves close and systematic analysis in future research of this sort.

Low rates (eight per cent) of previous convictions for violent and sexual offences were also found amongst men apprehended for kerb-crawling in Southampton (Shell, Campbell, Caren 2001). This also suggests that a small proportion of clients may be responsible for a large number of attacks. Data from the London Ugly Mugs List supports this hypothesis. Thirty per cent of attackers were known as clients, as having attacked other sex workers, or as being known to the police. The next section of this chapter will explore what we know about violent clients from press reports.

Media reports of repeat offenders (Kinnell 2004)

From media reports, examples of repeat offenders include:

- MO, who raped two sex workers in Coventry in 2000 (Coventry Evening Telegraph 19 June 2001), eight months after his release from prison for attacking another sex worker in 1996.

- ND, who stabbed a Bradford sex worker 43 times in 2000, had murdered a woman in Coventry in 1979 (Bradford Telegraph and Argus 6 November 2001).

- JW, convicted in 2001 of two rapes, four indecent assaults, four false imprisonments and other offences against sex workers in Plymouth (Plymouth Evening Herald 1 December 2001), had appeared in court on 56 previous occasions since 1962.

- DB, given a life sentence for sexual assaults on three Liverpool sex workers (Liverpool Echo 25 January 2002), had been convicted of rape in 1990, and of serious assaults on his partner in 1996.

- KS, who raped two sex workers in Aberdeen in 2000, had been convicted of four previous assaults on sex workers in 1997 (BBC News website 6 February 2001).

- VF, was given twelve years in 1988 for rape, false imprisonment, grievous bodily harm and unlawful wounding. Released in November 1995, the following month he attacked a sex worker in Hampshire, and six weeks later murdered another woman who was not a sex worker (BBC News website 29 January 1998).

- KV, convicted of murdering a Bradford sex worker in Bradford in 1996, was previously convicted of the manslaughter of another woman in Leeds in 1991, and for indecent assault, robbery and burglary (Yorkshire Post 27 March 1998).

- PB, who murdered a Wolverhampton sex worker in February 1999, and raped a 17-year-old shortly after, had served 15 years for beating a shopkeeper to death in Essex, and strangling a bus driver in Denmark (BBC News website 21 July 2000).

- DS, who murdered a London sex worker in April 1999, had previously raped a woman at knifepoint, in front of her children (1976), and had been acquitted of murdering another sex worker in 1993 (BBC News website 8 December 1999).

- AK, convicted in March 2000 of the murders of two women from the Midlands (December 1993 and March 1994), was serving seven years for rape when DNA linked him to the Midlands murders (Observer 19 March 2000).

Murder of sex workers

Information collated from sex work projects and press reports about 73 murders or unlawful killings of sex workers between January 1990 and December 2002 by Kinnell (2004) shows that 52 (71 per cent) were street workers and eleven (15 per cent) were indoor workers. The work style often is not known. In 46 of these 73 cases (63 per cent), it is known that charges have been brought or suspects named, and it appears that the majority approached their victims as clients (52 per cent), a similar proportion as found by Lowman (2000) in Canada (56 per cent). Nine (21 per cent) were partners, and in nine other cases (21 per cent), persons with other relationships to the victims were charged.[17]

Of 45 people known to have been charged or named as suspects,[18] 42 per cent (19 cases) have known previous or subsequent convictions for violence, including rape, manslaughter and murder. It is important to note that these previous offences were committed against non-sex workers as well as sex workers, and against both women and men. There is a common assumption that people who murder sex workers do not usually murder other people, that sex workers live lives which expose them to the criminally insane, and therefore that the rest of us are safe. It is perhaps far less comfortable to recognise that those who attack and murder sex workers frequently attack others, and are rarely classed as 'insane' by the courts, so are regularly released back into the community, where they re-offend.

Despite limited information about many of these deaths, available data appear to confirm the vulnerability of street workers, and patterns of repeat offending amongst aggressors. However, clients were not the only offenders. Both in the UK and elsewhere, killings have been attributed to partners, pimps, traffickers, drug dealers, other sex workers, acquaintances, robbers, vigilantes and homophobes. While sexual violence and partner homicide have been much studied, other causes of extreme violence towards sex workers are less understood. It may be that some aggressors are undeterred since they believe that police will not accord such crimes much priority, and perhaps, that acts which are normally considered crimes are not crimes if committed against a sex worker (O'Neill and Barbaret 2000 and Sanders 2001).

Violence and control policies surrounding street work

A few areas in the UK operate unofficial tolerance zones, but in most places police and courts harass, arrest, fine and imprison street workers and their clients.[19] These strategies increase the dangers of street work in several ways. Hostile policing reduces the vital assessment period when sex workers try to judge if a client may become violent, as one of Benson's interviewees explains:

> If the guy's driven around a couple of times, and he hasn't stopped and then he's come back round again, that sends a little signal to you, cause you think 'What's he keep driving round for? Why hasn't he stopped before?' Then when you open the car door … if they're tense, or too relaxed, you know, like 'Come on then get in I haven't got time to mess about' or even just the way he flicks his eyes at you, or you know like, if he's shuffling his legs, or he looks real sort of nervous and you think 'Well what's he nervous for?' that sort of sets your alarms off as well … (Benson 1998: 30)

To be told to get in the car quickly sounds reasonable if kerb-crawling measures are being enforced, instead of alerting the sex worker to potential trouble. A customer who is nervous, or looking over his shoulder, may also seem to be behaving reasonably under the circumstances. Police crackdowns mean fewer clients, so women spend longer in dangerous locations to make their money. Amongst women interviewed for a *Dispatches* documentary on Channel 4, 65 per cent worked longer hours, 71 per cent later at night, and 66 per cent earned less money anyway (Guardian, 16 September 2002). Reduced earnings leads to more violence: pimps may beat women for not earning enough; women made desperate may rob clients, who then turn violent: 'he thought the woman was someone who robbed him before ... he raped and assaulted [her]' (London Ugly Mugs List November 2001).

Anti-kerb-crawler policies disrupt sex workers' contact with regular clients, whom sex workers regard as less risky (Sanders 2001; Benson 1998): in the Channel 4 *Dispatches* sample 90 per cent said they had never done business before with the men who attacked them. However, regular clients are more vulnerable to anti-kerb-crawler initiatives than occasional visitors, leaving sex workers fewer 'regulars' to do business with.

Sex workers and clients are also likely to disperse from familiar areas during crackdowns, simply displacing problems to other neighbourhoods:

> Kerb-crawlers have been forced out of Hull, police chiefs claimed today ... A spokesman for South Yorkshire Police said officers had never before stopped such a significant number of motorists from East Yorkshire in Sheffield's red-light district. (*This Is Hull and East Yorkshire* website 20 January 1999)

The displacement effect of the 1998/9 Leeds Kerb-Crawler Rehabilitation Programme was acknowledged in the West Yorkshire Police evaluation:

> Intense high visibility policing of any problem that occurs in a public place will obviously have a displacement effect. This is clearly illustrated with the displacement that has been noticed in Chapeltown ... prostitutes have moved their business into surrounding divisions ... (West Yorkshire Police 2000)

Such displacement can have harmful consequences. During the anti-kerb-crawling activity in Leeds (April 1999), one local sex worker went to work in London, where she was murdered by DS, a convicted rapist (BBC News website 8 December 1999). DS was known to be dangerous by local women, but an outsider would not have known his reputation. A similar case occurred in Stoke-on-Trent in 1994, when a Wolverhampton woman was murdered by KW, known to local women as a dangerous client, but not to an outsider. Several more recent murders have occurred in places where hostile policing strategies have been adopted. Not only do such strategies increase sex workers' vulnerability and social stigmatisation, they also appear to interfere with police investigations of violence, by reducing the willingness of potential witnesses to come forward.

A Bradford sex worker was found murdered in April 2001. Within two weeks the senior vice officer was quoted as saying: 'I issue this warning to anybody who does undertake kerb-crawling or pimping – the police will always press for prosecution at court.' A week later the officer leading the murder investigation complained: 'We've had a disappointing response to our appeal so far ... Our detectives do not care under what circumstances you knew Becky, but if you did, please come forward ...' (Bradford Telegraph and Argus 8 May 2001 and 14 May 2001). The Bradford crackdown on street prostitution continued, but the murder is still unsolved, as are similar cases in Middlesborough, Stoke-on-Trent and Sheffield. There is then a contradiction in police work between their enforcement of anti-prostitution strategies which exacerbate violence against sex workers, and their duty to protect all citizens, including sex workers.

Police and judicial responses to violence

Sex workers are often unwilling to report violence to the police. They may not expect sympathetic treatment. Police may say they 'shouldn't be out there anyway' and refuse to take a statement. Women with outstanding warrants, those subject to Anti-social Behaviour Orders (ASBOs) or illegal immigrants may fear incarceration if they contact police. Those without prostitution-related convictions may hesitate to identify themselves as sex workers; indoor workers may not wish to draw attention to their working address. If they do approach the police, they may be detained for long periods, and questioned about unrelated matters. Government-set performance indicators for the police exclude violent crimes and sexual offences. Also, police efficiency is measured by the relationship between crimes reported and crimes solved, but no weighting is given to different types of crime. Consequently, solving a murder has no more importance than solving a theft, in this measurement system.

Encouraging the reporting of crimes that would otherwise go unreported, especially when the prospect of solving them is uncertain, would make police efficiency appear worse. From the police perspective, vigorous arresting policies towards sex workers and kerb-crawlers may be far more attractive options, since they produce good 'clear-up' rates and are cheap to run. Even when attacks are reported to the police, and arrests made, the judicial system can continue to expose potential victims to danger. The case of JW, eventually convicted of eleven offences against sex workers in Plymouth, illustrates the effect of failure to remand suspects in custody. JW was charged with indecent assault and false imprisonment in December 2000, but was not remanded in custody until arrested a fourth time. Had he been remanded in custody after the initial arrest, the subsequent offences, including two rapes, three indecent assaults and three false imprisonments, would not have occurred (Plymouth Evening Herald, 1 December 2001).

The decision to remand in custody someone who has been charged, though influenced by police advice, lies ultimately with the court. Decisions about what charges are brought depend on the Crown Prosecution Service (CPS). The record of the CPS for refusing to prosecute, or downgrading charges against those accused of rape, was documented by the English Collective of Prostitutes in 1995 (Women Against Rape and Legal Action for Women 1995) and there are still occasions when CPS decisions raise questions. For example, GA's attacks on two sex workers in Plymouth in 2000 made both women fear for their lives, but he was only charged with indecent assault and actual bodily harm, rather than grievous bodily harm or attempted murder. He was found guilty, but the charges brought limited the sentencing options available to the court (Plymouth Evening Herald, 9 December 2000).

The courts in England and Wales hand down swingeing sentences for property crime – one of those recently convicted for a failed robbery at the Millennium Dome, where no one was hurt, was sentenced to 18 years in prison, but sentences for violence against sex workers often seem inadequate. One of Benson's interviewees expressed the effect that lenient sentencing can have:

> I would never go to court again. I would never even make
> a statement to the police, I wouldn't go through with it

again, just for that, 'cause at the end of the day, they've only got four years and they're only gonna do two. What's that? I mean that's affected me for the rest of my life and all they get is two years. I don't think that's right. (Benson 1998: 45)

Several cases of rape and murder given above involve offenders released early from sentences for previous violent offences, including ND (Bradford Telegraph and Argus, 6 November 2001), JW (Plymouth Evening Herald, 1 December 2001), VF (BBC News website, 29 January 1998), KV (Yorkshire Post, 27 March 1998) and PB. The Chief Constable for the West Midlands attacked the decision to parole PB, saying:

> it seems inconceivable that a man who has previously been convicted for a litany of offences since 1968, including two counts of manslaughter and wounding for which he received three life sentences, can still be allowed to wander around the streets. (Guardian, 22 July 2000)

Failure to monitor violent offenders appropriately after release is also evident. KV, convicted of manslaughter in 1991 but released in 1995, had been rehoused in the Bradford street soliciting area, where he encouraged sex workers to use his flat for business. Here he murdered one sex worker, and when arrested, police found another woman imprisoned in his flat.

ND, a paranoid schizophrenic, having served 19 years for murder, was released on licence in 1998. In 2000 he stabbed a Bradford sex worker 43 times. At the time of the attack he was in breach of his licence conditions, having missed probation and psychiatric appointments (Bradford Telegraph and Argus November 2001). The judge at his trial said, 'the authorities' failure to trace him had enabled him to try to kill again'.

Vigilantes or respectable residents?

Some people are obsessively hateful of sex workers. But in England and Wales, more people opposed to prostitution join residents' groups to deter street prostitution than commit murder. However, the potential for such activities to turn into violent vigilantism is illustrated by a report from Bradford (1996). A woman told the local paper:

... the mob piled out of five cars and set upon the vice girl who fell into the pub ... the vigilantes demanded that we throw the prostitute back outside to them. Because we didn't, they got really nasty and were threatening to do things to the pub. They seemed to think that because she was a prostitute, she had no rights ... I've seen car loads of people who spit and throw things at prostitutes, and I've seen them trying to grab the women ... One day the vigilantes are going to pick on someone who isn't a prostitute ... Someone is going to get badly hurt. (Bradford Telegraph and Argus, November 1996)

Despite her opposition to violence, this woman's comment that, 'One day the vigilantes are going to pick on someone who isn't a prostitute' illustrates the automatic distinction made, even by well-intentioned people, between violence against sex workers and violence against others. The assumption that the former violence is legitimate is so widespread, it has even been incorporated into a popular computer game (The Independent, 9 January 2003). Lowman (2000) describes the 'rhetoric of disposal' used by Canadian media and action groups opposed to street prostitution. He draws associations between the intensity of such rhetoric and the incidence of murder of sex workers, arguing that the social acceptability of using language which equates sex workers with rubbish legitimises the actions of those who attack and kill them. Similar rhetoric has characterised innumerable press stories on street sex work in the UK, for example, in Hull where five sex workers have been killed since 1996:

Hull has declared war on vice girls operating on a city estate ... Humberside Police is launching a major new initiative to wipe out street prostitution. (Yorkshire Evening Post, 10 August 2001)

Police also make public statements that reinforce prejudice against sex workers. In November 1999, Aberdeen police warned clients that they risked being robbed by sex workers (BBC News website 25 November 1999). Not long after this, Kenneth Smith, convicted of four assaults against sex workers in Aberdeen in 1997, raped again, in February and in June 2000 (BBC News website 6 February 2001). Police in Wolverhampton used the arrest of a multiple rapist to raise fears about HIV:

A police force today warned men about the possibility of contracting HIV from prostitutes after a man with the condition was charged with rape ... A police spokesman said men who have had sex with prostitutes in the city within the past six months needed to be made aware of the situation. (Press Association News, 27 April 2001)

Politicians may also use fears of HIV to bolster support for punitive control measures. When the possibility of tolerance zones was discussed in Walsall in 2001, the MP told a local newspaper, 'Who is going to clean up the mess, the condoms and needles that are left behind? This could create a health epidemic (sic).' (Walsall Advertiser, 26 April 2001). The deliberate fomentation of public fears about the supposed dangers sex workers pose to the rest of society suggests there is a fine line between the self-justification of someone who attacks a sex worker, and the attitudes of some police, politicians, media, and residents' groups. Current state policies also show a similar disregard for sex workers' safety and could even be interpreted as legitimising violence (Kinnell 2004).

'Sex slavery' and the social and human cost of ignoring rights

The violence against sex workers is used by many religious and radical feminist groups (e.g. CHASTE, or members of the WNC–Womens National Commission) in order to try and abolish all sex work. Often it is linked rhetorically, using personal testimonies, to the concept of 'sex slavery'. Illogically, the violence that women can sometimes suffer in sex work is used to argue that they were not in sex work of their own volition. This is strange, because women can be working in sex work out of choice and be the victim of violence, just as a woman can work as a city trader, or cashier out of choice and be the victims of violence. The difference between the sex worker victim of violence and that of the female city trader is her access to, and protection by, the law. The city trader may leave court with her head held high having received justice from the legal system for whatever harassment she has suffered. The sex worker, however, will be branded a 'common prostitute', her testimony will be deemed unreliable, and if her picture is in the paper she may suffer from moralistic violence from vigilantes. This difference in rights is apparently accepted by those who would abolish sex work. By not supporting those who choose to sell sex those who would abolish sex work, conversely do not open the door of rights, or the right to legal recourse, for those who *are* enslaved.

Sadly many trafficking programmes do not seem able to accept that some women choose to sell sex and have trouble supporting those who do, preferring instead to use the violence, in the use of personal testimony, as a tool to pursue the impossible task of abolition at the expense of all in sex work. Personal testimony is typical of revivalist evangelical gatherings. Personal testimony turns personal suffering into performance art. It is significant that personal testimony is such an important tool in abolitionist tactics. The parallels with revivalist religion include emotional manipulation and hysteria, as well as the framing of conflicting ideas as a battle between the 'good' – those who accept their moral statements about sex work – and the 'evil' – those who don't. Personal testimony is open to abuse, since it is evident that women who are willing to testify in this way are given rewards, sympathy and protection which are not available to women who have a different story to tell.

The total disregard by many trafficking programmes (who refuse to differentiate between 'forced' and consensual sex work) has led to huge wastage of public money and continued stigmatisation, and increased vulnerability of those in the sex industry. For example, in Cambridge in 2005 a huge trafficking case was built on the fact that women were being held in a brothel against their will, but when the case came to court:

> Three Albanian men accused of holding a 29-year-old Russian woman captive and forcing her into prostitution were acquitted in July when the defence barrister proved the Russian had worked as a prostitute before. (Cambridge Evening News, 28 September 2005).

It was reported that the police were still praised for their police work 'despite the loss of £150,000 taxpayers' money when the case collapsed in court.' It is a simple fact that many women who migrate to England know they are going to work in the sex industry, and want to work in the sex industry. What they don't know is the conditions in which they will be kept once they get here. Had the narratives of 'forced' prostitution sexual slavery that have permeated public policy (through organisations such as the National Commission for Women) allowed the space for the woman to acknowledge that she wanted to do that sort of work, and had concentrated on giving her decent working conditions then whatever was done to her might not have gone unpunished. Thus the concept of 'sexual slavery' can be unhelpful to the empowerment of women in the sex industry.

Arguments for criminalising clients are based on assertions that sex work is intrinsically abusive. Yet such arguments deny the very women who are victims of violence rights of redress against oppressors (whether clients, boyfriends, pimps, or traffickers).

Empowerment, although being denied by trafficking organisations and abolitionists, is however moving along in the form of the unionisation. Sex workers in some parts of the sex industry are slowly being allowed their labour rights since their unionisation in the sex work branch of the GMB union in 2002. Yet these are in the minority with such powerful forces against them.

Chapter summary

This chapter draws together data on violence committed against sex workers from three sources: Ugly Mugs Lists, police data on criminal histories of kerb-crawlers, and information from sex work projects and press reports on repeat offenders against sex workers. It shows that levels of reporting of violence against sex workers are poor, despite the efforts of many sex work projects to improve matters. Failure to apprehend offenders, or to remand them in custody, has led to further violent crimes, including murder. Charges brought by the CPS may not reflect the seriousness of the offences, limiting the sentencing power of the court, if a guilty verdict is returned. At least 73 sex workers have been killed in the UK between 1990 and 2002, several by offenders with previous convictions for assault, rape, manslaughter and murder, against both sex workers and others. This suggests that current practice in sentencing violent offenders, the availability and efficacy of therapy when incarcerated, and their monitoring after release, are dangerously inadequate.

Sex workers experience violence from many sources, whether engaged in street soliciting or indoor work, but this violence is neither documented in official statistics, nor addressed by public policy towards prostitution. The deleterious effect of current law is acknowledged, if obliquely, in recent Home Office research on homicide: 'The feasibility of many preventive strategies depends largely on the legal position of prostitutes and police enforcement practices.' (Brookman and Maguire 2003: 11). Indoor workers are endangered by legislation which criminalises their working environments. The threat of brothel-keeping charges discourages those who work in groups from reporting crimes against them, and leads others to operate alone, which exposes them to greater violence.

Street workers are even more vulnerable. While some police and local authorities express interest in adopting 'tolerance' zones, these are officially opposed by central government and the Association of Chief Police Officers. Street prostitution is usually policed solely to remove sex workers and their clients from public areas. These control policies increase sex workers' vulnerability by increasing levels of client anger and public hatred towards them, and by decreasing their ability to limit their own risks. In several cases hostile policing has coincided with murder, or interfered with murder investigations, through decreased co-operation between sex workers, clients and police.

Politicians, police and the media routinely use 'the rhetoric of disposal' and that of 'sex slavery' to promote anti-prostitution policies, and deliberately foment public fears about the supposed dangers posed by sex workers to the rest of the population, without regard for the effect their words may have on public attitudes towards sex workers. Such rhetoric has coincided with serious violence against sex workers, including murder. This suggests that there is a fine line between the self-justifications expressed by those who attack and murder sex workers, and the attitudes of many in society towards sex workers. Since most public policy towards sex work in the UK reflects fear and hatred of sex workers, exacerbates their vulnerability, and hinders the investigation of crimes of violence against them, it is possible to conceptualise violence against sex workers as one aspect of public policy in the control of prostitution. The argument that policies and legal changes to promote safer working conditions are unacceptable, since they might 'encourage' sex work, demonstrates that violence is seen by many as a deterrent, as well as a punishment to those involved. Only a vigorous reshaping of public policy towards sex work, promoting safe working environments, and treating violent offences against sex workers with the seriousness they deserve, could alter this situation.

Notes

1 Some of the material in this chapter has been published in Kinnell (2004), and some of the material presented in Brooks-Gordon (1999).
2 Male sex workers also experience violence, as illustrated by the massacre of eight male masseurs in Cape Town in January 2003 (Guardian 21 January 2003).

3   Maids (who act as receptionists for sex workers), by definition, do not perform sexual services.

4   The term 'Ugly Mug' was coined by the Prostitutes' Collective of Victoria, Australia, in the 1980s for a report of an attack on a sex worker. The system of turning these reports into a flyer for distribution to other sex workers was taken up by UK projects from 1989 onwards, and is now common, though not universal, practice.

5   Birmingham data includes all violence at work, not only from clients.

6   Includes reports where robbery and/or other violence were combined with a sexual attack.

7   Figure in brackets is percent of all assaults by work sector.

8   See chapter 6 for full description of record categorisation and methodology.

9   From January 1996, driving offences became standard list offences (for example, driving while disqualified from holding a licence; driving or attempting to drive a motor vehicle while having breath, urine or blood alcohol concentration in excess of a prescribed limit; and dangerous driving) and are included in the police records, but summary driving offences are not included. Previously these had only been standard list when tried on indictment.

10 Markers were attached to people's names for a range of reasons, such as: being known to carry an offensive weapon, handling drugs, or for violence. The object of these 'markers' was to provide police with prior warning of a potentially volatile situation or person.

11 However, it is important to note that for the men whose kerb-crawling offence came near to the end of 1998, the period for which reconvictions could be explored was much shorter than for the men whose kerb-crawling offence was at the beginning of study.

12 This table excludes one case where the records had been transferred back to the court.

13 This term is used under the Home Office definition of the subset of standard list offences covering all indictable only offences which have a maximum sentence of life imprisonment. These are mainly offences of homicide, serious wounding, rape, buggery, robbery, aggravated burglary and arson endangering life.

14 Fare evasion.

15 The data is limited, for example, sampling is non-randomised and drawn from a sample of those men caught in the area, and those caught may be unrepresentative (for example, those who do not get caught may have better street knowledge to avoid surveillance, or be quicker at avoiding the police). The records are also subject to the vagaries of police targeting practices, and like many studies that use official records, the data relate only to known offenders, and reveal nothing about offenders who are not caught, or the perpetrators of offences that are not solved (Tarling 1995).

16 Records used here may not be a representative sample of kerb-crawlers in other cities throughout Britain, or indeed London. Whilst the areas of Mayfair, Paddington and Notting Hill represent a broad spectrum of the street prostitution economy in London, men with more violent criminal histories may be present in areas such as Kings Cross or Whitechapel. These are areas that are generally considered to have younger and more vulnerable prostitutes who are more likely to end up with violent or 'risky' clients. This data is based on cases looked up on PNC2. More comprehensive records could be gained by using the Offenders Index (OI) data which contain criminal histories of all those convicted of a standard list offence, from 1963 onwards, and is linked to the Prison Service records.

17 No information about person/s charged in four cases.

18 'Known to have' means known to Hilary Kinnell, from the sources stated in Kinnell (2004). In three cases police have named suspects but charges or prosecutions were not thought possible at the time of writing.

19 Imprisonment for street prostitution, discontinued in 1983, has been reintroduced through Anti-social Behaviour Orders, which ban the subject of the order from an area. If the order is breached, this can result in a prison sentence of up to five years.

Chapter 6

Methods, motives and morality[1]

> Let us consider the stratagems by which we were induced to apply all our skills to discovering its secrets, by which we were attached to the obligation to draw out its truth. (Foucault 1979: 159)

In the previous chapter the violence towards, and protection of, sex workers was explored. In this chapter I firstly describe the main research site and the functions, duties and routines of the vice unit where much of the case study material was gathered. I discuss the choice of site as well as the process of negotiating access to carry out the research. Secondly, I outline the theoretical orientation, choice and integration of methods, and describe the sampling selection, strategies and influences upon data-collection and analysis. I then describe various ethical problems encountered before concluding with some reflections upon the research experience.

Description of the research site

The case study material comes from data collected since 1997 and carried out over 300 hours of fieldwork observation with the Metropolitan Police Vice and Clubs Unit, the central unit policing kerb-crawlers and street prostitution, based at Charing Cross Police Station in London. The fieldwork involved 40 interviews, 21 focus groups, ethnographic observations, and documentary analysis of 518 police records.[2] It was carried out in two phases during both summer and Easter to capture the vagaries of street work. The Metropolitan Police Vice and Clubs Unit occupies the fourth floor of Charing Cross Station. The Unit was established in 1932 and is the oldest and largest of Britain's 30 vice-related specialist units (Benson and Matthews 1995). There are 80 officers attached to the unit, whose functions include the enforcement of legislation related to gaming, pornography and prostitution. The officers all belong to the uniformed branch of policing, but operate on this squad in plain clothes. As the central unit for policing prostitution in England, the Vice and Clubs Unit has a high profile both within and without the force. Two distinct squads carry out its operations – the Organised Vice Squad and the Street Offences Squad (SOS). Each squad is overseen by an Inspector who reports to a commanding officer of Superintendent rank.

Geographical location

The SOS patrols a wide range of red-light areas in central London. These range from Mayfair, where female (and transgender) sex workers in their own cars pick up street clients and sell expensive sex in hotels, to Leamington Road and the All Saints Road in Westbourne Park and Notting Hill, where the drug dealers sit outside to trade on the low garden walls of once-grand houses. At the time of the research, crack was £20 a rock on the street, and there was a large number of crack houses in this area. The sex workers are more likely to be drug-addicted in this area than those in other SOS patrol areas. In between these two extremes lies Soho, where the multiplicity of 'working flats' form part of the wider sex industry. Here in Soho, the activities of women and children selling sex along the sticky streets of Wardour and Berwick Street, compete with those of 'clippers', who make the pretext of offering sex for sale, but then defraud the prospective client of his money. One of the main areas policed is the Bayswater and Paddington Basin area, which also has an historical tradition of street sex.[3] Here, along Sussex Gardens and the Edgware Road, are cheap hotels with rooms that can be rented by the hour. These hotels neighbour expensive single-occupancy houses where the mews' garages and dustbin-sheds provide quiet corners for clients to be serviced by the women they have solicited on the street.

Organised Vice and the Street Offences (or 'Tom') Squad

The Organised Vice Squad comprises a team of 14 officers including one Inspector, one Sergeant and twelve constables. It is responsible for policing highly sensitive areas such as the sexual exploitation of children, pimping, and trafficking. These duties are London-wide, although many of the investigations have national and international aspects (Holmes 1999). The Street Offences Squad (SOS) is a larger unit and carries out more visible policing duties. It comprises one Inspector, four Sergeants, and 24 constables. Each of the four sergeants manages a team, A, B, C or D. Twenty-four-hour cover is provided in a three-shift system policing the whole area of London's West End. Because of the nature of the work and contemporary search laws, approximately half the constables are women.[4] This equal proportion of women provides an unusual critical mass of female officers and an interesting contrast to the vast majority of police teams.

Unlike regional vice squads, the SOS is a specialist department that is seen as a career choice. It is necessary to sit a police 'board' (an examination and interview) to get onto the squad, which is called the 'Tom Squad' in policing argot.[5] Promotional prospects are reported by the officers to be good, with many officers using operational experience on the Unit before joining other squads such as the Obscene Publications Squad, Drugs Squad, or the Organised Vice Squad. There are very close links between these squads, with many of the officers regarding the SOS as a training ground for the more complex, sensitive under-cover work carried out by the Organised Vice and the other squads. The SOS team members periodically help out in surveillance operations for the Organised Vice Squad on large operations that may encompass the trafficking or coercion of women and children imported into this country for sexual exploitation.

Functions and routines of the Street Offences Squad

During the day, the primary function of the SOS is juvenile protection. The secondary function is the policing of street offences committed by people seeking and selling (or purporting to sell) street sex. Juvenile protection takes place in a number of ways. Periodic juvenile 'sweeps' are carried out, in which all the teams patrol the places that children are drawn to, like Piccadilly Circus, Victoria, Leicester Square, Covent Garden, amusement arcades and large toyshops such as Hamleys or The Disney Store on Regent Street. The officers scour the London area looking for juveniles who are on the streets during school hours. The majority of children found are either truanting from school for a day out from the Home Counties or are runaways, often from other parts of England. Seventeen-to-18-year-olds are taken into police protection the first time they are found soliciting on the streets. Every child under 17 years old is taken into police protection every time they are found on the streets. The social services are contacted and the child handed over to social services or returned to the family home.

Juvenile protection is also carried out through regular supervisory visits to Soho flats. These are 'working' flats where off-street sex workers work alone apart from a 'maid'[6] who answers the door to clients and deals with payment. Routine visits to the Soho flats are undertaken in order to ensure that no one under-age is working in the flats, and that no one working there has been coerced. It also enables officers to obtain intelligence on any youngsters seeking work; on foreign nationals and trafficking for sexual exploitation; or on male clients who might be 'dodgy punters', that is men who have robbed the women, or requested the services of children. These visits are carried out to establish a working relationship, to elicit information, and to afford a degree of protection for the women working there. At the beginning of a shift, intelligence is passed on between officers verbally and is also recorded in an 'information folder' by those on previous shifts. In this way, teams coming onto duty are immediately updated about ongoing cases, and are able to catch up on the activities occurring on London's streets. Other duties include the prosecution of street sex offences. These include the prosecution of female sex workers for soliciting clients and the prosecution of clients under the 1985 Sex Offences Act. This is referred to in police officer argot as 'catching kerbies'.

Choice of research site and access

Contact with the Metropolitan Police Vice and Clubs Unit was made through the Divisional Commander of Senior Superintendent rank in the Metropolitan Police. The value of this recommendation was inestimable because the choice of data-collection method meant that I needed to be with the Unit for longer than any researcher had previously been. The recommendation of a senior officer therefore added substance to my request and meant an insider could vouch for me as a *bona fide* researcher. This was particularly important as the SOS receive requests daily from researchers, charities, journalists, documentary-makers and other political awareness groups for access.

Access was obtained at a single meeting at Superintendent level, which was left subject to agreement by the Inspectors concerned. The conditions of the research contract were structured around broad agreements made at that meeting. These were: a need to understand the nature of the 'problem' with prostitution, kerb-crawling, soliciting, the community, and to study the police perspective(s) and to explore the tensions between the policy and practice in the policing kerb-crawling – two of the main things that appear to cause the tensions between sex workers and residents. I wanted to go out on duty with a representative sample (in terms of age, gender, and length of service) of officers, a representative spread of teams and shifts, and cover the span of jobs and duties they had. I needed to gain an overview of different viewpoints on kerb-crawling: clients; sex workers; residents; and police.

The research process was to be an iterative one in which questions were constantly reformulated and refined as my understanding grew of the major issues; also, I offered to include police questions as the research proceeded. This factor was important in gaining access, as I was apparently the first researcher who had been prepared to do this. I gave assurances about what I was going to do with the information, how it would be stored, and promised a copy of the final thesis. From this meeting I was given an introduction to the Inspector at Paddington Police Station who was to provide introductions to community complainants in order for me to understand the nature of residents' complaints and the power dynamics behind the ongoing reactive policing. This recommendation was also valuable because the Inspector was not only helpful at that stage in the research, but later moved to the Vice and Clubs Unit to head the SOS. This meant that a good working relationship was already established with someone who understood and respected the research agenda. I appreciated my good fortune because the majority of decision-makers prefer research that has short-term instrumental utility rather than an in-depth long-term study (Lee 1993), which might not have been finished before they move to another operational role. Ease of access therefore influenced the choice of location, although social access had to be negotiated daily *in situ*.[7] This is not uncommon in field research (Burgess 1984) but more importantly, the role of the Unit, as the foremost in England, meant I could be guaranteed the variety and quantity of data required for such an in-depth study.

Negotiating access in situ

Whilst access had been granted at the higher levels, it had to be negotiated every day on the ground, it was apparent that true acceptance of the research would require careful negotiation. At the start of the first focus group, the team sergeant produced his own tape recorder to also record the session, and then sat upright in his chair with his arms crossed, maintaining his distance from me. Both his verbal and non-verbal behaviour communicated his suspicion of me to his team[8]. One team member, the only other male, a constable in his twenties, indicated his own anxiety at the beginning of the focus group. He said:

> Just before we start, what's is this going to be used for? ... We're not going to be quoted in the *News of the World* tomorrow or anything like that? If we are asked for individual opinions and we give those on the basis that it is going to be for research, but then if we find ourselves in the paper tomorrow, then there might be questions fired at us from people [upstairs]. (Focus group/ B Team/97)

Whilst this man's anxiety might be indicative of an organisational culture that relays only essential information to subordinates, the wall of defensiveness from the two men showed that access would have to be negotiated individually at every level. During the first phase of fieldwork, officers who lived near the neighbourhood where I stayed offered me lifts home in the early mornings following a nightshift. These lifts provided the chance to clarify many of the questions that emerged during a shift but I hadn't liked to ask about due to the interruption it might cause, and the extension of the researcher 'gaze' that constant explanation creates. The lifts also gave me a further degree of social access that was gained, to a degree, through interpersonal trust (Lee 1993: 123).

It was during these lifts home that the team sergeant who taped the first session explained his initial scepticism about the research. He said he had been reluctant to talk to me as he had become cynical through being 'stitched up' many times in the past. He felt this had happened in the past by a TV documentary team years ago when he was at another London station. His comments, however, betrayed a sense of vulnerability – well-founded, given his previous exposure. The television crew had taught this man a severe lesson, which still hurt. Clearly, the sense of threat, scrutiny and evaluation needed to be handled carefully and required open, honest interaction on my part with *all* the officers concerned. In time they revealed more and more to me about themselves, their working practices, their views on suitable responses in a sensitive policing area. The crews also took me to other areas in London such as Whitechapel to compare and contrast with what I saw in the West End.

Risks to access – the fear of scrutiny

It has been suggested that field roles are developed in at least five different phases: newcomer, provisional acceptance, categorical acceptance, personal acceptance and imminent migrant[9] (Burgess 1984b: 84); however, roles exist simultaneously and overlap occurs between roles (Burgess 1984b: 85). Although I later felt the focus group data was not as useful as data from observations or the records, for what it revealed about the behaviour of kerb-crawlers, the groups did provide me with a level of provisional acceptance as well as providing invaluable insight into the 'social organisation of the setting' (Hammersley and Atkinson 1995: 54). After taking part in one of the focus groups, which became called 'Belinda's social-worker-beanie-bag sessions', the majority of officers relaxed, felt they'd helped with the research, and that scrutiny was over. They felt I had collected the data I needed from them, and would turn my attention completely to the kerb-crawlers, rather than realising that my research is embedded in the social world it is seeking to study.

After acceptance at the provisional level, personal fear of scrutiny remained for some officers. This fear of scrutiny resurfaced in minor incidents. For example after one shift finished, I carried on scribbling notes while the officers had all finished their paperwork and were chatting. One of the male officers challenged me to show him what I had written. My notebook was full of descriptions, some them less than flattering. I looked him full in the face as he tried to decipher my tiny handwriting, and I said 'A sixteenth century scribe in her previous life'. This made everyone in the room laugh and offset the situation, but thereafter I made notes in the incident room only when they were all absorbed in their own paperwork.

Access from the ground up – categorical acceptance

I knew categorical acceptance had occurred when research access also began to work from the 'ground up'. The sergeant who spoke about his media experience did not want to subject his own crew to the same scrutiny nor bedevil them with the responsibility of my personal safety. At the same time he did not want to be seen to bar access, so he left the decision to his crew. He said he was unsure about letting me go along with them that shift as they were going to Soho to speak to a drug dealer on bail who failed to appear in court. He said he wasn't sure whether to risk letting me go as it might get a 'bit hairy'. He asked his team for their opinion, and only then agreed that I could go along.

Many officers were surprised I had such a long attachment because many of their colleagues from uniformed divisions who had requested week-long attachments to the SOS were denied it. This was not to give rise to any resentment; rather it served to confirm the quasi-official nature of my status. This popularity of the Unit also had advantages as far as researcher reactivity was concerned out on the streets. It meant that the crews were used to having strangers – both police and non-police outsiders – with them out on the streets at night. I was never complacent following the note-taking incident, although I learnt that it was acceptable to take copious notes out on the streets and at other stations, or if there was an 'offender' present, but in their own 'operations' room, it felt intrusive. Thus access of one sort or another was negotiated every day in a complex and dynamic world. For example, access had to be negotiated officially and unofficially at every station I went in with the team, and this served to both exemplify my outsider status and also illustrate how invisible I was becoming to observers.

Helpful gatekeepers – access at other stations

When people are charged for street offences, they are taken to the nearest station. These included Paddington, Bow Street, Harrow Road, and Notting Hill stations. As custody sergeants have a great deal of autonomy in their own stations, each custody officer at every different police station I went in to had to grant permission for me to remain with the squad. There were times, however, when I had become so familiar with the stations, their procedures and layouts, that I forgot to ask. Much to the squad's amusement, station sergeants assumed I was a police officer if I stood writing my notes besides the officers doing paperwork, or occasionally, a sex worker if I sat chatting or making notes beside a sex-working woman. On one such occasion I was asked to get an IP1 (the bag a charged person's valuables are put into). I looked confused and anxious in case the misunderstanding irritated the charging sergeant, but everyone laughed. When I explained I was a 'only a researcher on attachment', he smiled indulgently, and said 'you look like one of us.'

My clothes were not consciously picked to blend in with the officers, but the type of clothes I wore blended in anyway. I either wore a t-shirt and combat trousers, or jeans and shirts, with lots of pockets to hold notebook, tape recorder and pen, or carried a soft rucksack for these. It was usual for the female officers to have similarly bulging pockets or a soft rucksack as the equipment they carried included notebook, handcuffs, radio and an 'asp' (a small steel telescopic truncheon). They also carried the paperwork for dealing with sex offences, disposable rubber gloves, and mobile phone. One advantage about research with a plain clothes unit is that it is easier to transcend the 'outsider' barrier – although obviously it still exists.

Field relationships with key informants – the guides

The closest research relationships were developed with one male and two female officers. The male was a sergeant, the two females were constables, although one had passed her sergeants' 'board' and had begun to lead a team. This rapport was due to the proximity of my age with all three of them, but also due to gender and being a smoker. The two female officers and myself often went to a smoking room after break to have our cigarettes. With the male officer, connection came through lifts home. Subsequent field relations and the high degree of access I was allowed were due in part to similarities in what Banister et al. (1994: 39) have defined as culture power and personal style. My interpretative stance held multiple positions, firstly, as a woman identifying with female police officers. Although I recognised my privileged position as scholar, I identified with the economic struggle of the sex workers as I tried to support two children on student grants and scholarships. I identified with male officers as parents. I identified with officers of all levels and genders as observers of social life, and on the basis of class, sexuality, and my divorced status. Although I viewed the street social world predominantly from the police's angle (i.e. in the backs of their cars, overhearing the police view) I also identified with non-sex working women, and was able to capture their different perspective in unexpected ways – by being punted (i.e. solicited) myself.

The politics of observation

While my job was to observe I sensed that the officers felt less scrutinised if I was part of the scene rather than watching it as I shadowed them. There were times, too, when the decision to shadow was taken away from me and I was expected to do as I was told. The reason for such a directive was often personal safety, so I was happy to oblige. Usually, when a sex worker was taken into custody, we sat together in the back of the police car whilst the two officers sat in the front. One particular sex worker, Linda, who has known HIV positive status, keeps used needles with her for weapons against attack and to use against police officers to prevent arrest. Whenever Linda was wanted on warrant and taken into custody, it was considered too risky to allow me to remain in the back with her. Although to me she emanated vulnerability rather than danger, I did as requested. At other times the reason was a concern for the vulnerability of the sex worker in the back, especially when juveniles at risk were in the car. In these cases an officer sat in back to create a rapport with the child, as it could take over three hours to get a name or address from a child putting on a brave, aggressive front to an officer as he or she is taken into safe custody and returned to social services or the family home.

Questions driving the analysis were concerned with police interaction and attitudes to the kerb-crawlers, and how that is reported and then applied to the documents that are created. There are multiple ways of reading the reports. Clearly, the reading remains mine, and relevant constraints, limits and possibilities are wrought by my own position as analyst. But, given that there are no techniques or analytic strategies that escape the 'dangers of exploitation' (Banister *et al.* 1994: 66), consultation and feedback over interpretation of the transcripts was done continuously following entry to the field with each of the findings chapters (excepting the demographic data).[10] Given the highly charged political atmosphere surrounding the data-collection and analysis and the long-held sensitivity of the Metropolitan police with regard to race relations (for an early example, see Smith and Gray 1983), discriminatory practices of stop and search (Willis 1983, see Brogden, Jefferson and Walklate 1988 for an overview), and previous corruption in a squad now at Clubs and Vice (that is the porn squad, in Cox, Shirley and Short 1977), research findings emanating from this study may raise further questions.

Theoretical triangulation

The collection, analysis and interpretation of data are always carried out within broader understandings of what constitutes legitimate inquiry and warrantable knowledge (Henwood and Pidgeon 1993). The main theoretical stance adopted is what might be termed *interpretative social psychological* (Semin and Manstead 1983)[11]; this is especially pertinent to the accountability of conduct in social regulation and social control. It might also be called a 'critical' approach in the sense that it challenges absolutes in favour of multiple points of view and honours the contexts of observations by contesting objectivity about the 'way things really are' (Tiefer 1995: 37). Approaching data from multiple perspectives allows the researcher to understand the phenomenon (or phenomena), thus there is an anti-positivist rejection of the unity of science.[12] This research is thus within the post-empiricist paradigm and emphasises the importance of 'meaning construction' instead of uncovering 'hidden meanings' (Pujol 1999: 91). In deconstructing the discursive resources kerb-crawlers draw on when they construct their version of reality, my research is *social constructionist* in that interpretations and accounts that men give not only describe the world but construct it. This shows that these sexual acts are not the sole consequence of some cost-benefit analysis based upon an individual's social cognitions, but rather a way of positioning oneself within a network of social meanings and significations (Willig 1999). As well as the political world of the police stop, the wider theoretical framework for this analysis includes criminological as well as feminist theory, and the research is, above all, feminist in its theoretical orientation.

Methodological triangulation or 'convergent validation'

Qualitative methods have been employed throughout the study, but with an important quantitative component. Feminist researchers advocate the use of quantitative and qualitative data to develop, support, and explicate theory (see, for example, Jayaratne 1993). Such support is political, and underpins an assumption that the appropriate use of both these methods can help the feminist community to achieve its goal more than either method alone. These methods were chosen to be sensitive to research participants' experiences and enable me to represent people's meanings as well as interpret the documents to provide a 'thick description' (Geertz 1973) and rich understanding of the situation, they thus heighten validity of the findings (Banister *et al.* 1994). They were also the most suitable ones to answer the research questions, and generate theory in an under-theorised area.

The great strength in the use of documents and archival data is that this method is arguably unobtrusive and non-reactive (Marshall

Rossman 1995). Many important aspects of numerical data are easily lost in the retelling so I used the common practice in psychology of grounding the quantitative component by using qualitative data for the creation of a coding frame (Henwood and Pidgeon 1993).[13] Observation was used because previous research has shown that the interaction of the client and the sex worker (or police officer) can only be studied in an ethnographic, unstructured way (see, for example, O'Connell Davidson and Layder 1994).

A combination of different methods was used in order to counteract threats to validity in each on its own (Berg 1998). The use of multiple methods included informal interviews, participant observation, and focus groups, as well as documentary analysis and quantification. This provided both inter- and intra-method triangulation. By collecting documents from many sources, recording interactions, and then combining this with more directive interviewing, it is possible to build up a much fuller idea of the way participants' linguistic practices are organised, compared to one source alone (Potter and Wetherall 1987). There was also within-method triangulation and I used differing strategies within the same method, such as asking the same question in (specifically structured) different ways in interviews.

Sampling strategies and selection of informants

Selection of the participants (police, sex workers, and punters) was by judgement and opportunistic sampling. The residents' groups were all self-selecting. From the police officers, I collected accounts from a range of officers differently positioned in the organisation (inspectors, sergeants, constables), of different genders, and in terms of length of service, religions and ethnicity. There was judgement sampling, however, with the female officers, and when I had the choice, I chose to go out with teams of female officers. This is consistent with the recommendation of feminist and qualitative methodologists that interviewers and respondents are matched in terms of gender, age and ethnicity to set respondents at ease and encourage a good rapport to develop (O'Connell Davidson and Layder 1994). This is more likely to turn the research process into a more positive experience for the participants but is arguably likely to ensure better quality data.

Individual and officer-pair interviews

The 40 interviews were open and unstructured, taking the form of guided conversations; they were conducted at locations and times conducive to operations on the street. The interviews became collaborative and interactive, and interviewees were encouraged to discuss topics that had arisen during observation. They allowed for participants' views to be voiced and their own frame of reference to be interpreted. Topics covered in the interviews were kerb-crawlers, gendered experiences in police service, public indecency, sex-working women, pimping, drug addiction, juveniles at risk, and personal philosophies of paid sex. Successful interviewing arguably depends more on a complex interrelation between the relative structural position of the interviewer and interviewee and the interviewer's skill and personal style than a simple identity of gender (Wise 1987, cited in Lee 1993). The interviews carried out with women produced richer data, more interesting, sometimes counter-intuitive findings, and were more pleasurable to do than those with the male officers or residents. Rapport developed in these interviews, however, was not just the result of in-depth interviewing technique; it developed because a woman interviewing other women is arguably more 'conducive to the easy flow of information' (Finch 1993: 103).

Following Oakley (1981) and Finch (1993), the interviews were conducted within a non-hierarchical relationship. This was not only because of adherence to the moral position that giving part of oneself in this way is one of the ways to carry out ethical research, but also the experience of interviewing police officers, who are more used to the role of questioner themselves, amounts to being interviewed *by* them too. It is arguable that all interviews 'are interactions between embodied people' (Banister *et al.* 1994: 68) and issues of sexuality (money and gain) were very prevalent in the research. This was not surprising, given that many hours were spent watching the process of bargaining for, justifying, or, more rarely, the interruption of sexual exchange. Sitting in an enclosed, intimate space like a police car late at night watching the sale of sex go on all around, it is difficult for the subject of sex (and with it one's own beliefs, values, sexual politics and preferences) to be avoided, even if one wished it to be.

Interviews with officer pairs often took place with me in police cars while the officers looked out of the window, or turned round to explain a point. If two officers were present, then interviews would be interrupted by their talk to each other about what was happening on the street. This was like a non-interruption that occurs frequently in everyday life (see Wooffit 1996). I watched and interpreted the performance of the interviewees. Throughout the interview, the officers were wary of criticism and I was necessarily conscious of Goffman's (1959) 'deference ceremony' in order to let them understand how valuable their input was to me. One-to-one interviews, however, were more 'creative' or 'active': this type of interview creates an appropriate climate for informational exchanges and for mutual disclosure (Berg 1998).

Focus groups and group interviews

Twenty-one focus groups were held (consisting of three to six officers who worked together on each of the teams) to explore specific issues including knowledge of, and attitudes towards, male clients, kerb-crawlers, telephone-box carding, and risk assessment. One large focus group of seven female officers was held to specifically explore gender roles in this type of police work. This was considered necessary because although there is a body of knowledge on the attitudes of police men towards women (and its psychological impact upon them), within the police service (see, for example, Brown, Campbell and Fife-Shaw 1995; Brown 1999), and with female offenders (see, for example, Gelsthorpe 1989, Horn 1997), there is less information available on the attitudes of female police officers towards male offenders. Kitzinger (1994) suggests that the advantages of focus groups are that when one participant answers in a socially desirable manner (that is contrary to practice) or denies common frailties, they are often challenged by others. Such groups are also useful to highlight respondents' frameworks for understanding, identify group norms, gain insight in the operation of group process, examine the questions people ask each other to identify factors that influence individual assumptions, and the influence of models of thinking and moral values.

The focus groups were moderated by myself and were phenomenological in that they provided a means for bracketing topics such as sex worker cards, kerb-crawlers, sex workers, boyfriends, and pimps, which were removed from their natural world (Husserl 1913; 1961: 86). Discussion was facilitated by asking participants to carry out some activity (such as sorting the sex worker advertisement cards) and then discussing their perceptions of this activity in order to define and determine basic structures. Groups discussed all the elements of street sex work interaction, and bracketed, or held in exclusion, the demographics of kerb-crawlers, interaction with kerb-crawlers, interaction with sex workers, juveniles at risk, card boys, and other factors that lead to, or follow, episodes in the policing of street sex work.

Most researchers who use focus groups acknowledge that group influences can distort individual opinion (Berg 1998). This was certainly the case in a hierarchical organisation like the police force, and if a sergeant was present, views were, depending on leadership style, modified by them. These views were more often challenged by women than men, and these women had generally either already taken their sergeants' 'board' or policed 'vice' for a long period of time, or they were more able to empathise with the female sex workers.

The groups reflected collective notions and differed from individual data in some respects. Information gathered in the focus groups informed the research questions (and later informal interviews). The focus groups and individual interviews provided different perspectives on the same topics such as the sex workers and their clients. In individual interviews, for instance, there was more sympathy displayed for the sex workers, whereas in a larger group there was more conformity to pre-packaged, 'party line' attitudes displayed in answers. These focus groups generally yielded a 'quixotic' reliability whereby multiple observations by a single method of observation continually yield an unvarying measurement (Kirk and Miller 1986). However, during one focus group, the respondents positioned me as a *tertius gaudens*, a third party who benefits from the conflict of the other two groups due to their dissatisfaction with their sergeant, and perceived favouritism on his part to other pairings in his team (Lee 1993).[14] Whilst all interviews are arguably 'social performances' (Goffman 1959), organised around a 'dramaturgical model' (Burke 1966), the police cars sometimes became such personal, intimate spaces in which I was absorbed by the world of the sex trade, that I momentarily forgot my researcher status amongst the officers. Transcending the boundaries, however, between the researcher and the researched can often cause reactivity, and my research was no exception.

Rapport, reactivity and female bonding

The most extreme instance of reactivity during the course of my fieldwork was clearly gendered. The context for the interaction was during a night shift, when I accompanied three female officers. That evening, instead of using a police car, the officers used a transit van called the 'brothel wagon' by the squad. It was a hot night in early summer, and instead of taking a coffee break at a police station, we bought ice creams at the Haagen Daaz ice-cream parlour on

Edgware Road. For women in a culture that venerates thinness, the sharing of fattening foods is indulgent, and it provided the context for a bonding experience. In addition, the routine of watching the negotiation, purchase, and sometimes interruption of sex meant that it featured prominently in down-time talk. We discussed the fetish behaviour observed of male street clients (for example, those observed wearing women's clothes or bin liners). The conversation turned to our own individual personal predilections. This atmosphere of female bonding was the context in which a kerb-crawler was subsequently stopped, and our collective behaviour became the cause of an internal investigation. The man who was stopped had his shirt hanging out from his trousers and the two bottom buttons of the shirt were undone. He was wearing a toupée which was slightly askew. Following an initial denial, he decided to make a statement in overblown, old-fashioned English to explain his reason for being in the area (for example, his lines included 'heretofore I saw the young lady, whereupon I stopped my vehicle'). It became difficult to suppress a smile. Not only was his story ridiculous, and the language silly, but his reasons also included a rather busy mobile phone for the time of the night (4 a.m.). During this time, one of the women constables whispered to me, 'clock the syrup',[15] at which point I snorted with laughter, and we all stifled our giggles at his absurd hairstyle and absurd explanation. The man said he felt the officers had been very cheeky to him and would report them for it. As I left Charing Cross Police Station after the shift the man was already filing a complaint, in what apppeared to be a way to recover dignity after he had felt laughed at. This was not the only time when the men's interaction with the officers resembled a comedy of manners, although the absurdity of their excuses and picaresque behaviour was more easily recognised by the women than the men. An internal enquiry later vindicated the officers of the charge of unacceptable behaviour, and recognised they had found it hard to keep their amusement under control. I felt that my integration with the female officers had however, reactively generated the incident.[16] It is also possible that the measurement/research process had an impact on those who were observed in other ways. Given that I was looking at kerb-crawler behaviour, it was possible that the squad may have stopped more kerb-crawlers (and therefore fewer prostitutes) than they otherwise might have done had I not been with them. They did, however, continue to charge sex workers, and on some of these occasions, gender transcended the boundary between the researcher and the researched to incorporate the sex worker in a more inclusive way.

Transcending research boundaries

Whilst my identity as a researcher was as important to the research as my identity as a woman, there were times that gender transcended the boundaries between the researcher and the researched. In the incident below, this was due to a consensus of opinion amongst women:

> Jude asked in car if she could phone her next appointment – he didn't know she worked the streets as she met him through escort work. The two officers turned off the police radio and she moved the appointment later (to after midnight), which would give her time to be booked. She said the punter was old and would be grumpy about it. Later when the three of us women were in the charging room, I asked about the old punter. She reported that he was about 70 years old and that she visited him in his office after he has worked late. His home was a flat above his offices in an expensive part of North London. Then she gets a cab back to work on her corner near Sussex Gardens. She said it was embarrassing because he pays £200 for a blow-job but keeps going dead. She and I giggled and the wpc smiled. I asked if she would want to be kept by one such punter, and we all discussed the merits of being kept by old men in our various situations. The expressions on our faces expressed the unanimity of our thoughts. (Fieldnotes 98/27)

This incident highlighted, for me, that whatever the personal or social circumstances of women, the ridiculousness of men, and its ability to bond women, is something that can be generalised to all spheres from this research.

Selection of data for illustrative purposes

In the selection of data for illustrative purposes, I have tried not to make fools of, or to mock, the street clients – although as the previous examples show, I found some of them both amusing and foolish. Men's fear of being laughed at by women is matched only by women's fear of being raped or murdered by men. These men have the power over these women's bodies (and lives) in dark and deserted locations, and I witnessed for myself the most appalling effects of client violence. One sex worker, despite appalling injuries and sympathetic support from officers, would not bring charges against the punter who had put her in hospital. This was not unusual, and was because the process of using law inevitably stigmatised and criminalised aspects of the sex worker's life to the degree that she could not bear to go through the humiliation and pain of the system, even if it meant that her attacker would be punished. I had had an open mind before the research, but watching the process of cases like this led me to understand how the law contributes to the violence these women suffer. By criminalising sex workers the law has no muscle to punish the violent clients or pimps. Cases such as these, however, undoubtedly influenced the selection of case data and later led me to explore the criminal histories of these men. There were many sympathetic practical gestures shown by the officers towards the sex-working women. These included:

- inviting a rain-soaked and injured sex worker to sit in the car, telling her she wouldn't be charged but trying to persuade her to return to hospital from where she had just discharged herself, and offering a lift there;
- reminding sex workers to get their money 'up-front' during kerb-crawler initiatives so the sex worker had her money before the client got reported;
- reminding inebriated sex workers that it was not safe to work while drunk and persuading them to go home; and
- giving support, encouragement and praise to sex workers managing to stay off drugs.

Such humanitarian gestures within the boundaries of policy and discretion may have made me warm to certain officers and thus influenced decisions to pursue some issues rather than others. It also illustrated how ill at ease officers were with the policies that criminalise sex workers and how such policies effectively tie the hands of those who are otherwise ideally placed to help against the violence women suffer.

As the research progressed, my understanding increased of the situational context of street soliciting and the haste with which most client–sex worker negotiations are carried out in a high-tension atmosphere. I became interested in general patterns of the male clients' behaviour as they solicited for sex, and how they react when stopped. Questions emerged about the types of men who solicit. For example, who was most likely to get stopped for soliciting? I became more interested in the various client groups, and wanted to explore if any client group was being targeted for policing more than any other. The effects of client violence I witnessed made it necessary to explore any convictions street clients had in this respect. All these issues formed the basis for exploring the kerb-crawler documents.

Official records on kerb-crawlers

Police records of 518 consecutive cases of men coming to police notice for soliciting offences were used for an analysis of the demographics of kerb-crawling. These records were systematically cross-checked to verify that the type and number of clients I had observed were a representative sample of all those stopped and spoken to by the police in this area.[17] The sample of men stopped depended upon the search and patrol practices of officers, and practices that are important in understanding the sample composition are discussed in chapter 4. The records were depersonalised and then photocopied for the analysis. These were primary documents as they were written and collected by the people who actually witnessed the events they describe. Such documents are considered 'more likely to be an accurate representation of occurrences in terms of both the memory of the author (time) and their proximity to the event (space)' (May 1993: 136). These records are produced by the street offences officers, and record details of all kerb-crawling actions and allied offences. The records include some actions which are not offences, for example, the voyeuristic actions of men who 'persistently drive around a known red-light (prostitution) area without a good explanation'. For men who were reported for the offence, there was additional documentary information from another source – the 'process' books, which form part of the evidence for cases that go to court. The manifest content – that is, the elements that were present and countable (Berg 1998) – were analysed using standard guidelines for creating a statistical coding frame (Hoinville, Jowell and Associates 1978). These guidelines are based on two factors: the frequency with which different types of answer occurred and also the importance attached to a category for analysis purposes. Each case was allocated an individual ID number. The date, time, location of the incident, and location of the stop were coded. The variables for analysis were defined as follows:

Offence circumstances
Offence circumstances were coded on a five-point scale with the

section of the Sexual Offences Act 1985 within which they fell, for example, section 1: persistently soliciting a female from or near a vehicle, or causing annoyance by soliciting a female; through to section 2(1): persistently soliciting a woman on foot or persistently driving round a red-light area (RLA) without good explanation; to soliciting a woman on foot, not persistently.

Action taken

The variable 'action taken by the police' was coded on a six-point scale as follows:

1 'Reported for the offence
2 Letter sent
3 Verbal warning given
4 Caution/formal warning administered
5 Advised
6 No further action (NFA)

Whilst on the pro forma used at the start of the research in 1997, the action taken would appear to be straightforward, in practice 'Advised' and 'No further action' were sometimes synonymous in cases where a street client was advised to leave the area and there was no further action taken. In these cases the most serious or punitive action was entered. From 1998, however, officers were more likely to write 'verbal warning' as opposed to the more anodyne 'advised' on a pro forma that was modified and used in 1998.

Age

The man's age was coded using only the year he was born.

Ethnicity

Ethnicity was coded using the police IC codes from 1 to 6 as follows:

1 A white-skinned European appearance (for example, English, Scottish, Welsh, Norwegian, Russian)
2 A dark-skinned European appearance (for example, Greek, Cypriot, Spanish, Italian)
3 An Afro-Caribbean appearance (for example, West Indian, Guyanese)
4 A South Asian appearance (for example, Indian, Bangladeshi, or Sri Lankan)

5 Chinese or Japanese appearance, including South East Asian (for example, Malayan, Burmese)
6 Arabian or of Egyptian appearance (for example, Algerian, Tunisian, or North African)

Occupation
Occupation was coded using the Registrar General's classification of six classes. This, however, was expanded when it became apparent that there were more complex patterns emerging in the data, so these became:

1 Diplomatic
2 Professional A
3 Professional B (inc. media and marketing)
4 'White collar clerical' C1 (including restaurateurs and hotel managers)
5 Skilled manual C2 (including cab drivers)
6 Unskilled manual C3 (service industries)
7 Unemployed
8 Other (retired, student)
9 Declined to provide, or not known

Categories for social class are never rigid when based on occupation, and the classificatory system that evolved from coding the men's occupations is more closely related to the new classes system drawn up by the Office for National Statistics and Economic and Social Research Council for the 2001 census.

Distance from home address
The distance of the offence from offender home was calculated using Enroute software to calculate the distance between where a man was stopped and his home address. Although it is possible to calculate distances between points with a high degree of accuracy with Enroute, there is a margin of error with this variable as a small number of men were allowed to give company addresses rather than home addresses.

Temporary address
If the man provided a temporary or hotel address, the reason for doing so was coded as a discrete variable as follows:

1 Working away from home within UK Monday to Friday

2 Overseas tourist/business visitor (short stay)
3 Overseas expatriate working here (long stay)
4 Other (this included expatriates living abroad visiting the UK or those in social services bed and breakfast hostels)

Vehicle type
The vehicle type was coded as to whether the man used a bicycle, motorbike, car, minicab, hackney cab, small commercial vehicle, or other.

Vehicle ownership
Ownership of the vehicle was recorded to determine if it was owned by the man himself, a female partner, his company, a rental car, another male (for example, a cousin or friend), or in the cases of men soliciting a prostitute in her own car, the sex worker. There is a margin of error with this variable, as some company cars are leased from firms. In cases where the type of job and type of leasing firm made it apparent it was a company car, then this was entered into that category. All other leases went under rental category.

Vehicle value
The vehicle value was calculated using the year of vehicle registration, make and model, and pricing these in a second-hand buyers' guide, using a 1997 issue for 1997 offences, and a 1998 issue for the 1998 ones. Vehicles were coded on a five-point continuous scale: very cheap, cheap, mid-range, expensive and very expensive.

State of dress
The man's state of dress was coded on a four-point continuous scale:

1 Clothed
2 Doing up trouser flies
3 Partly undressed, for example with his trousers round his ankles
4 Totally naked

Sexual activity
Sexual activity was coded on a six-point scale:

1 Masturbating self through clothes
2 Reclined in car with sex worker
3 Touching or being touched by sex worker

4 Genitals being manually stimulated by sex worker
5 Engaged in oral sex with sex worker
6 Engaged in penetrative sex with sex worker

Attitude

A man's attitude following a stop was coded because this can often have important implications for how the police use their discretion to prosecute. This variable was coded on a five-point, continuous scale:

1 Declined to give details
2 Gave details reluctantly or declined to give them initially before co-operating/couldn't see what he'd done wrong
3 Co-operative
4 Appeared remorseful/embarrassed and apologetic
5 Showed genuine remorse or burst into tears

Admission

If the man admitted that he was looking for commercial sex this level was coded on a five-point continuous scale:

1 Admission to looking for prostitute(s) and attempt to justify actions
2 Immediate admission that he was looking for a woman/prostitute
3 Fully admitted arranged sex
4 Admission and that of previous behaviour
5 Admission of frequent behaviour

Cruising

If a man admitted to 'cruising' around the area but denied kerb-crawling, this was coded using three categorical variables, as follows:

1 Curious or admitted to being curious
2 Used driving round red-light area as form of entertainment activity
3 Admitted he was looking but wouldn't have used one

Denial

The denials were coded on a six-point continuous scale:

1 Denied offence giving a reason/justification for actions
2 Straightforward denial of not looking for a prostitute
3 Mildly confrontational, for example, taking of the officer's name and details
4 Became argumentative or verbally abusive
5 Aggressive
6 Failed to stop/had to be pursued

Sex worker present

If any prostitute(s) were recorded as being present at the time of the offence, the number of prostitutes present was entered.

Future behaviour

How the client talked about his future behaviour was coded on a three-point scale:

1 Stating he won't go near area again
2 May repeat behaviour
3 Whether he visits prostitutes on a regular basis

Type of sex

The type of sex the client had requested and price arranged was coded on a six-point scale:

1 'hand relief @ £30'
2 'topless hand relief'
3 'sex @ £40'
4 oral sex
5 s and m
6 other, such as 'just wanted someone to talk to'

This variable was used to compare with previous studies and to test a theory that men go to prostitutes for services non-paid sex partners are unlikely to perform.

Traffic offending

To explore any links with traffic offending, any traffic offences were coded:

1 Drink-driving under section 4 of the Road Traffic Act 1988
2 Drink-driving under section 5 of the Road Traffic Act

3 Driving without due care and attention
4 Dangerous driving
5 Other

Previous convictions and reconvictions
To explore any violent histories in the clients' backgrounds, the men's previous conviction history was recorded. In order to make meaningful analysis of these offences, exploration had to go beyond the original 518 kerb-crawling records up to 1,000 records to find the criminal conviction data of men coming to police notice for soliciting offences. These were scrutinised for those containing a Criminal Record (CRO), and then the men's previous conviction histories were looked up on the police national computer (PNC2), in court 'process' records and disposal documents. Police records are regarded by Denzin (1970, cited in Burgess 1984: 124) as public records, but extra permission was granted for this research. These men were followed up for up to two years following the kerb-crawling offence. The records of 22 men out of the 63 could not be traced. In 17 of these cases, the disposal summary was not updated when the police national computer record system (PNC1) was updated to a new system (PNC2) because they were considered 'old' convictions. Three records had been deleted because the offender was deceased, one offender was in prison, and one record had been mismatched. This left 41 cases, which were used for exploratory analysis into the previous criminal (mainly non-custodial) convictions of these men.

These men were followed up for up to two years following the kerb-crawling offence. Although there was a differential follow-up period for each person due to the cumulative nature of the sample, analysis of records in 11 cases where men were known to have reconvicted suggests scope for further analysis of this kind. Needless to say, future research should adopt a systematic two-year (or longer) follow-up period for each offender within the sample.

The distribution of variables

The range and grouping of all of the information from the documents was listed, taking into account the frequency with which variables occurred. Thus a process of induction, deduction and verification was carried out. To these documents, I also applied the quality control criteria of 'authenticity, credibility, representativeness and meaning' (Scott 1990: 19). They were certainly authentic – these were the records the officers wrote out, the handwriting was the same, and none had been altered. They were in slight disorder, and the question of how accurate and authoritative they are as records of who gets stopped was the next research problem.

Whilst the documents were reliable and accurate, they were not complete. Many variables were missing (but in a random, non-systematic way that did not skew the essential data), so all missing data were calculated. The distribution of variables was assessed graphically, and extremes were re-coded to the next value nearest the mean. The normality of residuals was assessed graphically.

Transferability and representativeness

Whilst some qualitative researchers actively reject the notion of generalisability (for example, Denzin 1983), others such as Henwood and Pidgeon (1993: 27) suggest 'transferability' instead. This refers to the application of the findings of a study in similar contexts. This is necessary to describe contextual features thoroughly.[18] The goal is to 'describe a specific group in fine detail and to explain the patterns that exist, certainly not to discover universal laws of human behaviour' (Schofield 1993: 201). On the issue of sampling, there are two questions: are the records themselves representative, and are the men they describe representative of the men stopped in other areas? Undoubtedly these records provide an accurate portrait of the men who solicit for sex in the London area. Given the size (and comparative resources) of the SOS, which is over four times larger than similar units in other forces, the unit stops many more men than any other force. The representativeness of the men described in these records as a sample of men actually soliciting sex-working women in the UK is hard to estimate as it is a highly mobile population, and a man soliciting in London may also solicit in his own suburb or home-town as well.

The documentation used by the Vice and Clubs Unit at this time was not representative or standardised. Letters sent to men following a kerb-crawling incident vary between force areas. For example the one sent out by the SOS in London is seemingly more polite and euphemistic compared to the more accusatory and confrontational letters sent out by other forces such as West Yorkshire. Interestingly, there are many more complaints from the men in London (and their solicitors) than in other areas such as West Yorkshire (Vice Squad Conference Proceedings 1999). This could be because there is a direct relationship between the 'softly, softly' approach letter and its response. It is possible that London males are professional and better resourced, have more to lose, better access to legal advice, are more affronted when stopped in red-light districts than men in other areas, and therefore more litigious complainants than in other areas. Thus, whilst the records of these men reflect the London population they may not be representative of England and Wales as a whole.

Documents as a representation of power

The document has been described as a text that expresses power relations at a particular time, and 'matters of detection, definition and police practices have now affected the production of crime statistics' (May 1993: 55). These records are no exception, and are the result of organisational polices and practices such as kerb-crawler initiatives and policies to tackle specific offences at different times of the year, and also discretionary procedures, such as who the officers stop. They are also subject to a range of other social and situational characteristics. Like Gelsthorpe (1989: 43), I found that reading files 'crystallized the images' the police officers had, in this case, of men who solicit for sex. Such documents, whilst not unproblematic, are very useful and provide an indication of the patterns that exist (for example, the number of men who come from within a community that deems kerb-crawling a nuisance). There is a tradition for this type of documentary analysis. Cicourel (1968), who explored the working of the police, courts, and probation service, and the documents produced by these, argued that these were fundamental to the construction and maintenance of delinquency. The existence of the kerb-crawling records serves to reinforce the legislation and illustrates that this legislation is upheld. Men are stopped (and prevented from buying sex) on a regular basis. These records, however, are not texts that have a meaning across time and space, for they could not have existed before 1985 when the kerb-crawling legislation came into effect. They do not exist across cultures, as Norway and Sweden are the only other European countries with kerb-crawling legislation, and in the Netherlands or Germany such records would not exist.

Analysis of qualitative data

Data from the interviews and observations were hard to separate methodologically. They were analysed at both the thematic and textual level in order to examine the processes by which people come to understand their world. My interpretations of both the observations and interviews were based on the 'cues, clues and encoded messages' offered by the 'participant/subject' which include communication of a variety of moods, sentiments, role portrayals, and stylised routines, which represent the subjects' 'script, line cues, blocking, and stage directions' (Berg 1998: 81). They also include facial expressions, hand gestures, body language (such as postural moulding to indicate the dyad were getting on well together), eye-gaze synchronisation – police officers have a lot of conversations without looking at each other, for example, looking out of car windows, or writing notes, yet when interacting with public maintain 'normal' eye contact to watch the suspect's non-verbal cues.

All the qualitative data from fieldnotes, interview transcriptions, focus-group transcriptions, and data from the official records was open-coded using Grounded Theory (Glaser and Strauss 1967). This generated the major theory and concepts that permeated the data as a whole. Core categories emerged, and the properties of these categories and dimensions were coded as they emerged, and re-categorised until no new dimensions were found and saturation was achieved. The analysis involved careful reading of the transcribed texts to discover discursive patterns of meaning, contradictions and inconsistencies.[19] At times there are contradictory discourses operating which both have implications for an understanding of the situation. Clichés, taken-for-granted assumptions, contradictions, absences, conflict and emotion surrounding the interaction, and police discussions of them, were also examined (after Crawford, Kippax, and Waldby 1994: 575 – except that Crawford *et al.* do not focus on the analysis of discourse, but rather consider the texts as accounts, like Harré 1983 and Shotter 1984), for constructions of lived experience (Haug 1984). I subsequently used discourse analysis to explore how the client discourse was constructed, its functions, action-orientation, and consequences (Potter and Wetherall 1987), and the use of argumentation and rhetoric for persuasive effect (Antaki 1987).

The discourse analytic technique

The discourse analytic technique is a particularly pertinent tool to use for such an exploration in this context. It has been argued that in the course of daily social interaction we carry out routine activities and practices based on common conventions and taken-for-granted assumptions (Garfinkel 1967). We do not usually question them, despite a human propensity for reflexively monitoring our own action and those of others, because our actions are known and understandable (Harré 1979) – until that is, something goes wrong. It is in problematic contexts, when a breakdown in the 'rules' between routine expectations or moral standards on the one hand, and conduct on the other, that the conscious reflexive monitoring of conduct occurs and explicit accounting is required (Semin and Manstead 1983: 143). This is either initiated spontaneously by the person who creates the 'fracture', or those who challenge the person in the form of direct inquiry. In the case of such fractured social interaction, the issue of 'impression management' (Tedeschi and Reiss 1981) or what Goffman (1959) has called 'identity management' or 'facework', becomes prominent.

In order to manage threatened identities, people use what Mills (1940) called 'motive talk'. When this happens, there are two alternative strategies open to the person (Austin 1961). They can provide either a justification or an excuse. The distinction between justifications and excuses is that justifications claim the act is good, or at least *permissible* in the circumstances, whereas excuses *acknowledge* the relevant act is bad in some way but claim they are due to external agency. Austin (1961) suggested that there are two reasons why the study of excuses is useful. Firstly, the reason for studying excuses is their significance for understanding the causes or motives of action. Austin suggests that instead of studying the perennial problem of free will in abstract terms, advances might be possible if we study how people account for freedom and constraint in cases where breakdowns occur, and excuses or justifications are required (see also Potter and Wetherell 1987). Secondly, as excuses occur in situations where there has been some failure or breakdown in human conduct, their study may clarify the nature of the 'normal', and some light might be thrown on the way social order is produced in society. Thus the study of fractures and their repair should illuminate how social frameworks emerge. In this way, such 'accountability of conduct' or defensive attribution is arguably at the basis of social and moral order.

The analysis of discourses produced in similar types of situational context was first developed by Sykes and Matza (1957), whose theory recognised that many offenders experience a sense of guilt or shame and 'its outward expression is not to be dismissed as a purely manipulative gesture to appease those in authority' (Sykes and Matza 1957: 665). It was suggested that delinquency is based on an unrecognised extension of defences to crimes, in the form of justifications for deviance that are seen as valid by the offender but not by the legal system or society as a whole. Five major types of neutralising technique were identified:

- denial of responsibility, whereby an offender came to be in a deviant situation due to forces outside his control;
- denial of injury, in which it is argued that the deviant actions don't cause harm even if they are against the law;
- denial of the victim, whereby the offender argues that his actions were a rightful retaliation;
- condemnation of the condemners, which occurs when an offender shifts the focus of attention to those who condemn him so that his own behaviour is more easily repressed or lost to view; and
- the appeal to higher loyalties, whereby the offender sacrifices the demands of larger society to smaller groups such as his friends.

These justifications or rationalisations not only protect the individual from self-blame and the blame of others after the act, but 'there is also reason to believe that they precede deviant behavior and make deviant behavior possible' (Sykes and Matza 1957: 666) and would thus provide an indication of the underlying motive for the act. Scott and Lyman (1968) later drew on these techniques to create a unified typology of accounts, and among the various types of excuse they distinguish the appeals to biological drives, appeals to accident, appeals to defeasibility and scapegoating. Typical examples of these subcategories would be:

- excusing one's amorous advances towards another person by claiming one has uncontrollable sexual drives;
- excusing one's lateness by claiming one's car had broken down;
- excusing one's upsetting behaviour towards another person by claiming lack of intent or lack of knowledge of the outcome; and
- excusing one's offensive behaviour by claiming it is a function of another person's pathology or deficiency.

Scott and Lyman (1968) also added two further types of *justification* to Sykes and Matza's (1957) original taxonomy. These are 'sad tales' and self-fulfilment.

In telling a 'sad tale', the person presents autobiographical evidence designed to justify the act. By invoking self-fulfilment the act is justified on the grounds that it leads to some enlightenment. Subsequent additions have been made to these techniques over the years by many others (most notably by Semin and Manstead

1983) to create a more comprehensive typology of justifications by adding:

- the denial of volition (for example, 'I did not want to perform this act, it happened through physical or psychological causes');
- the denial of intent (for example, 'I did not intend to produce these results: unforeseen circumstances or lack of skill led to the situation');
- denial of agency (such as mistaken identity: 'It wasn't me'); and
- the appeal to mitigating circumstances (for example, 'I am not entirely to blame', or 'sad tales').

Studying naturally occurring accounts

The methodology of studying naturally occurring accounts was used by Felson and Ribner (1981), who drew their sample of accounts from prison records kept of 226 males given sentences for murder, manslaughter and felonious assault. They examined the types of accounts, the extent to which the accounts related to characteristics of the offence, and the extent to which the account types were related to the severity of sentence received. Six 'account types' were distinguished:

- denial of guilt;
- admission of guilt;
- legal excuses (such as accidents);
- other excuses (such as drink, drugs, state of mind);
- legal justifications (self-defence); and
- other justifications (victim-wrongdoing, conflicts with victim, helping another).

Excuses were relatively infrequent, comprising 19 per cent of cases. Claims that the act was accidental were more frequent than other types of excuse. Justifications were much more frequent than excuses, and accounted for more than half the cases. The impact of account-type on severity of sentence was confined to the denial of guilt category.

Denial of guilt resulted in heavier sentences for those convicted of murder or first degree assault, but not manslaughter or second degree assault. It was assumed that because the difference between the degrees of each of these offences is intent, that admission and remorse are important to the consequences. Because Felson and Ribner's (1981) study was limited to investigation of cases where guilt was already determined, they suggested future research examine the effect of accounts given prior to and during trial, and that future research should also examine the antecedents, distributions and consequences of motive talk occurring naturally under a wide variety of circumstances. This was the rationale for using this method in my research.

Internal/construct validity

While many texts suggest ways of getting people to give truthful or sincere replies, less is said about how to tell if someone '*is* telling the truth or being completely frank and open' (O'Connell Davidson and Layder 1994: 116). To disentangle the meaning these respondents put on their acts, I had to decide whether or not they were telling the truth.[20] Indeed, establishing a good rapport is vital to the research relationship: 'rapport is tantamount to trust, and trust is the foundation for acquiring the fullest, most accurate disclosure a respondent is able to make' (Glesne and Peshkin, cited in O'Connell Davidson and Layder 1994: 122). It was also possible to check internal validity by examining data relating to the same construct across the different methods I had used. There was triangulation of what I saw, what the kerb-crawler said and did, what the sex worker said to me in the charging suite, and what the officers told me about each incident. All this I was able to compare with the written documents and records. I was also able to triangulate the attributional accounts the street clients gave police with what clients discuss with each other over the many expanding chat-lists and user groups on the internet where men discuss their experiences or fantasies of buying sex, (see for example, Soothill 2004; or http://www.worldsexguide. org/Manchester.txt.html). These provide a forum for men to discuss the services, the type of sex they can purchase for their money, with which type of women, and which streets to patronise. They also contain links to pages that describe how best to get round the laws in various countries in pursuit of sex to buy (for example, http://www. worldsexguide.org/uk_legal.txt.html). They are increasing at a rapid pace. During the research there was a 600 per cent increase in the amount of World Wide Web pages used by clients. Such techniques, however, for data-collection meant that the instrumental validity of the study was high.[21]

Time sampling and triangulation

I worked with different shifts on different weeks. As street offences are policed around the clock, I found myself working for an hour before the shift went out, and a few hours after they came in, and as new shift came on. This resulted in the sort of strategy whereby I observed on an afternoon shift for five days, a night shift for four nights, a day shift for five days until familiar with each shift. These shift-changes enabled the triangulation of views from each of the different teams. Returning to the field almost a year later was particularly useful to make a comparison across time and the similarity of observations through time illustrates the 'diachronic reliability', or reliability across time, of the findings (Kirk and Miller 1986: 46). The similarity (but not identicality) of observations within the same time period provided 'internal' or 'synchronic' reliability to the findings (Kirk and Miller 1986: 42). Both of these enabled me to carry out validity checks, and by testing the emergent model of client behaviour under different conditions I was able to ensure the high ecological validity of the findings. On multiple occasions throughout the research process I invited acquaintances, colleagues and students to challenge or comment on the research. This helped to illuminate blind spots and extend the framework I was working in. It was possible to triangulate how the different geographical areas (and thus the clients) were policed. Although the various teams and cars did not use geographical areas in the same ways, for instance, officers with Territorial Support Group (TSG) experience knew the various crack-houses and were more likely to police those areas more frequently, overall coverage and comparison of the main four red-light areas (Mayfair, Paddington, Soho and Notting Hill) was possible.

Ecological validity

Whilst the ecological validity of any naturalistic study is arguably high, observational methods have two main advantages over self-report methods in that they can often be made unobtrusively, and even when the participant knows that their behaviour is being observed, 'enacting the behaviour is typically quite engrossing, with the result that [they] have less opportunity to modify their behaviour than when completing a questionnaire' (Semin 1988: 96). This method has the advantage of being less susceptible to social desirability effects.

Feminist research methodology

From her analysis of previous scholarship on the question of 'What is feminist research?', Gelsthorpe (1990) cites four themes. The first is the choice of topic, which has to be relevant or sympathetic to women. The second is process, and an approach that acknowledges the 'subjectivity of the researcher and the researched' to expose 'unbiased subjectivity as a myth' (1990: 90). The third is the issue of power and control along with a rejection of the traditional relationship between the researcher and the researched. The fourth is the recording of the subjective experiences of doing research. Gender awareness can also mean analysing men in relation to women as well as in relation to other men (Gelsthorpe 1990: 99). By exploring masculinity and studying men it is possible also to acknowledge the power differential between men and women. A fifth element is the commitment to social action with the goal of bringing about change that improves the conditions under which women and the marginalised live (Cook and Fonow 1984, cited in Renzetti 1997). This study was grounded in these aims.

Ethics, principles and informed consent

Whilst mutual respect and confidence between myself and the participants in the research was possible with the officers, residents, and sex workers I interviewed, it was not possible between the kerb-crawlers and myself. The level of consent provided by each of these groups varied accordingly. To the police officers, there was open disclosure of my position and involvement as a researcher in the field. This included the purpose of the research; what would be involved; how it would be conducted; the time it would take; and what would happen to the material collected. The officers all gave informed consent; in the focus groups, officers soon declared any concerns they had. Arguably, for those who have enhanced rights, duties and obligations over and above those of the everyday citizen, then 'the moral right to be free from investigation is correspondingly reduced' (Jupp 1989: 156). For groups like the police, who have an important commitment to decision-making based on the principles of openness and impartiality, the power of this argument could be increased. Although in agreement with this philosophy, I felt, however, that the best way to build rapport and create a spirit of openness was to be absolutely open about the research myself.

These participants had the clear right to withdraw from the research at any stage, and one officer was tempted to exercise this right. She had been one of the 'guides' and someone with whom I had built up a close rapport. The officer complained to me when she felt I had recorded too much during one shift when there had been much self-disclosure from all the (female) officers. She told me that to tape-record during 'down time' was intrusive. She did, however, seem surprised by how seriously I took the matter of a research participant feeling I had taken advantage of the research relationship. I sent her a copy of the audio tape and the transcript on the basis that anything she wished could be deleted and not used. By this time, however, she had moved to another station, was carrying out different duties, and was unconcerned about the incident. She chose not to exercise her right to withdraw, but simply wanted to voice her dissatisfaction regarding the incident.

Sex workers and street clients

All the sex workers I spoke to and observed were told in full about the research, and I did not experience the lack of trust I had expected, or that to which other researchers refer (Ward and Day 1997). As soon as the sex workers heard I was a 'psychologist', they were keen to talk and wanted advice and information, or simply to be listened to. Despite full consent of all the officers concerned, the street clients did not know that I would be looking through their records. The level of power I had over the men who were on record caused me some disquiet. I found myself more troubled than O'Connell Davison by my intrusion into these men's lives via their files (O'Connell Davidson and Layder 1994). Any attempt to gain fully informed consent, however, such as writing a letter to the men whose records I used would cause them more problems individually than the use of their records collectively and anonymously. The behaviour of the street clients I observed was a different matter. All behaviour was observed in public places, and the majority of kerb-crawlers were told I was a 'researcher'. This was not possible with the minority, as they were too inebriated, or didn't understand English well enough to understand fully what was said to them regarding the research.

Full permission to look up the criminal records and use them in the research was provided by senior officers at both Charing Cross and Paddington police stations. Criminal records differ from records for soliciting, as they are more in the public domain. The Data Protection Act 1998 specifies that 'information obtained about a participant during an investigation is confidential unless otherwise agreed in advance', and confidentiality was maintained throughout. Historically, whenever street sex clients have been interviewed regarding violence to sex workers, the police have been overly sensitive to the partnered status and private lives of these men.[22] Indeed, the warning letter from this squad is often sent to a business or workplace address. Whilst I have some sympathy for men in less-than-satisfactory marital or sexual relationships, the safety of vulnerable sex-working (and non-sex-working) women took precedence in this study.

Confidentiality

To ensure the privacy of all the street clients, I removed sensitive identifiers such as name, house number and street name and postcode from the photocopies of their records. One solution to the problems of confidentiality 'is to obtain data which are anonymous at the point of collection or which are made so soon afterwards' (Lee 1993: 171). This I did with all the police documents, which I anonymised before photocopying and removing them from the station. As these documents were the social product of the interactions I had observed, they also contained all the officer's names, which were also removed. All interview material was anonymised afterwards on the typed transcript, and the records and tapes were kept in a safe that required two keys. These keys were stored in separate locations.

Personal reactions to kerb-crawlers

Prior to the research, kerb-crawlers were a population I regarded with a mild aversion, some fear, and considerable curiosity (like Van Maanen 1991: 33). Yet during the research, I was struck by the ordinariness of these men. This challenged my attitudes to those who buy sex, and mundanity of what they do. I was ever mindful, however, that their presence on the street at night exemplifies the power men have over women, and rather than feeling any degree of protection (as research participants) towards the few street clients who tried to solicit me, I felt mild disdain. Like Scully (1990), I did not feel I had to like them in order to do the research successfully. This contrasts with Kinnell (1998) who found that research on clients' questionnaires had a big effect on her view of the punters: 'instead of dismissing them as either pathetic or shits or both, I felt I was looking into a huge area of human sexual and emotional need which should not be trivialised or demonised' (Kinnell, personal communication). One cannot be in a research situation without changing things, and there is always danger of unintended consequences of social action (May 1993: 37). My disappointment, for example, that there were bits of information missing from the records may result in the maintenance of fuller records. Many officers never realised how valuable a research resource such records are and, as a matter of professional pride, may be likely to correct this in future. This has ethical implications in itself, if procedures become more coercive in order to gain fuller data on men stopped. My questions about kerb-crawlers, particularly about the violent ones, may have sensitised police attitudes to such harm.

Leaving the field

Although I have officially 'left the field', I remain available and contactable in person to senior officers via conferences and various policy meetings. At the start of the research, kerb-crawling was considered a marginal subject, a mere facet of prostitution that was thought to be ineradicable. By the end of the research period, it was, and remains, high on the Home Office agenda for reform (albeit with a view to increasing the penalties against kerb-crawlers once they had offended rather than looking at more constructive and effective ways of prevention). The accumulation of this knowledge, therefore, may become an instrument of change (Stavenhagen 1993: 61). This brings the question of how the research findings get used, by whom, and to what end. I clearly cannot alter the social forces that impel men to seek out sex workers, instigate the reinstatement of benefits to young people, nor change the poverty of women, but the findings have currency in illustrating that this social practice is not eradicable using the present policing methods.

Reflexivity, motivations and sisterhood[23]

The motivations and choice of research topic place the research within the tradition of feminist scholarship if one accepts that understanding client behaviour is important to sex-workers' well-being. Through the research, however, I understand better the immediacy of the sex worker's life, her finances, and her choices in life. I was interested in sex work *per se*, as a form of emotion work (Hochschild 1983). I had once worked as a beautician, and this increased my understanding and interest in emotional labour, as my work had involved tending and touching women's bodies, as well as being a salve and 'sounding board' for their minds. In recent critical feminist work on emotional labour and the sex industry, both Kane (1998) and Mattley (1998: 258) were made to suffer the indignities of the 'whore stigma' – Kane from hotel owners and porn-shop managers she encountered in the field and Mattley from male academic colleagues in her department. Towards her research on telephone fantasy workers, Mattley (1998: 152) found 'salacious curiosity', and men who were previously respectful would giggle, make double entendres and allude to things like pornographic films in her presence. She felt that she had become sexualised to male colleagues. My own field research association has resulted in a range of different reactions and effects on my own life. These have caused me to reflect not just about but also beyond the research, and for this the work of Michel Foucault is a useful frame. Foucault argues that there have been two procedures for producing the truth of sex. One is the *scientia sexualis*, or the sexual science, the tradition out of which this research has grown. The other is the *ars erotica*. The latter is common to numerous eastern societies: China, Japan, India and Islamic societies. In Eastern erotic art, the truth is drawn from pleasure, not in relation to the law of the permitted or the forbidden, nor by reference to utility, but in relation to itself, to the intensity of pleasure, its specific quality, its duration, its reverberations in 'the body and soul'. The Occident, however, is a place without an *ars erotica*, which leads Foucault to question whether: 'our *scientia sexualis* is but an extraordinarily subtle form of *ars erotica*, and that it is the Western, sublimated version of that seemingly lost tradition? Or must we suppose that all these pleasures are only the by-products of a sexual science ...?' (Foucault 1979: 72). To try and answer this, I will return to my own experience and to responses I received from interviewing participants, and also to my experiences when discussing my findings with other academics.

Interviewing within the *scientia sexualis* – a pleasure in itself?

Many of the men I interviewed (residents and some officers) said it was the first time they had discussed sex in an abstract way with a woman with whom they were not in a relationship. They reported that it was a liberating and refreshing experience for them to talk with a woman about intimately sexual issues that they would otherwise only have discussed in a safely male space. Whilst articulating their knowledge and feelings about kerb-crawlers, they became conscious of, and expressed, for the first time, personal philosophies regarding the purchase of sex, or of sex *per se*. To have their innermost thoughts listened to intently, and my desire for knowledge and earnest interest in their every speculation, combined to make the intellectual exercise a sensual one.[24] The interview situation when researching sexuality is, therefore, like Diderot's magical ring, something that is powerful and must be treated with care in the research process. To further reflect on the reasons *why* some of the participants felt as they did, my enthusiasm (infectious, I am told) for my subject, and my pursuit for a deep understanding of their views may have made me more attractive in their eyes and contributed to their perception.[25]

Or a pleasure drawn from the science?

Within the academic and wider social domain, I have found limitless desire in others to hear about the research. It is true that I enjoy the interest in the research, but I wonder if I also enjoy the simulacrum of myself in this situation as being invested with the 'fundamental secret of sex' by having studied the subject in such detail in the intellectual arena. Giddens (1992) points out that in previous cultures the *ars erotica* was a female specialty limited to specific groups, and erotic arts were cultivated only by concubines, prostitutes and minority religious communities. Yet we now live in a society where almost everyone has the chance to be sexually 'accomplished'. Not only does one 'become sexualised' (Mattley 1998) in such situations, but also the assumption of sexual accomplishment becomes projected onto one by others. I question myself whether I enjoy and therefore contribute to, this elevation of my science to an *ars erotica* in my own life in an attempt to make myself appear more attractive. I would not be the first to do so. Indeed, the historian Judith Walkowitz describes how the feminist intellectual and Fabian Olive Schreiner regaled her mentor Karl Pearson, the founder of the 'Men and Women's Club', with tales of her personal encounters with prostitutes (Walkowitz 1992).[26]

Reflections of pleasure and guilt

In their reading of Bachelard, Game and Metcalfe posit that 'shelter and protection make dreaming and remembering possible – daydreaming and imagining' (1996: 36). When I discuss the findings with the 'sensuality of the performative self' (Game and Metcalfe 1996: 30), whether in writing or in the construction of an individual *ars erotica*, I carry with me a degree of guilt for the shelter and protection I have. On more than one occasion the physical deterioration in the women sex workers, from the first phase of field work to the second nearly a year later, made me ponder on my own privilege by comparison. When showing off in writing, I find the 'performative self' mocking what I really feel and I am still trying to reconcile that self with this one with the humbling recognition that it is currently impossible to create an ideal feminist methodology which negates power differences.

Disciplinary reflexivity

As a white female single parent of two children closer recognition of, and empathy with, the lives of the working women developed throughout the entire project as I encountered, first-hand, the feminisation of poverty. This was when *'divorce* which is the trap-door through which women fall into the "new poverty"' (Beck 1992: 89) became lived reality. In evaluating my own contribution to the construction of meanings in this study, it is necessary to be constructively critical about relationships and research methodology in 'functional reflexivity' (Wilkinson 1988: 495) in this way.

In this chapter, I have explained the procedures and functions of the police unit in which the case study material was carried out. I have outlined the methods used to obtain and analyse the data, and have explored ethical issues which emerged during and beyond the research process. The following chapter draws together all the research findings and provides recommendations for future policy, practice and research.

Notes

1 Title used after Cassell (1978) *Motive, Method and Morality*, cited by Burgess (1984a).
2 This was extended out to 1000 records when scouring for those with criminal records.
3 One resident, an historian, explained that one of the reasons for this was architectural: the first residents of houses built from 1820 onwards complained there were no mews for the horses. Subsequent developers who had already begun work added mews, but it was not possible to run these the whole length of the terrace. As a result there are many quiet cul de sacs and spaces suitable for prostitutes to take their clients (ResInt 7: 11). I observed some of these, walled in at the back of buildings, such as Tenniel Close and Queensborough Mews.
4 It is specified in the Police and Criminal Evidence Act 1984, s. 55 that where a search is conducted for drugs or weapons it may only be carried

out by a nurse or medical practitioner or police officer of the same sex as the person to be searched.

5 Derived from the Cockney rhyming slang for Thomas More/whore (for the history and further details see Malcolm Young (1998)).

6 Maids are usually, but not always, retired sex workers (O'Connell Davidson 1994).

7 Formal access for the research had already been granted by senior police officers in Victoria and King's Cross in London, as well as Manchester. I spent several days at each of these sites, to appreciate the specific prostitution activities in each area, before limiting the choice of site to the Clubs and Vice Unit in London.

8 Analysis of three classes of hand and arm movement shows significant interconnection between non-verbal behaviour and spontaneous speech in conversation (Beattie 1983: 75).

9 This is not the definitive number of field roles; Spradley (1979: 83 cited in May 93: 99) for example, outlines four stages to establish rapport: apprehension; exploration; co-operation; and participation. At this last stage the informant accepts the role of the researcher who can start to explore a person's life in depth and/or examine and disconfirm ideas the researcher has.

10 The police requested the presentation of criminal career data in the form of a conference paper and received a draft of the data from the qualitative analysis as a validity check.

11 By 'interpretative social psychology' is meant those social psychological treatments of interpretation and understanding in everyday life that have been influenced by sociological considerations as exemplified by symbolic interactionism (Semin and Manstead 1983: 2).

12 Although it could be argued that the use of negative case analysis in my discursive analysis is similar to Popperian falsification.

13 This is evident in psychology where the fashion for using inferential statistical techniques by default rather than principled choice, and the common reliance upon statistical significance as the main criterion of interpretative worth, may well obscure many relevant features of data (Henwood and Pidgeon 1993: 28).

14 Whilst the information gathered was potentially useful for the team-building experience of sergeants, it would have breached the confidentiality of the participants so I chose not to use it.

15 Cockney rhyming slang: clock is short for 'clockface' and means 'look at', and 'syrup' is slang for 'syrup of fig', which means wig.

16 The Chief Inspector responsible for carrying out the inquiry told me months later that he had been so amused by my evidence, he had been 'dining out' on it ever since. I assumed from this that no long-term harm was done to any officer's career.

17 The men are stopped for offences covered by the Sexual Offences Act 1985. These include persistently soliciting a female from or near a vehicle

(s. 1(1)); causing annoyance by soliciting a female (s. 1(1)); persistently soliciting a woman on foot (s. 2(1). Men are stopped for soliciting a woman on foot (not persistently), and persistently driving around a known red-light (prostitution) area without a good explanation. The latter action, however, is not an offence.

18 Alternatively, generalisability is reconceptualised as 'fittingness' by Guba and Lincoln (1981), Goetz and LeCompte (1984) as 'translatability and comparability' (Guba and Lincoln, and Goetz and LeCompte cited in Schofield 1993: 207).

19 The term discursive is used to refer to common social meanings, metaphors and stories that underlie understandings.

20 Although it is accepted that what passes for truth at a particular time is bounded by the tolerance of the empirical reality and by the consensus of the scholarly community (Kirk and Miller 1986).

21 This is also known as pragmatic or criterion validity, which exists when a measurement procedure can be shown to produce observations matching those of alternative procedure (Kirk and Miller 1986).

22 During the Peter Sutcliffe investigation, enquiries made of some of the victims' clients, one officer distracted each respondent's wife by asking for a cup of tea, so concerned were officers for the men's marriages, while the other officer quietly revealed the real nature of the enquiries to the client. Such sensitivity to the men's relationships contrasted sharply with the contempt meted out to sex workers and their families (Smith 1989).

23 Whilst the term 'reflexivity' has had a variety of meanings (cf. Woolgar 1988; Steier 1991) I take it to mean my values, belief systems, biases, interests, predilections, values, experiences and characteristics.

24 As Frank Mort (Bland and Mort 1997) found in interviews with young male consumers in Soho, when the interviewee referred to cultural flashpoints, it forced some explicit reflection from him or the respondents 'about our sexual identities as men' (1997: 30). This occurred in my own interviews with male respondents. While I was seeking to understand the world of the male kerb-crawler, they would ask me questions 'as a woman'.

25 It was a perception that flattered then disturbed me, for 'Where there is desire, the power relation is already present' (Foucault 1979: 81), and I worried if I had negotiated power relations appropriately. Would the residents feel let down after I left the field? Would the officers feel resentful when my findings were not to their liking or maybe did not result in the practical policy changes they wanted?

26 It is noteworthy that Walkowitz adds that Schreiner's 'overidentification' and lack of 'scientific' distance must have appalled if intrigued Pearson (Walkowitz 1992: 292).

Chapter 7

Conclusion

This concluding chapter provides an overall summary of key findings and outlines the importance of these findings for our understanding of the behaviour involved in buying, selling and the policing of street sex markets. I also discuss the implications of the findings for theory, policy and practice. A brief research agenda for future lines of enquiry is provided and the chapter concludes by outlining what a law governing sex work should look like after consideration of appropriate interventions for men and women in the sex industry.

Key findings

Analysis of the changing trends and shifts in the legal construction of sex workers and clients shows that greater criminalisation of the client has occurred while the sex worker has increasingly become constructed as a victim. By looking critically at the changing nature of regulation it is apparent that change has occurred without reference to the empirical work on clients and street sex markets; an absence which is exemplified in the lack of attention to research evidence in the Government Consultation document *Paying the Price* and the subsequent *Strategy* on sex work.

The exploration of kerb-crawler characteristics has shown that 'catching kerbies' is no simple procedure. It is part of a range of policing duties, and the police have competing and seemingly conflicting demands on their time. From the research, it is apparent that officers responded to kerb-crawlers, sex workers, juveniles at risk and demands from residents, in different ways. Further, recognition of the pressures on sex-working women led to notional acceptance and sympathy from officers, who were reluctant to charge women – except where it was felt women abused the policy by waving the evidence that they had already been charged, as 'a warrant to work'. The police, therefore, denied the legitimacy of the law, which penalises sex-working women when they solicit.

Officers also questioned residents' demands that sex workers be cleared from the streets, and this further supported their somewhat low regard for the legitimacy of the law. Evidence in this study of over 500 clients shows no frightened residents in the records, nor the police being called out to such incidents of female fear. The Home Office consultation documents cite residents' fears of kerb-crawlers frightening non-sex-working women, but rather, it seems that the police insights show that residents' concerns revolve around the impact on property prices in this area rather than female safety.

Further complexity in the nature of policing is suggested in the fact that the time-consuming nature of duties, concerning the protection of juveniles at risk, may be offset against the actual numbers of kerb-crawlers stopped.

The findings show that the number of men stopped is nevertheless considerable; men of all ages are stopped by the police for kerb-crawling, though the mean age was 39 years (this is consistent with previous studies, such as Faugier (1995); Matthews (1993); and Benson and Matthews (1995a)). Also consistent with previous studies (Perkins 1991, and Kinnell 1989), is the finding that kerb-crawlers are from a broad range of occupational classes. Within these broad classes, however, new information was provided on specific types of occupation. This finding included a large group of men in skilled manual employment, of whom a large proportion were in the building, driving and catering trades. This was followed by men in professional occupations, nearly half of whom were in financial or accountancy-related professions. A small number of diplomats were found, a factor not evident in previous studies, though it can perhaps partly be accounted for by the location of the research.

The police charged a small number of hackney-cab drivers, and the findings illustrate that there was police antipathy towards them. This was because kerb-crawling by such men was considered to be an abuse of public trust. This has not been noted in previous research findings. More than half the men stopped were non-white, a finding which is contrary to findings in previous studies (including Cohen

1980; Holzman and Pines 1982; Van Wesenbeeck *et al.* 1993; Campbell 1997; O'Connell Davidson 1998; Monto 2000), all of whom found the overwhelming majority of clients to be white. A further key finding was that a significant number of Asian men were stopped when driving mini-cabs. Whilst these are mere speculations, the high number of Asian men stopped could be due to institutionalised racism in the Metropolitan police, or due to the strategies adopted by male Asian mini-cab drivers to follow one another when carrying groups of white male customers, in case of racist attacks (a factor which may lead to greater numbers of Asian men in the areas studied (Ahktar 2000)). Not only has this finding not been evident in previous research, but observation indicated that the number of men driving cabs was in excess of those in the records. It is also possible that the historical exploitation of Asian men described by Hubbard (1999), has led to large numbers of Asian men driving unlicensed cabs on the informal economy, some of whom may not be kerb-crawling, but rather, touting for casual cab business. In the light of these findings, it is possible to speculate support for the proposition of O'Connell Davidson (1998), who suggests that there is a parasitical relationship between cab drivers and sex workers. Alternatively, the findings may support the idea that strong social relationships develop between drivers and sex-working women, who use such cabs frequently.

The weekly distribution of men stopped for kerb-crawling was found to peak mid-week on Wednesdays, and this finding supported similar findings in Norway (Høigard and Finstad 1992).

The findings indicate that there was a high concentration of men living locally to where they were kerb-crawling. This concentration is higher than has been shown in previous research (Matthews 1993; Sharpe 1998), and perhaps suggests that many kerb-crawlers were kerb-crawling within their own communities. There was also a higher concentration of men living further than 50 miles away than has been shown in previous research (Matthews 1993; Kinnell 1989; Sharpe 1998), some of whom were recorded as working away from home in non-residential accommodation. Such men included those in the building trades, staying in nearby hotels, for example.

Many of the men who provided a non-residential address, however, were tourists or business visitors, light-skinned and European in appearance. The evidence of tourists in the records supports the findings of Cunnington (1979). These men were significantly less likely to receive the same charge (relative to the offence) as UK residents did, but a lower charge. In other words tourists were treated more leniently than UK residents.

A large number of men were found to be voyeuristically cruising the area. This finding of 'cruisers' supports the findings of McKeganey and Barnard (1996) and Høigard and Finstad (1992) on the behaviour of these men. While the majority of men solicited on their own, there were cases of men soliciting and cruising in pairs or groups. This has also been shown in previous research (Høigard and Finstad 1992; Boyle 1994; Monto 2000). However, a new finding in this study was that those men under 40 years of age were disproportionately represented.

The incidence of men with violent or criminal histories is lower than that in the general population. Examination of a sub-sample of kerb-crawlers with criminal records shows that these are also a very small minority of clients. As the first study to explore the criminal histories of these men, it should be considered preliminary research in this area. Whilst in the main, clients are generally law abiding, the situation in which the law places sex workers is what leaves them vulnerable to violence from a small number of serially violent men. Exploration of the context of violence shows that legal policy victimises sex workers and that rhetoric around 'disposal' and 'sex slavery' disempower those in the sex industry.

Implications for policy and practice

One of the main implications for policy and practice in this sphere concerns the tension between the law, which impels police officers to prosecute, and officers' private sentiments, which reflect sympathy for women sex workers. In effect, this results in a selective charging strategy, with officers only prosecuting (that is, recommending prosecution to the Crown Prosecution Service) when they feel they must. These circumstances appear to be dictated by the prevalence of sex workers on the street at any given period, and the frequency with which sex workers blatantly parade their trade – provoking the officers somewhat.

It might be argued that the officers lull the women into a false sense of security. Officers' sympathy towards, and interest in the individual women, with recognition of their vulnerability, perhaps leads the women to feel immune from prosecution, and yet any expression of this on the part of the women is taken to be a sign that officers' goodwill is being taken for granted – hence the move towards prosecution to mark the boundary. The uncertainty in policing practice here certainly raises questions about the comparative benefits of selective reluctance to prosecute and wholesale decriminalisation. The present policy is advantageous towards some women, but in an unpredictable way. It is arguable that consistency in policing is fundamental to the legitimacy of both the law and the agency which enforces the law. The majority of officers who police prostitution build up good relationships with sex workers and do not feel that increasing sanctions against sex workers and clients is effectual.[1] Indeed, such sanctions reduce the legitimacy of the law and greater sanctions might imperil the law's legitimacy further. For example, the ACPO strategy recommended an increase in police power.[2] ACPO strategists need to be educated to realise that greater police power is not a panacea for answering the problems associated with street sex work.[3] In addition the police do not have a vested interest in criminalisation of sex work as legislation currently affords them.

Another matter for consideration here revolves around the tensions between the priority status accorded by the police to juveniles at risk (that is, children involved in sex working) and recognition for police achievements in terms of prosecutions. Putting this crudely, there may be a need to give consideration to the value given to these competing tasks. The evidence from this study clearly suggests that such a tension weighs heavily in the everyday policing of street sex offences in the London area.

In relation to the policing of clients, there are several main issues to consider. The first concerns an apparent antipathy towards hackney-cab (black-cab) drivers – as expressed in officers' claims about drivers' 'abuse of public trust'. Whether or not this antipathy actually affects policing practice, of course, is difficult to say. Nevertheless, with general concerns about selective law enforcement in mind, there is sufficient evidence here to suggest that the issue of whether or not there is hostile policing towards such drivers perhaps deserves closer attention from both within and without policing organisations.

Another key policy issue concerns the treatment of tourists and UK residents. The evidence suggests the preferential treatment of tourists compared with UK residents (in terms of charge rates). Whilst this may in part be due to organisational expediency, given that officers exclaimed that it would not be worth pursuing prosecution because the man might well have left the country, or indeed because there was evidence to suggest that his departure was imminent, the differential response to men here raises questions about justice. As noted earlier, consistency in policing practice may be fundamental to the legitimacy of the Police Service and the law.

A further issue concerns the policing tactics employed against 'cruisers'. Evidence suggests that a number of men were stopped even when there were no apparent criminal offence committed. The absence of legal provision proved no bar. Police officers tended to level 'informal charges' against those observed in a red-light area where there was insufficient evidence to make a formal charge. As a consequence of the informal charge (the records indicate 'driving around a red-light area without an explanation'), men were frequently sent warning letters to their home or work address. Whatever the intention underpinning this police practice, it raises questions about civil liberties. This matter, as with others, deserves close attention.

The fifth issue concerns the weekly distribution of kerb-crawlers stopped. The key question here is whether or not the mid-week peak found in this study (and indeed in other studies), is a function of policing activity during the week. Again, this is a matter which deserves closer attention because of its implications for policing practice.

The main issue is essentially whether or not the criminalisation of clients is beneficial in terms of protecting those involved in sex working, or effective in deterring those involved. The research findings provide evidence of a very diverse set of client motivations, behaviours, and responses to the law in the face of police interaction that lead to a view that the criminalisation of clients neither protects those involved in sex working nor deters clients. It is hard to understand, from the empirical findings, what the justification is for the kerb-crawling laws at all. It follows that it is important to develop interventions to mirror and match the complexities of client behaviour, rather than simply relying on criminalisation and punitive responses. The evidence certainly supports a case for exploring effective alternatives to criminalisation such as safety parks/zones.

The research suggests, in the case of men for whom the 'risk' of visiting a sex worker is an erotic factor, that punitive measures against these men will only increase its attraction for them. Punitive measures will have the opposite of their intended effect on these clients.

Evidence on the context of violence provides a powerful adjunct to the argument for decriminalisation and empowerment strategies for sex workers such as a national database of difficult or dangerous clients, as well as legal intervention in the form of admissive statutes. It also shows that policy should consider the terms and language it uses as this rhetoric can be used in a way that is detrimental to the freedoms and rights of sex workers.

Implications for theory

The research findings on the occupational status of the clients challenge previous theory regarding a pyramidal model whereby the perceived social status of the sex worker would attract men from a certain occupational grouping (Perkins 1991). On the contrary, the research findings suggest no such alignment.

Similarly, the research findings here challenge previous theoretical and empirical assumptions that kerb-crawling is a 'casual matter' (Benson and Matthews 1995), in the sense of it being opportunistic. Rather, my findings, based on observation and data concerning routes and distances travelled from home, support Stoller's (1976) proposition that kerb-crawling (prostitute-use) is a purposeful activity in this respect, that is, it is 'sought out'. As a development of this issue, Stoller (1976) also proposed that voyeuristic behaviour and prostitute-use are closely related. Such a relationship raises theoretical questions with regard to whether this is the start, on a continuum of behaviour, that would build up to being a client. This is a matter for further research.

Whilst previous research has focused on men's accounts of kerb-crawling (Benson and Matthews 1995; Sharpe 1998), this has tended to be descriptive rather than analytical. My own research suggests that there is analytical utility in a four-dimensional model which accommodates admissions, admissions to 'cruising' but a denial of kerb-crawling, denials and excuses, and failure to stop. Moreover, analysis of the data suggests the existence of a continuum of compliance with the police. As one might expect, the continuum reflects admissions at the most compliant end and failure to stop at the least compliant end, but this belies a complexity in interactions with the police. Indeed, on the basis of my research findings, I have been able to suggest a sequential ordering of phases of interaction; these involve a bemused phase, an excuse phase, an indignant phase, a confrontational phase or pleading phase, which is followed in some cases by an indication of future intent regarding visits to the area.

My analysis here contributes not only to understanding of client behaviour but also broader theories concerning the accountability of conduct (Semin and Manstead 1983). Equally, analysis of gendered police responses to kerb-crawler accounts adds to understanding of the complexity of police–offender interactions.

Towards a new research agenda

Whilst there have been a number of research suggestions already mentioned in the text, there is perhaps need to highlight a number of these. I focus on two research priorities here. Firstly, there is perhaps a need to explore in what ways sex work may be conducted more safely, especially outdoors. Such research would lead to more informed debate about the most appropriate strategies for dealing with sex markets in order to ensure the protection of those at risk in a more realistic way than naïve strategies that assume eradication is desirable or even possible.

Whilst this research touches upon voyeuristic behaviour, it does not pursue this as far as being able to discern what the relationship is between this behaviour and the build-up to being a client. Given the interest accorded to voyeurism within the Sexual Offences Act 2003, this is an area which requires urgent attention. This is all the more so because policing practices regarding cruisers (who would often be labelled, or self-label, as voyeurs) appear to infringe civil liberties.

The exploratory examination of the criminal careers of kerb-crawlers certainly provides foundation for further research into finding ways of supporting sex workers' rights to work free of violence from the few serially violent men who become clients.

Most important of all, the discrepancy between the assumptions made in government policy documents about residents' views and the findings of this research about residents' actual concerns is essential to explore in detail. It is acknowledged that: 'many, if not most, decisions to criminalise conduct are simply a response either to pressure groups or to perceived public opinion' (Clarkson and Keating 2003: 3) and it is important that research explores what the public truly think and feel about sex-working practices and behaviours.

How should we decide which conduct should be criminal?

The findings in this book raise some important points about what is and what is not criminal. How should we decide which conduct should be criminal? Critics argue that there has been an alarming tendency 'on the part of the Government, in particular, to adopt the view that if there is a problem, an instant panacea is to [be] found by criminalising the conduct in question' (Clarkson and Keating 2003: 3). This has led some commentators to assert that there is no unifying thread in the criminal law at all. Yet on the matter of sex work, in the 1950s the Wolfenden Committee sought to provide a theoretical framework against which the decision to criminalise conduct should be made. And the thread throughout statutes on sex work should be based on the harm principle, a principle upon which it is argued that:

- conduct must be wrongful;
- it must be *necessary* to employ the criminal law to condemn or prevent such conduct; and
- it must also be permissible to criminalise the activity.

Conduct should not be prohibited unless it can be regarded as wrongful, that is if it causes harm or serious offence to others including 'the community spirit'.[4] It is not possible that the sale or purchase of sex can be criminalised on these grounds. Indeed, all around us sex is being sold in various forms. Sexuality is commodified and sold in various forms in every shop we go into and in every newspaper we buy. The commodification of sex is part and parcel of modern day community spirit.

The seriousness of the offensiveness would be determined by:

- the intensity and durability of the repugnance produced, and the extent to which repugnance could be anticipated in the general reaction of strangers to the conduct displayed or represented (conduct offensive only to persons with an abnormal susceptibility to offence would not count as very offensive);
- the ease with which unwilling witnesses can avoid the offensive displays; and
- whether or not the witnesses have willingly assumed the risk of being offended either through curiosity or the anticipation of pleasure (Feinberg 1985).

These factors would be weighed as a group against the reasonableness of the offending party's conduct as determined by:

- its personal importance to the actors themselves and its social utility generally, remembering always the enormous social utility of expression (in those cases where expression is involved);
- the availability of alternative times and places where the conduct in question would cause less offence; and
- the extent, if any, to which the offence is caused with spiteful motives.

In addition, the legislature would establish the character of various neighbourhoods, and consider establishing licensed zones in areas where the conduct in question is known to be already prevalent, so that people inclined to be offended are not likely to stumble on it to their surprise. The law should not treat the offence as if it is as serious as harm and where possible it should use other modes of regulations such as injunctions or licensing procedures (Feinberg 1985: 3).

The Law Commission sounds a note of caution that the offence principle must be qualified. The reason being that every activity might give offence to somebody, and everybody's autonomy would be severely and unacceptably curtailed if the criminal law routinely targeted offensive conduct. One can only countenance criminalising an offence which is extreme and unavoidable and 'this can never be said of activity which takes place in private' (The Law Commission 1995).

On the other hand, legal paternalism allows the criminal law to be used to protect a person from harm to themselves. Such a stance would suggest that the law is entitled to interfere with a person's autonomy for their own good and enhance their welfare. The legal paternalist is, however, only interested in enhancing the interests that a person actually has and not in protecting interests that a person ought to have. There are further problems with the paternalist approach. In 1995, the Law Commission undertook the task of examining the extent to which consent should be a defence to various activities such as sado-masochism and various types of fighting. Principles apply, therefore, that if one allows boxing (consent to self-harm) one must also allow people to consent to carefully controlled, planned, and consensual violence as part of a sexual encounter (in, for example, sado-masochistic encounters); many of us make lifestyle choices which do not promote our immediate or long-term interests and if these were all criminalised then 'sky-diving, mountaineering and most contact sports would have to be criminalised' (para. C.63). The Commission states:

It is a recognition of individual autonomy, the right of individuals of sufficient understanding to make their own decisions about what is good for them. In principle this should apply to people's sexual preferences. Indeed, it is hard to see how the interest (public or private) in allowing people to express their sexuality, which forms a fundamental part of people's personality, could be less important than the interest of allowing people to pursue sports. Sport is fun, but sex, for many people, is more than fun; it is a form of self-expression. (Feldman 2002: 716)

Is it necessary to employ the criminal law?

Assuming the conduct is wrongful, and the reasoning above shows that no case for this exists for sex work *per se*, then there is a further condition that must be established. It must be necessary to employ the criminal law. Before it is possible to criminalise the behaviour, that is, it must be necessary to invoke power of criminal law. It must be possible to show that criminalisation can condemn or prevent the behaviour. This is minimal, or necessary, but not a sufficient condition. This leads us to the final question: whether or not it is permissible to criminalise the conduct.

Is it permissible to criminalise the conduct?

Assuming the above two conditions have been met, i.e. that conduct is 'wrongful' and it is deemed 'necessary' to use criminal law, then a final condition must be met. Such criminalisation must not contravene the European Convention on Human Rights (in the Human Rights Act 1998). The importance of ECHR cannot be overestimated and Article 8 provides the right to a private life. The finding by the decision in *Niemetz v Germany* (1992) 16 EHRR 97 is that sex is the most intimate part of the private life to which one has a fundamental human right. This reasoning fundamentally supports the right to buy and/or sell sex between consenting adults. It is with the notion of rights to the fore that the next section explores how such rights can be protected for those in sex work by admissive statutes.

A legislative and policy framework: what laws on sex work should look like

What would good law on sex work look like? Legislation which respects the rights of sex workers, with the long-term aim of winning public recognition that respect for human rights of all is integral to a healthy society. Admissive statutes would offer guidance to organisations and institutions seeking to achieve equitable, non-discriminatory policy and practice. The Declaration of Rights of Sex Workers in Europe (2005) is not a legal document but is a synthesis of all the rights that have been agreed in international treaties and covenants, to uphold for all citizens, together with specific proposals to states for steps and policies that would ensure the protection of those rights for sex workers (2005: 4). The Declaration is based on the principle that selling sexual services is not grounds for sex workers to be denied the fundamental rights to which all human beings are entitled under international law (see www.sexworkeurope.org).

For example, if women were given the rights that natural justice demands, many of the cases the police bring under other laws, where for example sex workers have been coerced, sex workers could bring cases themselves under the Protection from Harassment Act 1997 (section 1, prohibition of harassment); this has civil remedies (section 3) and sections which deal with putting people in fear of violence (section 4) and restraining orders (section 5).

General framework for social policy on commercial sex[5]

Policy, including criminal policy, on commercial sex should be set within the framework of general codes of sexual behaviour and criminal law discussed above. Policy cannot be based on some romantic notion that sexual labour cannot be sold or the naïve assumption that sex work can be eradicated. Sex work is part of the wider sexual leisure industry and yet legislation does not reflect that. It has to be accepted that the sex industry exists at all levels. Psychosocial factors such as stigma have to be challenged. Public education has to take place to challenge the stigma and prejudice against sex workers so they are more likely to access services. There should be increased funding for NGO support and support for peer education amongst sex workers. There is a need for provision of non-coercive support that is truly voluntary for the sex workers who wish to exit sex work. Retraining programmes for sex workers who want to leave the industry and rehabilitation must be truly voluntary and not a stick with which to beat offenders. It must not include coercive tactics like those in Johns' schools; thus if drug rehabilitation is what is required by the person, the criminal justice system is not needed to 'support' it. The view that sex work is itself violent needs to be challenged, with local authorities enabled to uphold their duty of care to protect the welfare and safety of sex workers. Paying for sexual services is not an intrinisically violent behaviour. Specifically, legislation should enable:

1 The right to engage in sex work without coercion, and thus enable enforcement against coercion.

2 Provision to be made against harassment, fear, force or fraud.

3 Decriminalisation of all aspects of sex work involving consenting adults. One of the most important routes out of sex work is

265

decriminalisation. Historically, for many working class women, sex work was only one of a range of seasonable jobs such as fruit picking, that women would move in or out of (see Walkowitz 1992). Criminalising sex workers maintains women's outlaw status. Decriminalisation helps women to work legally and stay away from drug-dealers and pimps. This would mean those selling sex could report quite freely any coercion. Decriminalisation aids investigative practice and intelligence-gathering as sex workers are less frightened to report incidences of violence. Decriminalisation would also make the open promotion of safer sex and condom use easier, improving contact between health workers and sex workers.

4   Acknowledgement of the range of paid sexual acts and, in order to provide labour rights, sex work simply has to be classed as a 'special type of work'. This means incorporating a sex work discourse to ensure that the issues of labour rights, freedoms and working conditions do not slip off the agenda again in this country.

5   Entitlement to sick pay and parental leave for those working in the sex industry.

6   The right to work on the same basis as other independent contractors and employers and to receive the same benefits as other self-employed or contracted workers.

7   Legal support for sex workers who want to sue those who exploit their labour.

8   Clean and safe places to work.

9   The right to choose whether to work alone or co-operatively with other sex workers, and to pay tax.

10   Duty on public authorities to ensure fair working practices for those in sex industries.

11   Access for sex workers of social insurance that gives access to unemployment and sickness benefits, pensions and health care.

Off-street sex work

Legislation should be passed to enable:

1   Encouragement of small worker-run establishments.

2 A licensing system to ensure that children are not employed, employees are not in possession of drugs, and foreign nationals have work permits. Such policy on licensing is supported by those in the health field (for example, Cusick 2006).

3 Consideration given to licensing of larger, managed establishments, so that sex workers' rights can be protected by employment law, in premises that are compliant with health and safety regulations. In addition, planning regulations could stipulate that businesses offering sexual services should be situated a suitable distance away from churches or schools. By moving to a system of strictly regulated legal markets some MPs have argued that we might have a realistic chance of gaining some control of those markets which are currently under organised criminal control.

4 Reform of the laws that prevent women working together, allowing two or three women to work together from home. The problem of women being forced out on the street because they cannot fulfil the licence criteria of brothels would be averted by the legal option of two or three sex workers allowed to work from home. Sex workers would be encouraged by decriminalisation to move away from the black market, declare their earnings and pay tax and National Insurance contributions. It has been suggested (by MP Lynne Jones) that legal advertising would provide evidence for the Inland Revenue action on this.

5 Legislation that prohibits child working practices. Legislation already exists in other spheres (e.g. a child under 16 years can work in a delicatessen but is not allowed to operate dangerous machinery such as a bacon-slicing machine). There are age bars regarding certain types of job and family arrangements, for example a candidate must be 21 years to stand as an MP and in the domestic sphere it is necessary to be 21 years to adopt a child. Therefore, it is therefore possible to legislate that those working in parts of the sex industry should be of a certain age e.g. 21.

6 Employment contracts and all the protections that they can bring.

7 An occupational health and safety code to be set up with involvement from the sex industry.

8 Legal obligations on clients and establishment owners to ensure condom use and information on safer sex.

9 Brothels to be clean, hygienic, and free of fire risk.

10 Some of the onus for improving the safety of sex workers onto those who make money from advertising. For example, the media selling advertising space for sexual services could be obliged to ask advertisers to sign a contract stating that services are not sold by anyone under 18 years of age, and that those trading are voluntarily engaged in sex work etc. In this way, as with licensing laws, the retailer of advertising is involved in regulation.

11 The state should develop discussion with sex worker groups, for example the sex-work branch of the GMB union or the UKNSWP. This has clearly not occurred yet in the consultation process; for example, during a discussion with the then Under Secretary of State for the Home Office, Caroline Flint, Ms. Flint wondered why there weren't more sex workers at the consultation conferences. Yet the attendance cost of the conference was £250. Not all are as remote from the problem and some MPs, for example Lynne Jones, a scientist, who after reviewing the evidence, argued that: 'there should be a repeal of all laws which criminalise prostitution and that it should be regulated just like any other trading activity' (Lynne Jones MP at www.lynnejones.org.uk/prostitution.htm, accessed 22 June 2005). And in seeking to repeal the laws we should heed Mary McIntosh's wise words: 'Feminists should listen to the voices of organised prostitutes and other sex workers' (McIntosh 1996). This means free consultation, in every sense of the word.

12 That safeguards should include all usual health and safety regulations and planning regulations on businesses.

Street sex work

Statutes on street sex work should provide that:

1 Local authorities should be given the powers to set up safety zones for street work. This would enable local authorities to uphold their duty of care to the welfare and protection of sex workers. Zones could be in non-residential areas with proper lighting and adequate waste disposal facilities (such as Sharps boxes, and bins for condoms). Health and outreach would find it easier to build up contacts to ensure women are safe and have access to health services. These are put forward by the majority of researchers who

research street prostitution as they: 'have a social and political logic ... zoning involves a degree of formalisation and toleration ... [and] is gaining ground in a number of urban centres in Britain' (Matthews 2005: 887).

2 Areas would be identified in consultation with the communities concerned.

3 Safety zones should be monitored and measured with realistic success/fail criteria. Since 1990, 87 sex workers have been murdered and resource implications are worth every penny if they save just one life.

Clients

Particular statutes should place some responsibility on clients, so that:

1 Those who buy sex have the onus on them to use condoms.

2 Civil remedies are made available to sex workers so that they can bring cases against those who have harassed, stalked or been violent towards them. At present the law has little legitimacy with police when they have to prosecute sex workers and increasing the sanctions against sex workers will reduce the legitimacy of the law with the police 'on the ground' still further.

3 There is extension of the Ugly Mugs scheme and police intelligence networks to create a national database of dangerous clients, so that information can be coordinated and shared nationally of individuals who target sex workers.

4 Good practice guidelines are produced for police to address crimes against sex workers.

5 Civil remedies are provided, like those in German law, for sex workers and the freedom to refuse clients who are drunk or disrespectful.

6 Brothels can be pivotal in helping against trafficking and child abuse. By legitimising those who want to work in them, it paves the way not only for the workers to report, without fear of censure, any incidence of trafficking or child abuse, but guidance too could be given for clients to report anonymously if children are seen working in brothels, or women held against their will.

Clients actually have a lower level of criminal offences than the general male population and while some clients are abusive, the majority are not, and maintaining a non-judgemental tolerance would generate useful information.

The 'professionalisation process' of sex work has been lucidly described by Sanders (2004) who argues that any laws against the purchase and sale of commercial sex are out of step with the comprehensive and largely regulatory mechanisms that are evident within sex markets. Unionisation and joint collaboration at national level are key mechanisms of managing and professionalising. Sanders suggests that:

> official agencies that offer realistic solutions to managing the sex industry encourage a reciprocal flow of information between workers and law enforcement agencies that provides a key framework for maintaining regulation. (2004: 173)

This is the only realistic way for regulation to go, and I want to take forward Sanders' (2004) agency vision by outlining the form that such an agency should take. It should have an inspectorate (not linked to other forensic inspectorates like prisons but linked to a Home Office health-related model, that of veterinary medicine). The sex industry inspectorate would have a number of roles outlined below:

1 Scientific role – for the assessment of research programmes of research related to sex work.

2 Advisory role – as to whether licences should be granted.

3 Inspectorate role – maintaining programme of visits to establishments to check licencees and others are complying with the terms and conditions of licences, certificates, and maintaining standards of hygiene in line with published codes of practice.

4 Representative role – that intentions of Parliament are realised. They should be independent of all interest groups involved in the debate over sex work. Inspectors could advise potential applicants, licensees and others.

5 Provide policy support – to Home Office ministers, including preparation of responses to parliamentary questions, letters from MPs seeking advice from constituents, and public correspondence relating to commercial sex work.

6 Liaising with sex work health and outreach groups such as the English Collective of Prostitues (ECP) and the UKNSWP.

In many respects the health-related model of the veterinary inspectorate is the closest model to a sex industry inspectorate. Nobody denies that exploitation occurs in the sex industry, it goes on in every industry – even the most highly paid workplaces in the country, such as the City. The difference between the City trader and the sex worker is that the former can go to law for justice whereas the latter has all justice denied her as the law is used against her and increases the degree to which she is exploited. Because the sex industry is not subjected to same employment, trading and health and safety regulations as other businesses so trafficking, slavery, child abuse and problematic drug use have been able to proliferate. Criminals are able to hide vulnerable people in businesses where false identity is the norm, trade unions are poorly established and employment legislation is poorly enforced (Cusick 2005). A set of admissive statutes and a proper regulatory inspectorate based on a health-related model would help to remedy this.

Chapter summary

This study provides a deeper understanding of the behaviour of the sale, purchase and policing of sexual services and it is clear that the research findings are extremely pertinent to the future development of the law, policy and practice. As the theoretical gap widens between pro-criminalising feminists and those who believe in harm minimisation to sex workers, it has caused respected researchers to lament that focussing on health issues means that the 'political playing field has been abandoned to the idealogues of the abolitionist movement' (Day and Ward 2004: 8) – but the sex industry is not going to go away. Indeed it is becoming more and more a part of mainstream life, and decriminalisation could work if we admit the clear failings of prohibition and view prostitution as a service which is simply part of the wider sexual leisure industry, and as such should be tolerated.

At the time of writing, government ministers and senior police officers are travelling widely to promote the Government Strategy and have closed down consultation to announce that there will be disruption of indoor sex markets with a concomitant increase in street work, and zero tolerance on those who buy sex. The government's idiosyncratic attention to the evidence-base neglects a vast body of research which shows that Sweden's policy of criminalising buyers of commercial sex is not progressive but is retrogressive, dangerous, unworkable and expensive.

The extensive lobbying by the police for greater powers, an insidious trend seen in other aspects of policy, has already resulted in coercive statutes against sex workers such as the Criminal Justice and Police Act 2001, the Sexual Offences Act 2003, and the Serious Organised Crime and Police Act 2005, to name a few. There remains, however, a contradiction in police work between the enforcement of anti-prostitution strategies that exacerbate violence against sex workers and their duty to protect all citizens, including sex workers.

The Government Strategy now links any help to sex workers only to exiting sex work; and ties government policy to Christian morality and righteousness, and the unrealistic aspirations of the abolitionists, whose naïve belief that they can halt the ingrained commercialisation of sex in our culture with greater police power and campaigns against purchasers of sex is ill-advised.

What is needed are admissive statutes that place the onus for safety onto those who are engaged in commercial sex, such as brothel owners, advertisers, etc, and the progressive use of labour law, contract law, and human rights law such as those implemented in Europe since ECHR. The final section of this chapter has shown what statutes on sex work should look like. These include a set of principles that admissive statutes, labour law and employment law should take account of so that the civil liberties and human rights of sex workers are not breached. The section concludes with the recommendation for a Home Office sex industry inspectorate based on the health-related model that already exists in the Home Office.

As a final comment, I would suggest that government policy so far has only been reactive, that the policing of clients is too highly resource intensive and expensive and it has little legitimacy with officers on the ground. Such resources could be better used addressing the rights of sex workers and exploring incentives and exhortation to use a regulatory model rather than criminalisation. It is only with these to fore that any progress can be made.

Notes

1 Sharpe 1998 *op cit.*, n.23.
2 For example, Brain, Davis, and Phillips, *Policing Prostitution: ACPO's Policy, Strategy, and Operational Guidelines for dealing with exploitation and abuse through prostitution* (October 2004).
3 This is consistent with the Metropolitan Police Service stance on proceeds from child pornography where they would also like a share in the proceeds (see Appendix 2, para.28 HAC [HC 639])
4 This is not the same thing as sin, which has a religious connotation.
5 These statutes are drawn from those put forward over the past two decades and include recommendations put forward by ECP, UK NSWP, The International Union of Sex Workers, and The Declaration of the Rights of Sex Workers in Europe. They also emerged from conversations, either in person or by email with Helen Self, Hilary Kinnell, Linda Cusick, and Rosie Campbell.

References

ACPO (2000) Proceedings of the ACPO National Vice Squad Conference, Avon and Somerset Constabulary Headquarters, Bristol, 29–30 June 2000.

Ahktar, S. (2000) *Working With Black Sex Offenders*, HMP Training, Nottingham, 9 February.

Agustín, L. (2005a) 'Migrants in the Mistress's House: Other Voices in the "Trafficking" Debate', *Social Politics*, 12 (1): 96–117.

Agustín, L. (2005b) 'Helping Women who Sell Sex: The Construction of Benevolent Identities', *Rhizomes*, 10.

Agustín, L. (2004a) 'Alternative Ethics, or: Telling Lies to Researchers', *Research for Sex Work*, June, 6–7.

Agustín, L. (2004b) 'At Home in the Street: Questioning the Desire to Help and Save', in E. Bernstein and L. Shaffner (eds) *Regulating Sex: The Politics of Intimacy and Identity*, 67–81. New York: Routledge.

Allison, A. (1994) *Nightwork: Sexuality, Pleasure and Corporate Masculinity in a Tokyo Hostess Club*. Chicago: University of Chicago Press.

Antaki, C. (1987) *Explaining and Arguing: The Social Organisation of Accounts*. London: Sage.

Ashworth, A. 'Criminal Justice Act 2003: Criminal Justice Reform: Principles, Human Rights and Public Protection' [2004] Crim. L.R. 516.

Austin, J.L. (1961) 'A Plea for Excuses', in. J.D. Urmson and G. Warnock (eds) *Philosophical Papers*. Oxford: Clarendon Press.

Azevedo, J., Ward, H., Day, S. (2002) 'Health Risks for Sex Workers: Results of a European Study', Paper presented to Sex Work and Health in a Changing Europe Conference, January 2002.

Bainham, A. (2005) *Children: The Modern Law*. Bristol: Jordan.

Bainham, A. (2002) 'Sexualities, Sexual Relations and the Law', in A. Bainham, S. Day Sclater, and M.P.M. Richards *Body Lore and Laws*, pp. 193–210. Oxford: Hart Publishing.

Bainham, A. and Brooks-Gordon, B. (2004) 'Reforming the Law on Sexual Offences', in B.M. Brooks-Gordon, L.R. Gelsthorpe, M.H. Johnson and A. Bainham (eds) *Sexuality Repositioned: Diversity and the Law*. Oxford: Hart Publishing.

Bak, R.C. (1968) 'The Phallic Woman: The Ubiquitous Fantasy in Perversions', *Psycho-analytical: Study of Children*, 23: 15–36.

Banister, P., Burman, E., Parker, I., Taylor, M. and Tindall, C. (1994) *Qualitative Methods in Psychology*. Buckingham: Open University Press.

Barnard, M.A. (1993) 'Violence and Vulnerability: Conditions of Work for Street Working Prostitutes', *Sociology of Health and Illness*, 15: 683–705.

Barnard, M.A. (1996) 'Violence and Vulnerability: Conditions of Work for Streetworking Prostitutes', in H. Bradby (ed.) *Defining Violence*. Aldershot: Avebury.

Barnard, M., Hart, G. and Church, S. (2002) 'Client Violence Against Prostitute Women Working from Street and Off-street Locations: A Three-city Comparison', *Violence Research Programme: Research Findings*. Swindon: Economic and Social Research Council.

Barnett, T. (2004) *The Prostitution Reform Act: What is the Story One Year On?*. Available from UKNSWP.

Beattie, G. (1983) *Talk: An Analysis of Speech and Non-verbal Behaviour in Conversation*. Oxford: Blackwell.

Beck, U. (1992) *Risk Society*. London: Sage.

Bell, L. (1987) (ed.) *Good Girls/Bad Girls: Sex trade workers and feminists face to face*. Toronto: The Women's Press.

Benson, C. (1998) 'Violence against Female Prostitutes: Experiences of Violence, Safety Strategies and the Role of Agencies'. Leicestershire: Department of Social Sciences, Loughborough University (ISBN 0 907274 23 4).

Benson, C. and Matthews, R. (1995a) 'Street Prostitution: Ten Facts in Search of a Policy', *International Journal of the Sociology of Law*, 23: 395–415.

Benson, C. and Matthews, R. (1995b) *The National Vice Squad Survey*. Enfield: Middlesex University School of Sociology and Social Policy.

Benson, C. and Matthews, R. (1996) *Report of the Parliamentary Group on Prostitution*. Enfield: Middlesex University School of Sociology and Social Policy.

Berg, B.L. (1998) *Qualitative Research Methods for the Social Sciences*. Needham Heights, MA: Alleyn and Bacon.

Bindel, J. (1998) 'A New Way Forward in Tackling Prostitution: Kerb Crawler Rehabilitation Programme in West Yorkshire', Paper presented at the National Vice Squad Conference, Northumbria Police Headquarters, Ponteland, Newcastle, 10–11 June 1998.

Bindel, J. (1999) 'Kerb Crawler Rehabilitation Scheme', Paper presented at the National Vice Squad Conference, Avon and Somerset Constabulary Headquarters, Bristol, 29–30 June 1999.

Blackstone (1997) *Statutes on Criminal Law* (8th edn) P.R. Glazebrook (ed.). London: Blackstone Press.

Bland, L. and Mort, F. (1997) 'Thinking Sex Historically', in L. Segal (ed.) *New Sexual Agendas*. Hampshire: Macmillan.

Bonaparte, M. (1965) *Female Sexuality*. New York: Grove Press.

Boyle, S. (1994) *Working Girls and their Men*. London: Smith Gryphon.

Brain, T. (2002) Plenary Paper, 'Unguarded Passions: Policing Sexual Crime in the Twentieth Century', Conference held by Feminist Crime Research Network, British Energy, Gloucester, 15 May.

Brain, T., Davis, T. and Phillips, A. (2004) 'Policing, Prostitution: ACPO Policy, Strategy, and Operational Guidelines for Dealing with Exploitation and Abuse Through Prostitution', October 2004. ACPO.

Brain, T., Duffin, T., Anderson, S. and Parchment, P. (1998) 'Child Prostitution: A Report on the ACPO Guidelines and the Pilot Studies in Wolverhampton and Nottinghamshire'. Gloucestershire Constabulary.

Brandt, C. (1998) 'The Fine Art of Regulated Tolerance: Prostitution in Amsterdam', *Journal of Law and Society*, 25 (4): 621–35.

Brewis, J. and Linstead, S. (2000) *Sex, Work, and Sex Work*. London: Routledge.

Briggs, J., Harrison, C., McInnes, A. and Vincent, D. (1996) *Crime and Punishment in England*. London: UCL Press.

Brogden, M., Jefferson, T. and Walklate, S. (1988) *Introducing Police Work*. London: Unwin Hyman.

Brookman, F. and Maguire, M. (2003) 'Reducing Homicide: Summary of a Review of the Possibilities', January 2003, RDS Occasional Paper No 84, Home Office.

Brooks-Gordon, B.M. (1997) 'Media Representations of Homicidal Violence and the Woman on the Street', presented at British Psychological Society Division of Legal and Criminological Psychology Sixth Annual Conference, University College of Ripon and York St. John, 2–4 September 1997, *Proceedings of The British Psychological Society*, 5 (2): 66.

Brooks-Gordon, B. (1999) 'The Criminal Careers of Kerb-Crawlers', Paper presented to the National Police Vice Conference, 28–30 June 1999.

Brooks-Gordon, B.M. (2001) 'Prostitution in Public Space: Kerb Crawler Explanations and Malefactors', PhD thesis, University of Cambridge, Institute of Criminology.

Brooks-Gordon, B.M. (2003) 'Gendered Provisions in The Sexual Offences Bill 2003: Prostitution', *Criminal Justice Matters*, Gender and Crime, Autumn, 53: 28–33 (not consecutive).

Brooks-Gordon, B.M. (2005) 'Clients and Commercial Sex: Reflections on "Paying the Price": A Consultation Paper on Prostitution' [2005] Crim. L.R. 425–43.

Brooks-Gordon, B.M. and Gelsthorpe, L.R. (2003a) 'Prostitutes' Clients, Ken Livingstone, and a New Trojan Horse', *Howard Journal of Criminal Justice*, 42 (5): 437–51.

Brooks-Gordon, B.M. and Gelsthorpe, L.R. (2003b) 'What Men Say When Apprehended for Kerb Crawling: A Model of Prostitutes Clients' Talk', *Psychology, Crime and Law*, 9 (2): 145–72.

Brooks-Gordon, B.M. and Gelsthorpe, L.R. (2002) 'The Hiring and Selling of Bodies', in A. Bainham, S. Day Sclater and M.P.M. Richards *Body Lore and Laws*, pp. 193–210. Oxford: Hart Publishing.

Brown, J. (1999) 'Abusive Relationships at Work: Policewomen as Victims' *Criminal Justice Matters*, 35, Spring 22–23.

Brown, J.M., Campbell, E.A. and Fife-Shaw, C. (1995) 'Adverse Impacts Experienced by Police Officers Following Exposure to Sex Discrimination and Sexual Harassment', *Stress Medicine*, 11: 221–28.

Bullough, V. and Bullough, B. (1987) *Women and Prostitution*. New York: Prometheus.

Burford, E.J. (1976) *Bawds and Lodgings: A History of the Bankside Brothels – 1675*. London: Owen.

Burgess, R.G. (ed.) (1984) *Conducting Qualitative Research*. Greenwich, CT: JAI Press.

Burgess, R.G. (1984) *In the Field*. London: Routledge.

Burke, K. (1966) *Language as Symbolic Action: Essays on Life, Literature, and Method*. Berkeley: University of California Press.

Burn, G. (1985) *'... Somebody's Husband, Somebody's Son'*. London: Pan.

Burt, K. and Oaksford, M. (1999) 'Beyond Beliefs and Desires', *The Psychologist*, 12 (7): 332–35.

Cameron, S. and Collins, A. (2003) 'Estimates of a Model of Male Participation in the Market for Female Heterosexual Prostitution Services', *European Journal of Law and Economics*, 16: 271–88.

Campbell, R. (1997) 'It's Just Business, It's Just Sex': Male Clients of Female Prostitutes in Merseyside', report for Liverpool City Challenge and Liverpool City Centre Partnership.

Campbell, R. and Storr, M. (2001) 'Challenging the Kerb Crawler Rehabilitation Programme', *Feminist Review*, 67: 94–108.

Card, R. (2004) *Sexual Offences*. London: Jordan.

Carpenter, B.J. (2000) *Re-thinking Prostitution: Feminism, Sex, and the Self*. New York: Peter Lang Publishing.

Cassell, J. (1988) 'The Relationship of Observer to Observed when Studying Up', in R.G. Burgess *Conducting Qualitative Research*. Greenwich, CT: JAI Press.

Chapkis, W. (2003) 'Trafficking, Migration, and the Law', *Gender and Society*, Vol. 17, 6: 923–937.

Chibnall, S. (1977) *Law and Order News: An Analysis of Crime Reporting in the British Press*. London: Tavistock.

Chodorow, N. (1978) *The Reproduction of Mothering*. Berkeley: University of California Press.

Chodorow, N. (1994) 'Feminism and Psychoanalytic Theory', in *Polity Reader in Social Theory*. Cambridge: Polity.

Church, S., Henderson, M. and Barnard, M. (2001) 'Violence by Clients towards Female Prostitutes in Different Work Settings: Questionnaire Survey', *BMJ*, 322, 3 March 2001.

Cicourel, A.V. (1968) *The Social Organization of Juvenile Justice*. New York: John Wiley.

Clarkson, C.M.V. and Keating, H.M. (2003) *Criminal Law: Text and Materials*. London: Sweet and Maxwell.

Cohen, B. (1980) *Deviant Street Networks*. New York: Lexington.

Collier, R. (1998) *Masculinities, Crime and Criminology*. London: Sage.

Collison, M. (1996) 'In Search of the High Life', *British Journal of Criminology* 36 (3): 428–44.

Connell, R.W. (1987) *Gender and Power*. Cambridge: Polity.

Connell, R.W. (1995) *Masculinities*. Cambridge: Polity.

Connell, R.W. (1998) 'Masculinities and Globalisation', *Men and Masculinities*, 1 July, (1) 13–23.

Cooke, R. (1994) 'State Responsibility for Violations of Women's Human Rights', *Harvard Human Rights Journal*, 7: 125–75.

Copas, A.J., Wellings, K. Erens, B., Mercer, C.H., McManus, S., Fenton, K.A., Korovessis, C., Macdowell, W., Nanchatal, K. and Johnson, A.M. (2002) 'The Accuracy of Reported Sensitive Behaviour in Britain: Exploring the extent of the change 1990–2000', *Sexually Transmitted Infections*, Feb, 79 (1): 26–30.

Cox, B., Shirley, J. and Short, M. (1977) *The Fall of Scotland Yard*. Harmondsworth: Penguin.

Crawford, J., Kippax, S. and Waldby, C. (1994) 'Women's Sex Talk and Men's Sex Talk: Different Worlds', *Feminism and Psychology*, 4 (4): 571–85.

Criminal Law Revision Committee (1984) 'Prostitution in the Street' Sixteenth Report, Cmnd. 9329. London: HMSO.

Cunnington, S. (1979) 'Some Aspects of Prostitution in the West End of London in 1979', in D.J. West (ed.) *Sex Offenders in the Criminal Justice System*, Cropwood Conference No. 12, University of Cambridge, Institute of Criminology.

Cusick, L. (2006) 'Sex Workers to Pay the Price', *BMJ*, 28 January, 332: 90–191.

Cusick, L. (1998) 'Female Prostitution in Glasgow: Drug Use and Occupational Sector', *Addiction Research*, 6 (2): 115–30.

Cusick, L. and Berney, L. (2005) 'Prioritising Punitive Responses over Public Health: Commentary on the Home Office Consultation Document Paying the Price', *Critical Social Policy*, 25 (4): 596–606.

da Silva, C. (2000) 'Prostitution in the Nineties: Changing Working Practices, Changing Violence', MA Criminology dissertation, Middlesex University.

Day, S. and Ward, H. (eds) (2004) *Sex Work, Mobility and Health in Europe*. London: Kegan Paul.

de Graaf, R., Vanwesenbeeck, I., van Zessen, G., Straver, C.J. and Visser, J.H. (1995) 'Alcohol and Drug Use in Heterosexual and Homosexual Prostitution, and its Relation to Protection Behaviour', *AIDS CARE*, 7 (1): 35–47.

Denzin N.K. (1983) 'Interpretive Interactionism', in G. Morgan *Beyond Method: Strategies for Social Research*. California: Sage.

Deutsch, H. (1945) *Female Sexuality: The Psychology of Women*. New York: Grune and Stratton.

Dinnerstein, D. (1976) *The Mermaid and the Minotaur: Sexual Arrangements and Human Malaise*. London/New York: Harper and Row.

Dworkin, A. (1987) *Intercourse*. London: Secker and Warburg.

Dworkin, A. (1997) *Life and Death*. London: Virago.

English Collective of Prostitutes (ECP) (1997) 'Campaigning for Legal Change', in G. Scambler and A. Scambler (eds) *Rethinking Prostitution*. London: Routledge.

Edley, N. and Wetherell, M. (1995) *Men in Perspective*. Hemel Hempstead: Harvester Wheatsheaf.

Edlund, L. and Korn, E. (2000) 'A Theory of Prostitution', *Journal of Political Economy*, 110 (1): 181–214.

Edwards, S.S.M. (1993) 'England and Wales' in N.J. Davis (ed.) *Prostitution: An International Handbook on Trends, Problems and Policies*. West Port: Greenwood Press.

Edwards, S.S.M. and Armstrong, G. (1988) 'Policing Street Prostitution: The Street Offences Squad in London', *Police Journal*, 209–217, July.

Edwards, S.S.M. (1993) 'England and Wales', in N.J. Davis *Prostitution: An International Handbook on Trends, Problems and Policies*. West Port: Greenwood Press.

Edwards, D. and Potter J. (1993) 'Language and Causation: A Discursive Action Model of Description and Attribution', *Psychological Review*, 100 (1): 23–41.

Elias, N. (1994) *The Civilizing Process*. Oxford: Blackwell.

Ellis, H.H. (1911) *Sex in Relation to Society*, cited in Segal (1994).

Ellis, H. (1918) *The Objects of Marriage, The Erotic Rights of Women*, cited in Hall (1991).

Ellis, H. (1921) *The Play Function of Sex*, cited in Hall (1991).

Europap (1995) 'European Intervention Projects Aids Prevention for Prostitutes', Final Report 1994. Gent, Belgium: University of Gent.

Everett, F. (2005) 'Girl', *The Guardian*, 22 July 2005, pp. 3–10.

Farley, M., Baral, I., Kiremire, M. and Sezgin, U. (1998) 'Prostitution in Five Countries: Violence and Post-traumatic Stress Disorder', *Feminism and Psychology*, 8 (4): 405–26.

Farrington, D. (1994) 'Human Development and Criminal Careers', in M. Maguire, R. Morgan and R. Reiner (eds) *The Oxford Handbook of Criminology*. Oxford: Oxford University Press.

Faugier, J. (1995) *Looking for Business: A Descriptive Study of Drug Using Prostitutes, Their Clients and Their Health Care Needs*, PhD thesis, University of Manchester.

Faugier, J. and Cranfield, S. (1994) 'Making the Connection', School of Nursing Information Pack. Manchester: University of Manchester.

Faugier, J. and Sargeant, M. (1997) 'Boyfriends, 'Pimps' and Clients', in G. Scambler and A. Scambler (eds) *Rethinking Prostitution*. London: Routledge.

Feinberg, J. (1985) *The Moral Limits of the Criminal Law: Offence to Others*, pp. 1, 2, 26. New York/Oxford: Oxford University Press.

Feldman, D. (2002) *Civil Liberties and Human Rights in England and Wales* (2nd edn). Oxford: Blackwell.

Felson, R.B. and Ribner, S.A. (1981) 'An Attributional Approach to Accounts and Sanctions for Criminal Violence', *Social Psychology Quarterly*, 44: 137–42.

Finch, J. (1993) 'It's Great to Have Someone to Talk to', in C. Bell and H. Roberts (eds) *Social Researching: Politics, Problems and Practice*. London: Routledge.

Fischer, B., Wortley, S., Webster, C. and Kirst, M. (2002) 'The Socio-legal Dynamics and Implications of "Diversion"', *Criminal Justice*, 2 (4): 385–410.

Foucault, M. (1979) *The History of Sexuality, Vol 1: An Introduction*, trans. R. Hurley. London: Penguin.

Franks, L. (1999) *Having None of It: Women, Men and the Future of Work*. London: Granta.

Freeman, M. (1997) The Moral Status of Children. Martinus Nijhoff.

Freud, S.E. (1910–19) papers cited in *The Complete Psychological Works of Sigmund Freud* (Standard ed.), trans. J. Strachey. London: Hogarth Press.

Frosh, S. (1994) *Sexual Difference: Masculinity and Psychoanalysis*. London and New York: Routledge.

Game, A. and Metcalfe, A. (1996) *Passionate Sociology*. London: Sage.

Garfinkel, (1967 [1984]) *Studies in Ethnomethodology*. Englewood Cliffs, NJ: Prentice-Hall.

Geertz, C. (1973) *The Interpretation of Cultures*. New York: Basic Books.

Gelsthorpe, L.R. (1989) *Sexism and the Female Offender*. Hants: Gower.

Gibbens, T.C.N. and Silberman, J. (1960) 'The Clients of Prostitutes', *British Journal of Venereal Diseases*, 36: 113.

Giddens, A. (1992) *The Transformation of Intimacy*. Cambridge: Polity.

Glaser, B. and Strauss, A. (1967) *The Discovery of Grounded Theory*. Chicago: Aldine.

Glazebrook, P.R. (2005) *Blackstones' Statutes on Criminal Law 2005–2006* (15th edn). Oxford: Blackstones.

Glendinning, C. and Miller, J. (1992) *Women and Poverty in Britain: The 1990s*. London: Harvester.

Goffman, E. (1959) *The Presentation of Self in Everyday Life*. Garden City. New York: Doubleday.

Golding, R. (1986) 'Prostitution in Holland', *Policing*, 18: 48–57.

Gusfield, J.R. (1966) *Symbolic Crusade: Status Politics and the American Temperance Movement*. Illinois: University of Illinois.

Gusfield, J.R. (1981) *The Culture of Public Problems: Drink Driving the Symbolic Order*. Chicago: University of Chicago Press.

Hall, L.A. (1991) *Hidden Anxieties, Male Sexuality, 1900–1950*. Cambridge: Polity.

Hammersley, M. and Atkinson, P. (1995) *Ethnography*. London: Routledge.

Hansard Parliamentary Debates (6 July, 1990), col.1291. London: HMSO.

Hanson, R.K. and Harris A.J.R. (1997) 'Voyeurism: Assessment and Treatment', in R.D. Laws and W.T. O'Donohue (eds) *Sexual Deviance: Theory, Assessment and Treatment*. New York: The Guilford Press.

Harre, R. (1979) *The Social Being*. Oxford: Blackwell.

Harre, R. (1983) *Personal Being*. Oxford: Blackwell.

Haug, F. (1984) *Females Sexualisation*. London: Verso.

Havelock Ellis (1899) *Studies in the Psychology of Sex: Volume 1: The Evolution of Modesty; the Phenomena of Sexual Peridiocity: Auto-Erotism*. Leipzip and Watford.

Henwood, K. and Pidgeon, N. (1993) 'Qualitative Research and Psychology', in M. Hammersley *Social Research. Philosophy, Politics and Practice*. London: Sage.

Hester, M. and Westmarland, N. (2004) *Tackling Street Prostitution: Towards a Holistic Approach*. London: Home Office.

Hochschild, A. (1983) *The Managed Heart*. California: University of California Press.

Hofstadter, R. and Lipset, S.M. (1969) *Sociology and History*. New York: Basic Books.

Høigard, C. and Finstad, L. (1992) *Backstreets*. Cambridge: Polity Press.

Hollway, W. and Jefferson, T. (1997) 'The Risk Society in an Age of Anxiety: Situating Fear of Crime', *British Journal of Criminology*, 48 (2): 255–66.

Holzman, S.H. and Pines, M. (1982) 'Buying Sex: The Phenomenology of Being a John', *Deviant Behaviour*, 4: 89–116.

Home Office (2006) 'A Co-ordinated Prostitution Strategy and a Summary of Responses to Paying the Price' (ref. 272136), January 2006. London: COI on behalf of Home Office.

Home Office (2004) 'Paying the Price: A Consultation Paper on Prostitution', July 2004. London: Home Office Communications Directorate.

Home Office (2004) 'Solutions and Strategies: Drug Problems and Street Sex Markets'. London: Home Office.

Home Office (2000) Review of Sex Offences 'Setting The Boundaries: Reforming the Law on Sex Offences'. London: HMSO.

Home Office (1999) 'Statistical Bulletin', Issue 19/99, 25 October 1999.

Home Office (1998) 'Guidelines for Responding to Juveniles Under Children Act 1989'. London: HMSO.

Home Office (1997) The National Police Records (Recordable Offences) (Amendment) Regulations 1997 (Statutory Instrument 1997, No. 566). London: HMSO.

Home Office White Paper (1996) 'Protecting the Public', Cmd. 3190. London: HMSO.

Home Office (1995) 'Criminal Careers of those Born between 1953 and 1973', *Home Office Statistical Bulletin*, Issue 14/95, 5 July 1995.

Home Office (1994) 'Criminal Statistics. England and Wales'. London: HMSO.

Home Office (1986) 'Criminal Statistics. England and Wales'. London: HMSO.

Home Office (1984a) 'Prostitution: Off-street Activities', Criminal Law Revision Committee, Seventeenth Report. London: HMSO.

Home Office (1984b) 'Prostitution in the Street', Criminal Law Revision Committee, Sixteenth Report. London: HMSO.

Home Office (1984c) Circular No. 52/1985.

Hope, T. (2005/06) 'Things can only get better', *Criminal Justice Matters*, Winter, pp. 37–39.

Horn, R. (1997) 'Not "One of The Boys": Women Researching the Police', *Journal of Gender Studies*, 6 (3): 297–308.

Hubbard, P. (1997) 'Community Action and the Displacement of Street Prostitution: Evidence from British Cities', *Geoforum*, 29 (3): 269–86.

Hubbard, P. (1999) *Sex and the City: Geographies of Prostitution in the Urban West*. Aldershot: Ashgate.

Humphreys, L. (1970) *Tearoom Trade*. London: Duckworth and Co.

Humphries, S. (1988) *A Secret World of Sex: The British Experience 1900–1950*. London: Sidgwick and Jackson.

Husserl, E. (1913 [1961]) *Ideas: General Introduction to Pure Phenomenology*. New York: Collier.

Hutton, I. (1923) *The Hygiene of Marriage*, cited in Hall (1991).

James, T.E. (1976) *Prostitution and the Law*. Altrincham: William Heinman.

Janus, S., Bess, B. and Saltus C. (1977) *A Sexual Profile of Men in Power*. New York: Warner Books.

Jeffreys, S. (1997) *The Idea of Prostitution*. North Melbourne: Spinifex Press.

Johnson, A.M., Mercer, C.H. *et al.* (2001) 'Sexual Behaviour in Britain: Partnerships, Practices, and HIV Risk Behaviours', *Lancet*, 358: 1835–42.

Johnston, L. (1997) 'Policing Communities of Risk', in P. Francis, P. Davies, and V. Jupp (eds) *Policing Futures: The Police, Law Enforcement and the Twenty-First Century*. Basingstoke: Macmillan.

Jones, H. and Sagar, T. (2001) 'Crime and Disorder Act 1998: Prostitution and the Anti-Social Behaviour Order' [2001] Crim. L.R. 873–85.

Jones, L. MP (2004) at: www.lynnejones.org.uk/prostitution.htm accessed 22 June 2005).

Jordan, J. (1997) 'User Pays: Why Men Buy Sex', *Australian and New Zealand Journal of Criminology*, 30 (1): 55–71.

Jouve, N. (1986) *The Streetcleaner*. London: Marion Boyers.

Jukes, A.E. (1999) *Men Who Batter Women*. London: Routledge.

Jupp, V. (1989) *Methods of Criminological Research*. London: Routledge.

Kane, B. (1998) 'Reversing the Ethnographic Gaze', in J. Ferrell, and M.S. Hamm *Ethnography at the Edge*. Boston: Northeastern Univeristy Press.

Kantola, J. and Squires, J. (2004) 'Discourses Surrounding Prostitution in the UK', *European Journal of Women's Studies*, Vol, 11, 1: 77–101.

Kaplan, R.B. and Krueger, M.S. (1997) 'Voyeurism: Psychopathology and Theory', in R.D. Laws and W.T. O'Donohue (eds) *Sexual Deviance: Theory, Assessment and Treatment*. New York: The Guilford Press.

Karras, R.M. (1996) *Common Women: Prostitution and Sexuality in Medieval England*. Oxford: Oxford University Press.

Kenworthy, T., Adams, C., Bilby, C., Brooks-Gordon, B. and Fenton, M. (2004) 'Psychological Interventions for those who have Sexually Offended or at Risk of Offending', *Cochrane Review*, The Cochrane Library, Issue 3, 2004. Chichester: John Wiley.

Kesler, K. (2002) 'Is a Feminist Stance in Support of Prostitution Possible? An Exploration of Current Trends', *Sexualities*, 5 (2): 219–35.

Kinnell, H. (2002) 'Violence against Sex Workers in London: The London Ugly Mugs List', Europap-UK, February 2002, unpublished paper.

Kinnell, H. (2000) 'European Network for HIV/STD Prevention in Prostitution: 1998–2000 Final Report', European Commission Programme of Community Action on the Prevention of AIDS and certain other Communicable Diseases (SOC.98 200582 05F02/ 98F02PF017). London.

Kinnell, H. (1999) 'Europap Annual Report' (European Network for HIV/ STD Prevention in Prostitution). Europap.

Kinnell, H. (1998) 'Personal Communication', 10 October 1998.

Kinnell, H. (1994) 'Prostitutes' Exposure to Rape and Other Violence as an Occupational Hazard', European Conference on Methods and Results of Psycho-Social Aspects of AIDS – AIDS in Europe – The Behavioural Aspect, Berlin, Germany, September 1994.

Kinnell, H. (1993) 'Prostitutes' Exposure to Rape: Implications for HIV Prevention and for Legal Reform', Paper presented to VII Social Aspects of AIDS Conference, South Bank University, London: June 1993.

Kinnell, H. and Griffiths, R.K. (1989) 'Male Clients of Female Prostitutes in Birmingham, England: A Bridge for Transmission of HIV?', 5th International Conference on AIDS, Montreal, June 1989.

Kinnell, H. (1989) 'Male Clients of Female Prostitutes in Birmingham, England: A Bridge for Transmission of HIV?', Report of 5th International Conference on AIDS, Montreal, June 1989.

Kinsey, A.C., Pomeroy, W.B. and Martin, C.E. (1948) *Sexual Behaviour in the Human Male*. Philadelphia and London: W.B. Saunders.

Kippax, S., Crawford, J., Benton, P., Gault, U. and Noesjirwan, J. (1988) 'Constructing Emotion: Weaving Meaning from Memories', *British Journal of Social Psychology*, 27: 19–33.

Kirk, J. and Miller, M. (1986) *Reliability and Validity in Qualitative Research Methods*. London: Sage.

Kitzinger, J. (1994) 'Focus Groups: Method or Madness?', in M. Boulton *Research Methods*. London: Taylor and Francis.

Klein, M. (1928) 'Early Stages of the Oedipal Conflict', *International Journal of Psychoanalysis*, 8: 25–37.

Knox, E.G., MacArthur, C. and Simons, K.J. (1993) *Sexual Behaviour and AIDS in Britain*. London: HMSO.

Kuo, L. (2002) *Prostitution Policy*. New York: New York University Press.

Kureishi, H. (1997) *Love in a Blue Time*. London: Faber.

Kulick, D. (2003) 'Sex in the New Europe', *Anthropological Theory*, 3 (2): 199–218.

Krafft-Ebing, R.C., cited in L. Segal (1990) *Slow Motion: Changing Masculinities, Changing Men* (1st edn). London: Virago.

Lacey, N. (2001) 'Beset by Boundaries: The Home Office Review of Sex Offences' [2001] Crim. L.R. 3.

Larsen E.N. (1996) 'The Effect of Different Police Enforcement Policies on the Control of Prostitution', *Canadian Public Policy*, XXII: 1, 40.

Laskowski, R.S. (2002) 'The New German Prostitution Act – An Important Step to a More Rational View of Prostitution as an Ordinary Profession in Accordance with European Community Law', *The International Journal of Labour Law and Industrial Relations*, 18 (4): 479–91.

The Law Commission (1995) 'Consent in the Criminal Law' (Consultation Paper No. 139, Appendix C, para. C.41).

Lawless, S., Kippax, S. and Crawford, J. (1996) 'Dirty, Diseased and Undeserving: The Positioning of HIV Positive Women', *Social Science Medicine*, 43 (9): 1371–1377.

Lea, J. and Young, J. (1993) *What is to be Done About Law and Order?* London: Pluto Press.

Lee, R.M. (1993) *Doing Research on Sensitive Topics*. London: Sage.

Lee, M. and O'Brien, R. (1995) *The Game's Up: Redefining Child Prostitution*. London: The Children's Society.

Lemoncheck, L. (1997) *Loose Women, Lecherous Men: A Feminist Philosophy of Sex*. Oxford: Oxford University Press.

Liberty (2004) 'Liberty's Response to the Home Office Consultation Paper: Paying the Price: A Consultation Paper on Prostitution', November 2004.

Lieberman, B. (1982) *Contemporary Problems in Statistics: A Book of Readings for the Behavioural Sciences*. New York: Oxford University Press.

Lloyd, C., Mair, G. and Hough, M. (1994) 'Explaining Reconviction Rates: A Critical Analysis', Home Office Research Study 136. London: HMSO.

Lofland, J. (1971) *Analysing Social Settings*. London: Wadsworth.

Lombroso, C. (1885) *The Criminal Woman and the Prostitute*, trans. L. Melville, M. St. Auben (Milan, 1997).

London Ugly Mugs List, November 2001 'Sex Worker's Report of Attack, September 2001'.

Lopez-Jones, N. (1990) 'Guilty Until Proven Innocent', *New Law Journal*, 11 May 1990.

Lowman, J. (1993) 'Canada', in N.J. Davis *Prostitution: International Handbook on Trends, Problems and Policies*. London: Greenwood Press.

Lowman, J. (2000) 'Violence and the Outlaw Status of (Street) Prostitution in Canada', *Violence Against Women*, 6 (9).

MacKinnon, C. (1987) *Feminism Unmodified: Discourses on Life and the Law*. Harvard: Harvard University Press.

Maher, L. (1997) *Sexed Work, Gender, Race, and Resistance in a Brooklyn Drug Market*. Oxford: Clarendon Press.

Mancini, J.G. (1963) *Prostitutes and Their Parasites*. London: Elek Books.

Marshall, C. and Rossman, G.B. (1995) *Designing Qualitative Research* (2nd edn). London: Sage.

Mass Observation (1949), cited in Stanley (1995).

Mattley, C. (1998) (Dis) 'Courtesy Stigma: Fieldwork among Phone Fantasy Workers', in J. Ferrell and M.S. Hamm *Ethnography at the Edge*. Boston: Northeastern University Press.

Matthews, R. (1993) 'Kerb Crawling, Prostitution and Multi-agency Policing', Police Research Group, Crime Prevention Unit Series, Paper 43.

Matthews, R. (2005) 'Policing Prostitution Ten Years On', *British Journal of Criminology*, 45: 877–95.

May, T. (1993) *Social Research: Issues, Methods and Process*. Buckingham: Open University Press.

McDowell, L. (1998) *Gender, Identity and Place*. Cambridge: Polity.

McIntosh, M. (1979) 'Who Needs Prostitutes? The Ideology of Male Sexual Needs', in C. Smart and B. Smart (eds) *Sexuality and Social Control*. London: Routledge and Kegan Paul.

McIntosh, M. (1996) 'Feminist Debates on Prostitution', in L. Adkins and V. Merchant *Sexualising the Social*. Basingstoke: Macmillan.

McKeganey, N. and Barnard, M. (1996) *Sex Work on the Streets: Prostitutes and their Clients*. Buckingham: Open University Press.

McLeod, E. (1982) *Women Working: Prostitution Now*. London and Canberra: Croom Helm.

Messerschmidt, J. (1997) *Crime as Structured Action*. London: Sage.

Michael *et al.* (1992), cited in Monto (2000).

Miller, J. (1997) 'Researching Violence Against Street Prostitutes', in M. Schwartz (ed.) *Researching Violence Against Women*. Thousand Oaks, CA: Sage.

Millet, K. (1975 [1971]) *The Prostitution Papers*. Hertfordshire: Paladin.

Mills, C.W. (1940) 'Situated Actions and Vocabularies of Motive', *American Sociological Review*, 5: 904–13.

Money, J. (1996) *Lovemaps: Clinical Concepts and Sexual/Erotic Health and Pathology, Paraphilia and Gender Transposition in Childhood, Adolescence, and Maturity*. New York: Irvington.

Monto, M. (2000) 'Why Men Seek Out Prostitutes', in R. Weitzer (ed.) *Sex for Sale*. New York: Routledge.

Nash, M. (1999) *Police, Probation and Protecting the Public*. London: Blackstone Press.

Oakely, A. (1981) 'Interviewing Women: A Contradiction in Terms', in H. Roberts (ed.) *Doing Feminist Research*. London: Routledge.

O'Connell Davidson, J. and Layder, D. (1994) *Methods, Sex and Madness*. London: Routledge.

O'Connell Davidson, J. (1998) *Prostitution, Power and Freedom*. Cambridge: Polity.

O'Neill, M. (1997) 'An Overview', in G. Scambler and A. Scambler (eds) *Rethinking Prostitution*. London: Routledge.

O'Neill, M. (1991) *Routes to Prostitution: Poverty, Homelessness and Leaving Care*. Nottingham Trent University.

O'Neill, M. and Barbaret, R. (2000) 'Victimisation and the Social Organisation of Prostitution in England and Spain', in R. Weittzer (ed.) Sex for Sale. London: Routledge.

Ormerod, D. (2005) *Smith and Hogan Criminal Law*. Oxford: Oxford University Press.

O'Sullivan, J. (1998) 'A Prostitute is not a Rapist', The Independent, 23 July 1998, p. 9.

Os Stolan, L. (1995) 'Changing Faces of Prostitution', Conference Proceedings Helsinki, 3–5 May 1995.

Otis, L.L. (1985) *Prostitution in Medieval Society: The History of an Urban Institution in Languedoc*. Chicago: University of Chicago Press.

Outshoorn, J. (2001) 'Debating Prostitution in Parliament: A Feminist Analysis', *The European Journal of Women's Studies*, 8 (4): 472–90.

Outshoorn, J. (*ed*.) (2004) *The Politics of Prostitution*. Cambridge: Polity.

Parris, M. (2002) *Chance Witness*. London: Penguin.

Pauw, I. and Brener, L. (2003) '"You are just Whores – You can't be Raped": Barriers to Safer Sex Practice among Women Street Sex Workers in Cape Town', *Culture Health and Sexuality*, 5 (6): 465–81.

Pearce, J.J., Roach P. *et al.* (1997) 'Report into the Links between Prostitution, Drugs and Violence', A SOVA publication in collaboration with Middlesex University (ISBN 185924 1565).

Pease, P. and Pringle, K. (2002) *A Man's World: Changing Men's Practices in a Globalized World*. London: Zed Books.

Perkins, R. (1991) *Working Girl: Prostitutes, their Life and Social Control.* Canberra: Australian Institute of Criminology.

Phoenix, J. (1999) *Making Sense of Prostitution.* Hampshire: Macmillan.

Phoenix, J. (2004) 'Regulating Sex: Young People, Prostitution, and Policy Reform', in B. Brooks-Gordon, L. Gelsthorpe, M. Johnson and A. Bainham (eds) *Sexuality Repositioned.* Oxford: Hart Publishing.

Plumridge, E.W., Chetwynd, S.J., Reed, A. and Gifford, S.J. (1996) 'Patrons of the Sex Industry: Perceptions of Risk', *AIDS Care*, 8 (4): 405–16.

Potter, J. and Wetherell, M. (1987) *Discourse and Social Psychology: Beyond Attitudes and Behaviour.* London: Sage.

Prieur and Taskal (1989) in Hoigard and Finstad (1992) *Backstreets.* Cambridge: Polity.

Pujol, J. (1999) 'Deconstructing and Reconstructing', in C. Willig *Applied Discourse Analysis.* Buckingham: Open University Press.

Reiner, R. (1993) 'Race, Crime and Justice: Models of Interpretation', in L.R. Gelsthorpe (ed.) *Minority Groups in Criminal Justice System*, Cropwood Conference Series. No. 21. University of Cambridge: Institute of Criminology.

Renzetti, C.M. (1997) 'Confessions of a Reformed Positivist', in M. Schwartz *Researching Sexual Violence Against Women.* Thousand Oaks, CA: Sage.

Ringdal, N. (2004) *Love for Sale: A Global History of Prostitution.* London: Atlantic Books.

Ritzer, G. (1998) *The McDonaldization Thesis: Extensions and Explorations.* London: Sage.

Roberts, N. (1993) *Whores in History.* London: Harper Collins.

Roberts, J.V. and Hough, M. (2005) *Understanding Public Attitudes to Criminal Justice.* Maidenhead: Open University Press.

Roiph, C.H. (ed.) (1955) *Women of the Streets.* London: Secker and Warburg.

Rossiaud, J. (1988) *Medieval Prostitution*, trans. L.G. Cochrane. Oxford: Blackwell.

Sagar, T. (2005) 'Street Watch: Concept and Practice: Civilian Participation in Street Prostitution Control', *British Journal of Criminology*, 45 (1): 98–112.

Sanders, T. (2001) Female street sex workers, sexual violence and protection strategies, *Journal of Sexual Aggression*, 7 (1).

Sanders, T. (2004) *Sex Work: A risky business.* Cullompton: Willan.

Scambler, G. and Scambler, A. (1997) (eds) *Rethinking Prostitution.* London: Routledge.

Schofield, J.W. (1993) 'Generalisability of Qualitative Research', in M. Hammersley *Social Research. Philosophy, Politics and Practice.* London: Sage.

Scott, J. (1990) *A Matter of Record.* Cambridge: Polity.

Scott, M.B. and Lyman, S.M. (1968) 'Accounts', *American Sociological Review*, 33: 46–62.

Scully, D. (1990) *Understanding Sexual Violence*. London: Harper Collins.

Seabrook, J. (1996) *Travels in the Skin Trade: Tourism and the Sex Industry*. London: Pluto Press.

Segal, L. (1990) *Slow Motion: Changing Masculinities, Changing Men* (1st edn). London: Virago.

Segal, L. (1994) *Straight Sex*. London: Virago.

Segal, L. (1997) *Slow Motion: Changing Masculinities, Changing Men* (2nd edn). London: Virago.

Segal, L. (1997) 'Feminist Sexual Politics and the Heterosexual Predicament', in L. Segal (ed.) *New Sexual Agendas*. Hampshire: Macmillan.

Seidler, V. (1992) (ed.) *Men Sex and Relationships*. London: Routledge.

Self, H. (2006) 'Regulating Prostitution', in B. Brooks-Gordon and M. Freeman *Law and Psychology: Current Legal Issues*. Oxford: Oxford University Press.

Self, H. (2005) 'Lies, Damned Lies and Prostitution Statistics', unpublished article.

Self, H. (2004) 'Response to Paying the Price', personal correspondence.

Self, H. (2003) *Fallen Daughters of Eve: Prostitution, Women and Misuse of the Law*. London: Frank Cass.

Self, H. (1999a) 'Fair Game', *Police Review*, 21 May 1999, pp. 26, 27.

Self, H. (1999b) 'Trade Barrier', *Police Review*, 19 November 1999.

Selfe, D. and Burke, V. (2001) *Perspectives on Sex, Crime and Society*. London: Cavendish.

Semin, G.R. and Manstead A.S.R. (1983) *The Accountability of Conduct*. London: Academic Press.

Sharpe, K. (1998) *Red Light, Blue Light: Prostitutes, Punters and the Police*. Hampshire: Ashgate.

Shell, Y., Campbell, P. and Caren, I. (2001) 'It's Not a Game: A Report on Hampshire Constabulary's Anti Kerb-Crawling Initiative', Hampshire Constabulary.

Sherman, L.W. (1992) *Policing Domestic Violence: Experiments and Dilemmas*. New York: Free Press.

Shotter, J. (1984) *Social Accountability and Selfhood*. Oxford: Blackwell.

Simon, W. and Gagnon, J. (1973) *Sexual Conduct*. Chicago: Markham Publishing.

Smith, D.J. and Gray, J. (1983) 'Police and People in London': London: Policy Studies Institute Report 1–4.

Smith, J. (1989) *Misogynies*. London: Faber.

Soothill, K. and Sanders, T. (2004) 'Calling the Tune? Some Observations on Paying the Price: A Consultation Paper on Prostitution', *The Journal of Forensic Psychiatry and Psychology*, 15 (4): 1–18.

Stanko, E.A. (1994) 'Men's Individual Violence', in. T. Newburn and E.A. Stanko (eds) *Just Boys Doing Business?* London: Routledge.

Stanley, L. (1995) *Sex Surveyed, 1949–1994: From Mass-Observation's 'Little Kinsey' to the National Survey and the Hite Reports*. London: Taylor and Francis.

Stanton, M. (1990) *Sandor Ferenczi: Reconsidering Active Intervention*. London: Free Association Press.

Stavenhagen, R. (1993) 'Decolonizing Applied Social Sciences', in M. Hammersley *Social Research: Philosophy, Politics and Practice*. London: Sage.

Steier, F. (1991) *Research and Reflexivity*. London: Sage.

Stein, M. (1974) *Lovers, Friends, Slaves: Nine Male Sexual Types: Their Psychosexual Transactions with Call Girls*. Berkeley and New York: Berkeley Publishing Co. and Puttnam and Sons.

Stoller, R.J. (1976) *Perversions: The Erotic Form of Hatred*. New York: Harverster Press in association with Pantheon.

Stoller, R.J. (1979) *Sexual Excitement: Dynamic of Erotic Life*. New York: Pantheon.

Stoller, R.J. (1985) *Observing the Erotic Imagination*. New Haven CT: Yale University Press.

Stone, L. (1977) *The Family, Sex and Marriage in England 1500–1800*. New York: Harper and Row.

Stopes, M. (1918) *Married Love: A New Contribution to the Solution of Sex Difficulties*. London: A.C. Fifield.

Sullivan, B. (1997) *The Politics of Sex: Prostitution and Pornography in Australia since 1945*. Cambridge: Cambridge University Press.

Sykes, G. and Matza, D. (1957) 'Techniques of Neutralization. A Theory of Delinquency', *American Sociological Review*, 22: 664–70.

Tarling, R. (1995) *Analysing Offending: Models and Interpretations*. London: HMSO.

Tedeschi, J. and Reiss, M. (1981) 'Verbal Strategies for Impression Management', in C. Antaki (ed.) *The Psychology of Ordinary Explanations of Social Behaviour*. London: Academic Press.

Tiefer, E. (1995) *Sex is Not a Natural Act*. Oxford: Westview Press.

Trott, L. (1979) 'An Understanding of Prostitution, With Particular Reference to Mayfair, London', in D.J. West (ed.) *Sex Offenders in the Criminal Justice System*, Cropwood Conference No. 12, University of Cambridge, Institute of Criminology.

Van Bruschot, E.G. (2002) 'Community Policing and "John Schools"', *CRSA/ RCSA*, 4 (2): 215.

Van Maanen, J. (ed.) (1991) *Representation in Ethnography*. Thousand Oaks, CA: Sage.

Vanwesenbeeck, I., de Graaf, R., van Zessen. G., Straver, C.J. and Visser. J.H. (1993) 'Protection Styles of Prostitutes' Clients: Intentions, Behavior, and Considerations in Relation to AIDS', *Journal of Sex Education and Therapy*, 19 (2): 79–92.

Viney, E. (1996) *Dancing to Different Tunes*. Belfast: Blackstaff Press.

Walkowitz, J. (1992) *City of Dreadful Delight*. London: Virago.

Walters, R. (2005/06) *Criminal Justice Matters*, Winter 2005/06, pp. 6, 7.

Ward, H. and Day, S. (1997) 'Prostitute Women and Public Health', *British Medical Journal*, 297: 1585.

Wasik, M. (2001) 'Legislating in the Shadow of the Human Rights Act: The Criminal Justice and Police Act 2001' [2001] Crim. L.R. 931–47.

Weeks, J. (1977) *Coming Out: Homosexual Politics in Britain from the Nineteenth Century to the Present*. London: Quartet.

Weeks, J. (1985) *Invented Moralities*. Cambridge: Polity.

Weitzer, R. (ed.) (2000) *Sex For Sale*. New York: Routledge.

Wellings, K., Field, J., Johnson, A.M. and Wadsworth, J. (1994) *Sexual Behaviour in Britain: The National Survey of Sexual Attitudes and Lifestyles*. London: Penguin.

Wellings, K. (2000) 'National Sexual Attitudes and Lifestyle Survey' (NATSAL), UK National Survey of Sexual Attitudes and Lifestyles (NATSAL, 2000), *Lancet* (2001), 358: 1835–42.

West Yorkshire Police (2000) 'The Kerb-Crawlers Rehabilitation Programme: An Evaluation from the Police Perspective'.

Westmarland, L. (2001) *Gender and Policing: Sex Power and Police Culture*. Cullompton: Willan.

Whittaker, D. and Hart, G. (1996) 'Managing the Risks: The Social Organisation of Indoor Sex Work', *Sociology of Health and Illness*, 18 (3): 399–414.

Wilkinson, S. (1988) 'The Role of Reflexivity in Feminist Psychology', *Women's Studies International Forum*, 11: 493–502.

Willig, C. (1999) 'Discourse Analysis and Sex Education', in. C. Willig (ed.) *Applied Discourse Analysis*. Buckingham: Open University Press.

Willis, C. (1983) *The Use, Effectiveness and Impact of Police Stop and Search Powers*. London: Home Office Research Unit.

Winick, C. (1962) 'Prostitutes' Clients' Perception of the Prostitute and Themselves', *International Journal of Social Psychiatry*, 8: 289–97.

Winick, C. and Kinsie P.M. (1971) *The Lively Commerce*. Chicago: Quadrangle.

Women Against Rape and Legal Action for Women (1995) 'Dossier: The Crown Prosecution Service and the Crime of Rape'.

Wolfenden Report (1957) 'Report of the Committee on Homosexuality and Prostitution', Cmnd. 247. London: Home Office.

Wolff, J. (1994) *Feminism and Modernism: In The Polity Reader in Social Theory*. Cambridge: Polity.

Wooffit, R. (1996) *Telling Tales of the Unexpected: The Organisation of Factual Discourse*. Hemel Hempstead: Harvester Wheatsheaf.

Woolgar, S. (1988) *Knowledge and Reflexivity: New Frontiers in the Sociology of Knowledge*. London: Sage.

Young, A. (1996) *Imagining Crime*. London: Sage.

Young, M. (1998) Personal communication, November 1997.

Zamble, V.L. and Quinsey E. (1997) *The Criminal Recidivism Process*. Cambridge: Cambridge University Press.

Newspaper articles

'Party Horror after Vice Girls Attacked', Bradford Telegraph and Argus, November 1996.
Bradford Telegraph and Argus, 8 May 2001 and 14 May 2001.
'Double Life Term for Knife Maniac', Bradford Telegraph and Argus, November 2001.
Bradford Telegraph and Argus, 6 November 2001.
Coventry Evening Telegraph, 19 June 2001.
'Chief Constable Attacks Jail System', Guardian, 22 July 2000.
'Law Increases Danger, Prostitutes Say', Guardian, 16 September 2002.
'Sex Beast Preyed on Vice Girls', Liverpool Echo, 25 January 2002.
'Midlands Ripper Unmasked', Observer, 19 March 2000.
Plymouth Evening Herald, 1 December 2001.
Plymouth Evening Herald, 9 December 2000.
'HIV Warning to Men Using Prostitutes', Press Association, 27 April 2001.
N. Walker 'All Victims of Murder should be Treated Equally', The Independent, 9 January 2003.
Walsall Advertiser, 26 April 2001.
'New Drive to Keep Vice Girls off Streets', Yorkshire Evening Post, 10 August 2001.
'Minimum of 22 years for Prostitute's Killer', Yorkshire Post, 27 March 1998.

Websites

BBC News website, 29 January 1998 'Rapist gets Life for Murder': http://news.bbc.co.uk/1/hi/uk/51747.stm (accessed 17 March 2003).
BBC News website, 25 November 1999 'Sex Clients' Robbery Risk': http://news.bbc.co.uk/hi/english/uk/scotland/newsid_536000/536141.stm (accessed 17 March 2003).
BBC News website, 8 December 1999 'Prostitute Murderer gets Life David Smith': http://news.bbc.co.uk/1/hi/uk/552350.stm (accessed 17 March 2003).
BBC News website, 21 July 2000 'Freed Killer Murders Again': http://news.bbc.co.uk/1/hi/uk/845211.stm (accessed 17 March 2003).
BBC News website, 6 February 2001 'Rapist Jailed for Prostitute Attacks': http://news.bbc.co.uk/1/hi/scotland/1156724.stm. (accessed 17 March 2003). This is Hull and East Yorkshire website, 20 January 1999, link no longer available (accessed by H. Kinnell 20 October 2000).

Index